Larry Flynt

June 20, 1996

Dear Tonya,

Maybe I haven't been much of a father, but you and I both know the accusations of physical and sexual abuse are a lie. I have never layed a hand on you physically or sexually in your entire life. I don't know what your motivation is for doing and saying the things you have done, but go ahead and enjoy your fifteen minutes of fame because people will soon grow tired of you.

I want you to know that in the process of all of this, you have forever burned any bridges between us. I will ensure that you will never benefit one penny from of my estate.

I don't want to hear from you, see you or speak to you as long as I live.

Your father,

P.S.   Publish this letter in your book.

8484 WILSHIRE BOULEVARD • EXECUTIVE OFFICE • BEVERLY HILLS, CALIFORNIA 90211 • PHONE 213-651-5400 FAX: 213-651-2936

HUSTLED

HUSTLED
My Journey from Fear to Faith

Tonya Flynt-Vega
with Ted Schwarz

Westminster John Knox Press
Louisville, Kentucky

Some of the names in this book have been changed to protect the parties involved. In several instances, teenagers with whom I was associated during a period of great rebelliousness and inappropriate action for us all are now adults who have changed. They are leading rich, productive lives, morally upright and totally different people from the teens we all were so many years ago.

Book design by Jennifer K. Cox
Cover design by Kim Wohlenhaus
Cover photograph by David Howard

First edition
Published by Westminster John Knox Press
Louisville, Kentucky

Published in association with the literary agency of Wolgemuth & Hyatt, Inc., 8012 Brooks Chapel Road, Suite 243, Brentwood, Tennessee 37027.

This book is printed on acid-free paper that meets the American National Standards Institute Z39.48 standard. ♾

PRINTED IN THE UNITED STATES OF AMERICA
98 99 00 01 02 03 04 05 06 07 — 10 9 8 7 6 5 4 3 2 1

Library of Congress Cataloging-in-Publication Data

Flynt-Vega, Tonya.
    Hustled : my journey from fear to faith / Tonya Flynt-Vega, with Ted Schwarz. — 1st ed.
        p.   cm.
    Includes bibliographical references and index.
    ISBN 0-664-22114-9
    1. Flynt-Vega, Tonya. 2. Flynt, Larry. 3. Hustler (Columbus)
4. Christian biography—United States. I. Schwarz, Ted, 1945-
II. Title.
BR1725.F524A3   1998
362.76′092   98-14880
[B]—DC21

This book is lovingly dedicated to the Father of the Fatherless,
without whom I would not have survived;
all the women and children who suffer because of our blindness and sloth;
my supporter and friend, my husband, Lawrence Vega;
our precious gift from God, Marilyn;
and my beloved mother.

Contents

Introduction

It was an unusually frenzied morning. My husband had left for work and my daughter, Marilyn, was still gathering her things for school. I was working feverishly to get my hair just right, to find the perfect outfit. Right after I dropped my daughter off at school, I would be meeting with a reporter and television crew from the syndicated television program *Day & Date*. They were conducting the first broadcast interview I had ever given concerning my life and the world of my father: Larry Flynt.

The publicity had been building for months. Everyone wanted to know about my stand against pornography, about my faith, about my convictions that pornography damages individuals, families, and society as a whole. Both *U.S.A. Today* and the *Washington Times* had discussed my concerns as a result of the release of the movie *The People vs. Larry Flynt*. Now a television crew was coming.

Naively, I thought little about the full impact of what I was doing. I had seen the results of pornography addiction up close and personal. I had been addicted to pornography myself at one highly troubled time of my life. I knew pornography raised serious First Amendment issues that were being debated all over the country. I knew there were controversies over community standards. I knew there were marketplace concerns. And of course I understood the moral issue of producing and selling exploitative material that degraded women and children. Yet I did not fully understand the passions of men for whom the use of pornography is so critical that they would do anything to get it.

My daughter and I left our house, got in our car, and prepared to leave. As we pulled out, I noticed a plain white Chrysler sedan parked nearby. Inside was a well-dressed man in a suit sitting with the ramrod straight appearance of one of my father's bodyguards. Not that this man worked for my father. I had never seen him before and doubt that he had any connection with Larry Flynt Enterprises. But his dress and posture were just unusual enough for laid-back Jacksonville, Florida, to make him conspicuous.

I pulled onto the road leading to Marilyn's school, and suddenly the Chrysler was on top of me. The driver floored the accelerator. His tires squealed. I glanced in my rearview mirror and saw the man was inches from my bumper. He was speaking intently into a phone or something like a CB, keeping exact pace with me.

This guy was good. If I sped up, he was right behind me; if I slowed, he decreased his speed to match mine.

I knew I had to get to an open area, a public place where I could get help. I turned corners where I normally went straight and went straight where I routinely turned corners. I finally reached my daughter's school and pulled into the parking area, a place with lots of students and children milling about. It was only then that the man backed off and sped away.

I have not seen that man since. But immediately after that incident the telephone calls began. Obscene calls. Threatening calls. Calls that told me I would think differently about pornography if I had one really good sexual experience.

Not that such a polite term was used, of course. I heard the "f" word more times than I could count.

There were also more serious threats, both directly to me and through a friend of mine who was warned that I had better back off speaking against pornography, otherwise I would be hurt—or worse.

It was then that I began to realize that I had no choice. I had to speak out. I had to dedicate my life to eradicating a scourge on our moral landscape.

There are cigarette addicts, alcohol addicts, drug addicts. And then there are pornography addicts. They are different. After talking with thousands of college students, I have learned that domestic violence, date rape, and similar crimes are integrally related to pornography. Incest, child abuse, spouse abuse, and the destruction of families stem from the use of pornography. There are other causes of these horrors, of course. But when pornography is eliminated in a community, violent crimes are cut by more than half.

I have also learned that to stand against pornography often means to stand alone, in the midst of threats and physical danger. In 1997, in Columbus, Ohio, I brought criminal charges against my father for sexual molestation, realizing that I might be destroyed in the process. For months I had been telling young women that in order to heal they must also bring charges against the man or men who molested them. Certainly the women need their day in court. They need to have the courage to confront their abuser and publicly denounce his actions. It is like a ritual cleansing so often practiced in the Old Testament. The women have never been evil or dirty, yet they have been seduced into feeling shame rather than outrage, fear rather than empowerment. Bringing well-deserved charges is an act of purification, of rebirth, of moving forward.

Equally important is the fact that most incestuous molesters who are not stopped will continue to physically act out their fantasies. Their actions within their families will obviously be limited, but studies quoted by the National Coalition for the Protection of Children and Family indicate that a molester who is not stopped will, within his lifetime, molest an average of 380 children.

The women who came to me were adults. They usually had left home. Certainly they were in positions where their fathers, grandfathers, or others were never going to be able to molest them again. But that did not mean the men had stopped.

There were other little girls—in the family, in the neighborhood, in any place the molesters might travel. Such men have the instincts of predators, sensing when a child is feeling sad, lonely, vulnerable. They learn how to give just enough appropriate pleasure to a child to gain the trust necessary for acts so unspeakable, everyone connected with the victim often goes into denial.

My father, Larry Flynt, molested me. I am certain I was not unique, either in my family or in the world at large. From time to time one or another of my sisters has lost her inhibitions from a combination of exhaustion and alcohol. She has told stories that revealed she, too, had lived in the dark side of my father's life. These have been stories as yet unproven which I believe because of my own experiences. And if us, then why not others, either near where he lives or during his trips abroad? To prosecute would be to heal, but it would also mean that girls like my daughter would be safer for the action. Even if I lost. Even if nothing changed when the notoriety died down. Standing up meant that other victims might have the courage to come forward. They would not see what happened as a disgrace. They would not feel themselves to be betrayers of family secrets. They would walk into court with their heads held high, comfortable with the knowledge that justice, not fear and self-loathing, would be a part of their future.

Standing up was a way of putting the molester and his apologists on record that such behavior would not be tolerated. And by law, I had to do it in Columbus, the location of the criminal action.

For me and my family there is no turning back. Larry Flynt is my father, and his empire is the enemy. I am fighting what may be the greatest menace in America today, one that threatens women, children, and, ultimately, the soul of our society. My journey has been long, and it has not been easy. I have been threatened. My faith has been challenged. But I have persevered.

I am the pornographer's daughter. And this is my story.

1

The Country Roads of My Mind

Sometimes we never know the full meaning of our dreams. Mine involved country roads, carpets of green grass, quiltlike patches of wildflowers luminous in the late afternoon sun, and rocky mountains, where you could refresh yourself from a lake whose water was so pure, it seemed to have been poured from a heavenly chalice. It was a world of peace, where darkness was no more fearful than daylight, and birds performed lullabies to comfort you until morning.

Not that I had ever seen such a land. I was a city girl, the middle child in a family of four being raised by an overworked, always exhausted, sometimes severely depressed single mother. We lived in public housing, but because my mother held as many different jobs as she could find, we were what is now called working poor. Those without any ability to pay were apportioned apartments according to the size of their families. The working poor were more limited. We were in a tiny apartment where there was a bedroom for my older sister, Judy, a bedroom my mother shared with my baby brother, Shawn, and a walk-in closet.

The walk-in closet was where I slept, where I listened to music, wrote poetry, and dreamed my dreams of a land in which only my father had been raised.

That closet was special to me. I had a mattress on the floor flush against the back wall. It was covered with a sheet and served as bed, desk, and couch. On one side I had pictures cut from magazines—John Denver, Shaun Cassidy, and the other heartthrobs I found in the teen magazines kids shared at school. Books, a handful of John Denver records, and a cheap, well-used record player rested at the foot of the bed. My "night table," actually a scavenged box covered with a well-washed, rather tattered rag on which I had set a candle, was at the other end. And above my head was a round magazine snapshot of my dad. I had carefully clipped it from the first publication he gave me on one of my visits with him in Columbus. It was a publication he seemed to know would make him rich and famous one day. The magazine was for the regulars at the string of nightclubs he owned in Ohio, seemingly a million miles away from the inner city of Jacksonville, where I lived with Mom and my half-brother and half-sister. It bore the same name as the clubs, and as he anticipated, it would make him wealthy. The magazine was called *Hustler*.

And like the John Denver song "Country Roads" I so adored, Dad had come from the same type of place where the singer talked of his Rocky Mountain high. What I did not realize was that instead of being a location of serenity and joy, Dad was raised amid abject poverty, alcoholism, adultery, casual sex, and incest. Even worse, when he left that world behind him, educating himself to a level rarely exceeded by the most scholarly of university graduates, he continued to perpetuate his past. Nothing was taboo if it gave him pleasure, and as I was to find when I reached puberty, this included bringing me deeply into the world of America's most controversial empire of pornography.

They were children when they met. Mom was barely a teenager. Dad, a half-dozen years older, was still in the throes of adolescence.

I am certain they did not see themselves that way back then. Mom had physically matured quite young. At ten she had learned how to fix her makeup and clothing so she could pass for sixteen. Three years later, in a fit of rebellion against a hard-drinking mother she felt was too strict and abusive, she had run off with a young man who took her to Texas. She fancied herself a woman in love. He saw her for what she was, physically mature yet naive enough never to suspect he was using her, paying for their travels through a series of robberies. The man was caught, tried, and convicted for his crimes. Mom was cleared of any wrongdoing, then returned to her mother. Grandma was outraged by Mom's behavior and the way she let the man lie to her. She continued to believe that hers had been a true love affair, that she had meant more to the man than a diversion while committing crimes.

By fourteen, Mom had to go to court, hear her mother and others describe outrageous, out-of-control behavior, then listen as the judge declared her "incorrigible."

Not that the label was undeserved. Mom frequently waited until the often nightly rages of Grandma subsided, then dressed to look older than her years and sneaked out of the house to run with a crowd of kids who had already graduated from her high school. She lived for the moment, trying to experience the forbidden fruits of the adult world other girls her age only fantasized about.

Dad was equally wild, though in a different way. He lied about his age in order to enter the Army in August 1958, when he was just fourteen. He had a ninth-grade education and the arrogant attitude of a kid who decided he knew all that was necessary to get through life before he had barely experienced any of it. As a result, he was unable to handle most of the basic training. He was discharged six months later, by his own admission having been classed as "too dumb" for the military life.[1] He wasn't, of course. He had just failed to realize how much education was needed to get along in life.

The reason for the discharge was shattering for Dad. It was an embarrassment he has hidden or lied about over the years, trying to elevate his importance to our nation during those years of rebellion. Regardless of the problems, though, he managed to falsify information concerning his prior service and enlist in the Navy in 1960, serving a full four years.

Dad was actually not stupid, something he began to prove in the Navy. By the time he entered the service, he had traveled far from the Kentucky hill country where he was raised. Then, while on the ships, he developed a more cosmopolitan lifestyle. He read voraciously, paid for the favors of a variety of women in numerous ports of call, and usually had a pocket full of cash from the high stakes gambling he won more often than not.

Mom met Dad strictly by chance during those years. My grandmother took her to one of the family bars that served their neighborhood. Mom should not have been served because she was too far underage. But Mom looked older, and Grandma was more comfortable being with a drinking buddy than a kid sipping on a soft drink. The two of them ordered beers or stronger drinks, the staff probably knowing the truth yet not willing to offend a couple of good neighborhood customers.

Dad was the most worldly man Mom had ever met. He could talk about places Mom had only heard about in romantic movies. The fact that his sophistication had more to do with a knowledge of brothels than museums, concert halls, and architectural achievements meant nothing to her. She saw a handsome man, who seemed to know a little about everything. Seemingly everyone else in town saw just another uneducated dropout who stayed in the military until he was too old for some judge to send him to reform school.

Dad had come a long way from his place of birth, but he still seemed destined to be like all the other young men who comprised so much of the laboring class in Dayton, Ohio. Ultimately they got shift jobs at The Inland, the local General Motors plant where unskilled laborers could receive on-the-job training, increasing their pay as they moved to more sophisticated assignments on the assembly line. If anyone had to guess about Dad's future back then, he or she probably would have seen him as one of the multitude of anonymous Ohio youths who would go from the military to the assembly line to the nursing home to the grave. Only his children would be his legacy, and even they would be hard-pressed to think of anything that might class him as special.

Except to Mom, and even she had no real sense of the future.

Before she met Dad, Mom's world had been defined by what she felt was verbal abuse at home, school classes for which she had the intelligence to excel yet no interest in doing so, and bars whose bouncers never should have allowed her to enter. The latter had a sameness to them in those days. The jukeboxes held a mix of popular songs for the younger customers and country western tunes for those who had moved to Dayton from the mining towns and hardscrabble farms of West Virginia, Kentucky, and the foothills of the Alleghenies. In darker corners, lovers and drunks filled the tables. The lovers spoke quietly, held hands, or fondled each other in the shadows. The drunks filled the air with a thick haze of tobacco smoke and their ashtrays with squashed butts. Sometimes the drunks fell asleep at the tables. Sometimes they wept over songs about lost loves, lost dogs, and lost pickup trucks. A few became belligerent, the reason there was usually a baseball bat or "Texas sapper" hidden behind the bar.

Men working for The Inland, and that meant just about every male in the area, would come by for a beer and a shot after work. They were often boisterous, lying about how hard they worked and how often they had sex. They were only honest about the dream that their kids would somehow escape the assembly-line life that had prematurely aged their grandfathers, fathers, and, if they ever gained the courage to look in the mirror, themselves.

Young adults who had graduated from high school would hang out, listen to music, dance where possible, and see who was willing to leave long enough to enjoy a few minutes of acrobatic passion in the backseat of an old Chevy, DeSoto, or Ford. Movies, dancing, alcohol, and sex served as entertainment, fellowship, courtship, and foreplay for kids with neither the knowledge, the ambition, nor the courage to seek the greater world around them.

Children frequently mixed with the adults in what the locals considered to be family bars. They drank Cokes or Shirley Temples. They played pool when their parents would let them; SkilBall if the bar was big enough to have one of the games. They also were bored a lot, usually being dragged into that environment by parents who wanted to escape the chores at home when they earned a day off.

Wages were up in those days, and the union had negotiated a few benefits, but hourly workers never could get very far ahead before layoffs, strikes, and similar problems ate up their savings. The family bar was the only consistent source of inexpensive entertainment, and frequently it was owned by someone with whom they had once worked the assembly line.

Dad's mother and aunt were among the luckier entrepreneurs in Dayton. They owned one of the neighborhood bars which provided an adequate living when run "straight." This meant the liquor wasn't watered, the prices were fair, and anyone who looked old enough was served, even if the server knew the drinker was underage. The cops also left the bar alone because they were more often than not local "good old boys" who considered free drinks and a weekly envelope of cash more than enough reason to look the other way.

It was as a result of friendships made in such a bar in such a world that my mom, grandmother, and a mutual friend would sit down together with Larry Flynt. For Mom it was love at first sight, or at least what passes for love when you're fourteen and still think every man who physically arouses you has somehow been predestined to be your mate forever. Dad seems to have felt the same way, perhaps the only time in his life when he experienced genuine passion for another human being.

Dad and Mom must have talked that night, though I doubt either of them remembers what was said. What matters is that he began calling her on the telephone, liking what he heard, then asking her for a date.

As wild as they all were, there was a hesitancy to that first stage of courtship. Dad knew Mom wanted to go out with him, would probably do anything with him he asked. But he was still a country kid at heart, someone who had been raised in an area where you could walk for miles without seeing a neighbor. He was insecure in the city, even after his time in the Navy. He was also a romantic, a kid who had discovered poetry and literature with the same intensity that he had discovered "professional" sex. Rather than asking Mom directly or joining her when she sneaked out of the house, he asked a mutual friend of my grandmother, another worker at The Inland, if he would intercede.

As we kids later heard the story when we were old enough to understand, Grandma said, "Hell, no, Larry. All you want to do is get into her pants."

There is some irony in the fact that it was a movie that started me on a crusade which eventually came to the attention of Rosemary Meyer, a longtime pornography opponent and Cincinnati, Ohio, city council candidate. She and her followers paid for my trip to objectively discuss the story of my father and his empire. *The People vs. Larry Flynt* had been released some months earlier and it had turned Dad into a folk hero. Mostly fiction, the film told producer Oliver Stone's version of Dad's defense against the libel suit brought by the Reverend Jerry Falwell.

With all the hype Hollywood can produce, it revealed my father's and the screenwriters' version of Dad's past. This meant the wild living, and the "love affair" with his fourth wife, Althea Leasure, a teenager my Uncle Jimmy hired to dance in one of Dad's clubs. Dad promoted the movie on talk shows in major cities throughout the United States, proud that the film was the "truth" about his life, including the embarrassing moments of his naive youth. His television performance was folksy, friendly, kooky, and a delight to watch if you didn't know him, just as pretentious as the film if you did. He seemed the wiseacre kid you knew from high school, the boy whose rebellious attitude and naughty pranks masked great intelligence. He was the type who knew the principal's office better than the classroom, and while teachers despaired of ever having him as a student, boys secretly envied him and girls were intrigued. No one was surprised if he lived fast and died young. And no one was surprised if he found a special interest, rising to great heights in whatever field he eventually focused his attention.

That was Dad's image, and the fact that he was confined to a wheelchair as a result of an assassination attempt almost two decades earlier made him even more sympathetic. Some television reviewers and many television watchers not familiar with the real Larry Flynt loved that man when he was on television. They delighted in his wit and the naughty sparkle in his eye, never realizing, as I did, that it was an evil heart shining through for its own devious ends.

I knew the truth as I both read the screenplay and watched an advance copy of the movie. I studied it scene by scene and line by line. I was horrified to find that my father was lying to the American public through the screen portrayal of which he approved in the same manner that he had lied to me for so many years of my young life.

Since the founding of *Hustler*, my father's world had been narrowed to obsessive involvement with images and stories objectifying women and children. He hid behind what I consider a distorted version of the First Amendment, his words strengthened by a brilliant, well-funded publicity campaign. At the same time he was being corrupted in the same manner as others who are addicted to pornography. He was also attempting to justify his actions as voluntary pleasures while seeking endless sex partners both in and out of marriage. And when adults failed to fully satisfy him, he turned to his own children, bringing them into a world of perversion that is an abomination to the family, society, and God.

Perhaps all of our lives would have been different had Mom and Dad's families been more traditional. But as I mentioned, they were children who had been raised by children. Mom's mother was still in high school when she got pregnant, a child having a child who, in turn, would give birth to me before she could legally take her first drink. The only difference in Dad's family was that they were hill people, education frequently ending when a boy could pick cotton and make salable moonshine, and a girl could get herself pregnant.

Dad always had a love/hate relationship with the Cumberland Mountain land where he was born. To a city kid like myself, his Kentucky was the object of childhood fantasies. In my mind's eye, nurtured by John Denver song lyrics, there were trees whose summer leaves formed a canvas as thick as carpet sheltering the ground below. I imagined roaming the rolling hills and drinking from the myriad rivers and streams. The grass was lush, and frequent rain enriched the soil. Roads were typically little more than well-trodden paths, the sound of horse hooves more familiar than the honking of a car's horn. And entertainment came from the Technicolor sunrises and sunsets that enveloped days of listening to song birds, tilling the land, and being in harmony with God's handiwork.

Denver's songs evoked a world of love for me. I made it Dad's world, and love, especially from my father, was what I desperately sought.

In truth, such a fantasy was only partially correct. The insular area was so hate filled, Dad would later proudly comment that there wasn't a black or a Jew in the entire county because they had killed them all.

For whites, Magoffin County, Kentucky, was more fortunate than most isolated areas frequently unrecorded on maps until Eleanor Roosevelt made a concerted effort to help the rural poor. Prior to her efforts during her husband's administration, some communities' last contact with the society at large had been so far back in time that residents still spoke Elizabethan English. Inbreeding of a handful of families resulted in damage to everything from intelligence to the immune system. Mild retardation was common, and most families had some of their children die in childbirth or within the first four or five years of life.

Magoffin's approximately five hundred people had come from a variety of places in the early years of settlement, a fact that delayed any degeneration of the area's gene pool. Dad's great-great-grandfather, for example, was a West Virginian married to a Scottish woman. Other families came from the North and East. For several generations it was still possible to fall in love and marry without the type of genetic mixing common in similarly isolated areas. At least until Dad was born on November 1, 1942.

By the time of the war years, Magoffin County, and especially the community of Lakeville (population fifty, and then only if someone from out of the area was having an extended visit), was a land of poverty, alcoholism, incest, and violence.

The coal mines were the largest employer of Magoffin men. The work was labor intensive, being able to use shovel, pick, and dynamite a rite of passage into manhood that lured the area's teenage boys. Youths loaded coal onto railcars, building rock-hard muscles on their thin bodies. The dust blackened their skin, kept their eyes tearing, and aged their lungs. Youths in their twenties frequently had rotting teeth, brittle hair, and a chronic cough. By thirty-five many of the miners were old men who had searing pain with each breath and found themselves exhausted when trying to walk from their shack homes to the outhouse and back. No one identified the problem as black lung disease back then. The women simply knew that if their husbands worked in the mines, they would be young widows. And if their husbands did not want to work in the mines, the choice often meant having to leave the area completely, moving to factory and mill towns such as Dayton, Cleveland, Akron, Pittsburgh, and Detroit.

The Lakeville area was near the county seat. This meant that there was not only a general store but also a handful of what, anywhere else, would be white-collar jobs. By the time Mom paid her first visit to Dad's grandparents in Lakeville, the county seat had a five-and-dime, a coffee shop, and some small offices. This downtown development was no more than a block in length, but it brought more of a sense of the world to the area.

Paved roads had begun to enter the area in the 1950s, the result of President Eisenhower's effort to have a national highway system that could transport soldiers and equipment across the nation. Electricity and some indoor plumbing also arrived. But well into the 1960s, Magoffin County was mostly scattered lean-tos, shacks, log cabins, and a smattering of more traditional homes. Rich and poor were relative; almost everyone in Lakeville earned so little money that having surplus crops and the ability to occasionally sell some of your livestock without going hungry was wealth.

Dad's family was as sophisticated as you could get in the Lakeville area. There were carpenters, blacksmiths, and even a schoolteacher. His father was in the South Pacific during World War II, falling in love with the stimulation and more rapid pace of real cities. He chose to stay in Lakeville, becoming an alcoholic who seldom worked more than a few weeks at a time.

Dad tells a story of the reason he was determined to leave the region. There was a day when he was out picking cotton. Not yet a teenager, he was doing what most of us would consider a man's job. The work was hot, tiring, dirty, and low paying, but it was the work he had to do, the work so many of the kids had to do for their families to survive.

As Dad picked the cotton, some outsiders drove through the area in a big white car. There were people in the front and back seats, though how many and how old I do not know. What Dad remembered, what he told so vividly years later, was that they were mocking his legitimate labor. They pointed their fingers at him. They ridiculed him. They blew their horn so he would know he was the object of their derision. They made him feel he was worth less than the dirt staining his pants as he stooped and rose, stooped and rose, sweating, straining, growing more tired by the minute.

Dad watched that big white car move on down the road, the passengers gradually becoming distracted by other scenery. He made a vow that his own children would never have to live as he did. They would never be poor. They would never have to labor in the fields. Theirs would be a life of luxury, of respect, free from the ridicule of others. And when he achieved that dream, the first car I remember him buying was a big, white Lincoln Continental.

(Many years later, when preparing to write this book, I discovered that my perceptions of the amount of alcoholism in Lakeville were not accurate. Because of all the heavy drinking among my grandparents, as well as Dad's admitted substance abuse long before a would-be assassin left him partially paralyzed, I thought he was raised in a community of drunks. However, after talking with people who had been there, I learned that drinking was prevalent, alcoholism was not.)

There were only three activities to vary the pace of life when Dad was growing up. The first was drinking moonshine. Whiskey was too expensive to buy but easy to make. Bootlegging was common, and every evening after work, the men in the more isolated areas of Magoffin County would gather in someone's home, barn, or outbuilding to drink and talk about the day. The jug would be brought out, some people sharing it, others using cups of one sort or another. The idea was not to get drunk. In fact, those who did lose control were frequently not respected. Instead they engaged in what today might be called a rite of male bonding, sipping the liquor and sharing the news that affected their lives. Theirs was an oral tradition, story serving in place of a newspaper few would have been able to read.

Sex was also a popular male-initiated activity. Relations might be with your own wife, someone else's wife, or even your own daughter. Neither incest nor adultery were taboo subjects in Lakeville. Girls were raised to never say "no."

Dad has proudly repeated his own early sexual history. He claims that his first experience was at the age of seven when a neighbor girl of thirteen sought to end his virginity. Nothing happened, of course—he was far too young. But as he later discussed in his autobiography, he thought he had achieved the essence of manhood.

Later he experimented in a way I have since learned is not unusual for rural farm boys in many parts of the country. At the suggestion of a friend, he had sex with a chicken. Scared to let anyone know what he had done, he wrung the chicken's neck, then threw the dead bird in the creek. Although such activities were never repeated, he was amused enough by the experience that he had a stuffed chicken adorn the recreation room of his first mansion in suburban Columbus, Ohio. I find it ironic that Dad, a man who has made millions in part by depicting sexual violence, also murdered his first "lover."

It is impossible for me to fully understand such a culture. As an adult I have come to understand that a woman has the right to choose what happens to her body. Girls, including my own daughter, are taught to be independent, to respect sexuality as a gift from God ideally to be saved for marriage.

Not that I wasn't wild during my teen years. I did my own rebelling against a home life often filled with neglect and verbal abuse. It is just that a woman forever at the sexual mercy of all the men in her community is incomprehensible to me. Yet Dad was shown by frequent example that women were meant for the sexual pleasure of men.

CS

Sex addiction is multigenerational. I learned this when I finally had to admit to the nightmares I was having. Reading about Dad's upcoming movie, eventually obtaining a script and prerelease video copy of the feature, I was troubled by the hero worship. There was something wrong, something I had tried to repress over the years. It was only at night, when I had fought going to bed as long as possible, when my husband was worried about my health and my daughter despaired of my being too tired to play with her because of lack of sleep, that I would finally let myself remember. There was the time in the Columbus, Ohio, apartment when I was around the same age as my own child. There was the time in the rented mansion in Palm Beach, Florida. There was . . . .

My stomach began to ache and the color drained from my face. I had been speaking out against pornography's impact in society for more than a year. I had talked with thousands of college students, many of whom had brothers, fathers, or other relatives obsessively hooked on magazines such as were produced by Larry Flynt Publications. They shared their stories of shattered marriages where negative fantasy prevented true commitment. They told of neglect by a parent whose free time was spent looking at magazines or searching for sexual images on the Internet. And they told of incest, gently committed, by fathers and grandfathers who first convinced them that inappropriate touching was the loving way for a parent to show a daughter how to love.

The stories were ones I knew well. The stories were ones I had lived. My grandfather. My father. My Dad's own parents, my paternal grandparents, were like characters from a parody of a country western song turned soap opera. Dad's mother was fourteen when Dad's father took a liking to her. He went to his future father-in-law and together they decided on Grandma's worth if Grandpa was to be given her hand in marriage. Great-grandpa got a jug of moonshine and Grandpa got Dad's mother. In the land Dad always called the "holler" (the hollow or valley in which Lakeville was situated), marriage was at least as much about property rights as it was about commitment.

There is no question in my mind that Dad's understanding about sexuality and interpersonal relations was horribly skewed by the world in which he was raised. However, my compassion for his past ended when I realized he knew how wrong it was in the eyes of the greater society. Long after escaping Lakeville, long after his period of self-education while in the Navy, long after he had experienced a real marriage and success in the business world, he consciously chose to be a man without sexual boundaries. If it felt good to him, he would do it, even if he dared not admit to such desires and actions in any public forum. But that story will be told later in this book.

Dad was raised in the manner of many boys with the misfortune of being conceived during wartime. His father was drafted a month before Dad's birth and did not come home to spend time with him until October 1945, when Dad was almost three years old.

The following year Judy Flynt was born, a child who died of leukemia five years later. And in 1948, Jimmy Flynt became part of the family. There had been one other child, a girl, but she was dead at birth.

Money was always scarce. Dad's father worked as a sharecropper, a plumber, and a handyman. In a county of just five hundred people, with many of them living in relative isolation, most of the men could claim to be a jack-of-all-trades. My grandfather's abilities were thus in limited demand, daily life always a struggle for enough food.

Perhaps it was the alcoholism of Dad's father. Perhaps it was the brutality, both Dad and his mother being beaten with some frequency. Perhaps it was the death of his sister in a tiny county hospital with few more amenities than a well-stocked first-aid station. Or perhaps there was truth to the rumors that Dad's mother was seeking men outside her marriage. All I know is that there was a time when his parents had had enough of each other. She found a waitress job in Hammond, Indiana, taking my eleven-year-old father with her while leaving Jimmy with his paternal grandfather.

The violence and alcoholism in the home, the loss of his sister to death, the loss of his brother, Jimmy, to their grandparents, and the loss of all that was familiar through the move to Indiana, were heart-wrenching for Dad. He developed a love/hate relationship with his mother. He also acted out in many different ways, biting his nails, having violent stomach pains, and wetting his bed until he was thirteen years old. There were times he tried to run away, but when he was twelve and a half, his mother having divorced his father and remarried, it was obvious the situation was out of hand. Dad went to live with relatives, then managed to enlist in the Army.

Years later Dad would care for his dying mother in his Bel Air mansion. He loved her deeply and was determined to ease the suffering of her final days. Yet there was great anger, too. Later he would talk of her being promiscuous. He resented her many lovers and several husbands. He called her a "whore," yet she was also the type of woman to whom he was attracted during many of his extramarital affairs.

I understood that men such as my father did not get rich creating pictures and cartoons for a man or woman who might look at such things every few years. Just as beer companies love Joe Six-Pack, the alcoholic whose habit does not yet interfere with his work, so Dad and others only desire the addict. Pornography can create an insatiable curiosity and desire for ever more distorted, violent, and/or sexually abusive images, and pornographers do all they can to ensure that the casual viewer becomes the steady user. When people do become addicted, as Dad is, as I was, they eventually are desensitized to what they see, craving more and different material. They are desensitized to the joys in healthy relationships. They may act out in obviously horrible ways, though most are personally destructive of all they once valued, all they once cherished.

Two of Dad's wives are dead from overdoses of drugs. My family includes both substance abusers and at least one sex addict. And I was almost broken by a father who wanted me to relate love with incestuous child molestation.

All because of pornography.

In the Army, Dad's true age was never discovered. Eventually he went from Fort Jackson, South Carolina, to Fort Leonard Wood, Missouri. For some reason he was enrolled in engineering school there. I don't know whether he was placed there by random selection or if he had to take some sort of test to get that assignment. His exposure to math, surely a basic for such training, had been limited at best. I doubt Dad had the equivalent of first-year high school algebra by the time he joined the military. And certainly his service record, including the fast discharge, indicated he couldn't bluff his way through the training.[2]

Years later Dad would admit to psychologists that the Army discharge was his one secret in life, his one true shame.[3] Certainly it was not something he has revealed in either his magazines or his autobiography. I can only imagine that he has never put the situation in perspective, never admitted that any fourteen-year-old school dropout whose earliest education was in a community primarily peopled by semiliterates, would have had an equally hard time.

Dad already knew he could pass as being older than his years and chose not to return to school when he was tossed out of the Army. Instead, he moved to Dayton, where his uncle lived. He found a room he could rent for $7 a week, a dishwashing job that paid 95 cents an hour, and settled down to the good life. He bought beer and chased girls, presumably finding little resistance to his pursuits.

Next came a job at The Inland, a position that briefly brought him more money. However, he was unskilled, and the job was one that just needed a warm body to handle. As a result, he was in the first wave to be let go when a steel strike idled many of the plants supplying parts for automobiles.

Dad was overwhelmed with emotion. Everything he was doing had not worked. Yet he could not understand how that could be.

Mom told me that during this time Dad was idealistic. He had dreams, plans, the belief that if he set his mind to a task, he could achieve it no matter what the odds. Yet suddenly that sense of self had been shattered. He felt he had lost all self-respect, his life in constant turmoil.[4] He felt he had to return to the military, had to succeed at something.

Dad entered the Navy with the attitude that nothing was going to stop his success. He admitted on enlistment to having a limited education, willingly completing his GED in the service before going on to specialized training. He was assigned to the Great Lakes Naval Training School, never mentioning his prior failure in the Army. (This was an era when computers were too unsophisticated for tracking current and former military personnel. His past was never uncovered.) After finishing boot camp, Dad returned to Dayton, where he was briefly married.

According to the often repeated story, he wanted sex with this first wife, nothing more. Although she was allegedly quite experienced, something he claims to have learned later, she seemed to be a woman who only believed in sex after marriage. She refused to go to bed with Dad unless he was honorable. Dad had no respect for virgins saving themselves for marriage, but he apparently wanted to have sex with her enough to have a ceremony.

Once again nothing went as planned. She had the financial stability of being a Navy wife, receiving an allotment check that eased her life. He had a willing bedmate. Yet it was not enough to keep them together. When Dad also heard that she had allegedly been quite promiscuous with other men prior to him, they separated after two weeks and were divorced after six months.

That was his story, anyway. I have since learned that whenever Dad wants to get out of a relationship, he will either lie or convince himself that the woman is or was promiscuous, even if there is no proof. He fantasizes the woman is going to be the way he viewed his own mother after her divorce from his dad. I don't believe his version of the truth about some of these women. I think his statements are often just self-serving ways to displace his anger toward his own mother.

The incident made Dad mistrustful of women. He may have been raised in a community with no taboos, but when living in Dayton, Dad expected women to be morally upright when they married. He was confused, angry, and frustrated, and it was with this background coloring his thinking that Dad was set up to meet Mom.

The date occurred in the home of my Great-Grandma Jackson. She was a gentle, loving soul according to everyone who knew her. She was also someone who would have been morally outraged had she known much of what was eventually to take place.

Both my mother, who was fourteen, and my grandma were living in Great-Grandma Jackson's house at the time. Grandma and her boyfriend knew Dad and decided to bring him over to introduce him to Mom.

Oddly, despite what happened during his brief first marriage, Dad was a romantic back then. He had discovered both poetry and the power of the poetic image in the Navy during his period of self-education through endless reading. He also enjoyed sharing what he read with my mother, enhancing his image in her eyes.

While Mom may have experienced lust at first sight of Larry Flynt, there was always some sort of tension between my maternal grandmother and my father. Perhaps it was sexual. Dad's picture from those days shows a handsome, lean young man with a wholesomeness that seems right out of one of the Mickey Rooney/Judy Garland movies periodically shown on late-night television. He had a combination of aw-shucks bashful folksiness with a glint in his eye that hinted at trouble in a way that just might be fun. It was an image I could see being very appealing to women in those days.

Or perhaps Grandma simply saw in Larry Flynt the end of her daughter's teenage innocence, or what was left of it. Her youthful efforts to experience adult pleasures aborted her childhood, forced her to parent long before she was ready, and left her unable to nurture as we kids desired. When Grandma felt like going to a bar and didn't have one of her regular drinking buddies available, she would take Mom. She acted in much the same way as less dysfunctional mothers might go with their daughters to Scout meetings, school activities, and family-oriented health clubs.

All I know for certain is that Larry Flynt became a symbol of something beyond the adolescent young man that he was. He was a focus for Grandma's rage, and when she attacked him for loving Mom, it was with an act that should have been unimaginable for a healthy mind.

Dad and Mom were sexual during those first days of dating. The nation was in the midst of the Cold War. The Soviet Union was an enemy who was quietly changing the balance of power by shipping atomic weapons to Cuba, ninety miles off the Florida coast. While missiles coming from Europe and Asia might be difficult to target, having a Cuban launch site guaranteed that, if used, they could accurately destroy such critical cities as New York and Washington. All the men and women in the military, including Dad, were on alert for what they knew might become war.

Mom was both deeply in love with Dad and not a virgin when they met. Dad considered sex a natural part of any date, and Mom was a willing partner, both of them convinced, at least in the eyes of their friends, that they would be together "forever."

Dad had another reason to live as though there might be no tomorrow when the United States experienced what became known as the Cuban Missile Crisis. He was ordered to go from where he was—in Mom's arms, as it turned out—to the USS *Enterprise*, which would take him and others to the Caribbean.

There was going to be a showdown before even one missile could be launched.

For several days the nation was prepared for a war that would have brought nuclear destruction to the North American continent. Observation plane photos, spies working from Cuba, and others provided constant information about the actions being taken. A blockade of the island country was begun, American ships sent to interdict anyone challenging the blockade. Many were also equipped for attack, the nation in a deadly state of preparedness.

Eventually, of course, the Soviet Union backed down. Dad's ship returned to the United States, where he was granted shore leave to visit Dayton. What he did not expect was that Mom had gotten pregnant.

Pregnancy in the 1960s was a very different matter than it is today. Abortion was not legal and few skilled doctors would even consider performing one. When they did, it was usually for someone in a family they had known both personally and professionally for many years. Some girls resorted to home methods that ranged from the useless and the bizarre, such as intense exercise to create a spontaneous abortion, to the deadly, such as using a coat hanger to kill the fetus. The latter frequently brought about internal bleeding that could leave a woman sterile, if she survived.

Other girls went away to homes where arrangements were made to deliver the baby at term, then give it up for adoption before anyone learned she had been pregnant. And still others used illegal abortionists—skilled neighbors, some of whom were nurses. The availability of their services was spread by word of mouth.

Mom might have used any one of them. Certainly within a plant as large as The Inland, women occasionally became pregnant against their will, had abortions, and became the subject for gossip. Grandma might have known of someone who could perform such an act for just that reason, though I never asked how it all came about. I do not want to know the details of an act my mother would never consider today. It was a traumatic and shameful time for her.

All that is certain is that Grandma took Mom to an abortionist. The abortionist was apparently the lowest kind because there was no effort to remove the fetus, no effort to protect Mom. Instead, the abortionist killed the fetus in the womb, after which Mom passed it in the toilet. In great physical and emotional pain, horrified by what had happened, Mom learned shortly thereafter that instead of what might pass for humane disposal, Grandma took the fetus from the toilet and saved it in a jar with a preserving chemical.

The fetus was probably taken at the end of the first trimester, just late enough to be fully formed on the outside. Grandma was determined to show it to Dad when he returned from sea duty because she was outraged with him for not marrying my pregnant mother.

What is unclear to me was whether or not Dad even knew she was pregnant. Given how long he was at sea, and since I didn't think I might be pregnant with my own daughter until my period was two weeks late, Dad may not have known what happened. Certainly Mom would not have gone to the doctor. She probably would have waited until she was scared by missing two periods in a row before she faced Grandma's potential wrath. This would have made Grandma's anger at Dad even more outrageous.

It was on that first date following his return from the waters off Cuba that Dad was shown the jar with the fetus. Grandma carefully pointed out the tiny eyes that were just forming, the hands, the tiny penis that proved the child would have been Larry's first son. Dad began hyperventilating and consumed a large glass of whiskey. He must have been in shock, outraged, horrified; he ended up having to be treated in the hospital. Dad did not believe in abortion. Grandma did not believe in pregnancy without marriage. Mom emotionally withdrew, hating her mother, desperate for the man she loved, not knowing what to do about anyone or anything.

Incident after incident was piling up on Dad. He had been writing to Mom quite regularly, frequently including copies of poems he had read that he felt would touch her heart. Some she believed he wrote himself. Other poetry he found in books and magazines. There had been a gentleness to him, a love for Mom and a genuine friendship with Grandma that transcended their frequent arguments and hostile banter.

Now nothing was right. He had been hurt by his mother, hurt by his first wife, hurt by my grandmother, and because of the abortion, hurt by Mom. He was in a daze, and though he claimed he quickly recovered from the incident, I have my doubts.

When Dad finally returned to the USS *Enterprise* for a six-month deployment in the Mediterranean, he read voraciously on his own and studied hard in his classes. Thirty-nine sailors were going through Navy training with him, and when graduation came, he was seventh. For a youth who had dropped out of ninth grade in a community where education was little better than the one-room schoolhouse days, this was a remarkable feat. For Dad, it was what was necessary to restore his self-esteem. After that triumph, nothing was going to stop him. Certainly not a woman.

"Dear Peggy," Dad wrote to Mom. "I have decided to break off with you. I need to go on with my life."

Dad eventually exaggerated his importance about this time. He would later make clear that the captain of the ship so relied upon his expertise that he would not launch a missile unless Larry Flynt was on board. ("There's something special about me," he wrote in a letter. "The U.S. Navy had to depend on an enlisted man. . . . I learned all the jobs on the ship. I had my hands into everything on the ship."[5]) While Dad deserved respect for his achievements

("... excellent Petty Officer and Radarman ... extreme willingness and shows ... initiative ..." according to his record), this was the Cold War. He was on a ship that was still primed for war. To think that someone of Dad's age and experience could become so important to the seasoned captain was nonsense. It was also the first hint of the manic character Dad would exhibit many times in more extreme ways in the future. Eventually he would be diagnosed as a manic-depressive, a more likely reason for his bragging than deliberately lying.

While Dad was elated, Mom was devastated. She had little self-esteem, no goals, no thought beyond the day. With Dad so prominently in her life while they were dating regularly, Mom at least could share what she felt was his dream of the little white house with the picket fence and children playing happily in the yard. Without Dad, with no interest in education, no support from her mother, no friends beyond ones with whom she had gone barhopping, Mom became severely depressed. Experiencing all the intense emotions only a teenager in the throes of adolescence can endure, she took to her bed, wanting to die. Grandma, never much of a success with men herself, finally convinced Mom to escape in the manner that was all too familiar. She asked Mom to go to the Sip-N-Nip bar in Dayton where Mom could drink away her pain.

It was at the Sip-N-Nip that Mom was introduced to Frank Reed, one of Grandma's drinking buddies. Frank was single, not that much older than Mom, and Grandma thought they should go out together. Depressed, drunk, and feeling as though there would never be another man in her life who mattered as much as Larry Flynt, the one she had just lost, Mom agreed.

Mom was a beautiful woman in those days, her soft, sensual voice as erotic as her excellent figure. Frank fell in love with Mom, and though she did not love him, he seemed her only hope to have someone care for her. On one of their dates they went to bed together and Mom got pregnant with my older sister.

And then the letter came.

It was not from Dad, of course. Even back then he tried to avoid admitting to having intense emotions about another person. Instead he had a friend write to explain how upset Dad was. The friend wrote that Dad thought about her all the time, that he knew Dad really loved her. He suggested that Mom write directly to Dad, telling him she wanted him back in her life. Dad loved Mom so much he wanted her to make the first move.

As usual, the letter was manipulative and almost demeaning in hindsight. As would become routine, Mom overlooked the negatives and was thrilled. However, she did not write the letter.

Instead, Dad was in Greece when he got the courage to directly contact Mom. He telephoned her, asking her to marry him when he returned to the United States. Naturally, she accepted.

Mom was not totally naive. She was certain Dad had probably cheated on her, something to which he later confessed. She was pregnant with another man's child, determined that this one would not be aborted as Dad's son had been. In the throes of teenage love, she was both terrified of his finding out and elated that he was coming home. Larry Flynt loved her. Larry Flynt was returning to her. Perhaps Larry Flynt loved her as much as she loved him. They could work it out. . . . They could. . . .

Mom started taking diet pills during this period. These were prescription amphetamines, known as "black beauties" when purchased underground. Back then doctors were more casual about a woman's health, including during pregnancy, which is why Mom had such an easy time getting what is now known to be dangerous. I suspect she was trying to lose body fat as she gained pounds with the baby growing in her womb. There was never any question about having sex with Dad when he returned, and I think she planned to try to convince him the baby was his. So long as it arrived full term, she could either get him to think it was premature or hope he loved the child and her so much it no longer mattered who was the father.

As it turned out, the diet pills affected the pregnancy in ways Mom had not anticipated. My sister Judy was born premature and weighed a little over three pounds, just large enough to survive. At birth she fit in the palm of the nurse's hand.

As I understand it, Dad and Mom were intimate when he realized she was in the early stages of pregnancy. He found the bulge in her belly and freaked out. Mom, in tears, tried to explain about the impact of Dad's first letter, about her devastation that Dad had told her they were finished. She tried to explain about the severe depression, about taking to her bed, about Grandma endlessly prodding her to go out with Judy's father. Dad would hear none of it. He told her he could not take it. He had to get away. He fled from the hotel room, leaving Mom hysterical.

Later, calmer, Dad decided he loved Mom enough to take a chance with her. He would not let anything happen to Mom or the growing baby inside her womb. He said he would marry her and give the child a good name, that of his beloved baby sister who died of leukemia at age five: Judy Flynt. What he did not say was that he would also go out and beat up Frank Reed so severely that Reed was left with a permanent limp.

The marriage to Mom was everything she ever wanted in life. Larry was her beloved, her once in a lifetime chance for all the happiness for which she had ever dreamed. No matter what had happened before, no matter with whom she had been involved, her one aspiration from the moment she met Dad was to be Mrs. Larry Flynt.

The fact that Dad would give Judy his name proved his love. The fact that she became pregnant with me meant there would be a new generation of "pure" Flynts. Yet while there should have been at least some rejoicing, Mom quickly realized that the heaven she fantasized was, in reality, increasingly a nightmare she did not know how to change or escape. It was a remarkable period of tension, violence, and madness, all of which Mom, knowing no alternative, chose to ignore.

Mom briefly moved to Virginia Beach, where Dad was stationed. Grandma decided to visit them, her departure ironically occurring on November 22, 1963, the day John Kennedy was assassinated. Dad did not want to see his mother-in-law, did not want her in his home, and the stress was compounded by the horror of that day. Grandma later commented to me, "I flew down for a visit. The day I got there and Larry saw that I was there, Peggy and Larry went to his friend's house and Peggy called me and told me to go back to Ohio. Larry didn't want me there."

Dad constantly hounded Mom about getting pregnant, even though all of us kids thought Judy was Dad's daughter. For years he never said anything different. In fact, there would be times when Judy was the favored child, especially by Dad's fourth and most famous wife, Althea. However, in hindsight I realize that perhaps the favoritism was precisely because she was not Dad's daughter.

Grandma made it very clear that she hated my dad. She also seemed to hate me during the years when I was growing up, something I could not understand. Finally I asked her why she was always so mean to me, why she seemed to despise my very existence when I had done nothing to earn her wrath. She told me it was because every time she looked at my face, she saw the mirror image of my father.

In the beginning of our relationship, Althea was often vicious to me as well, and perhaps she, too, did not want me being so obviously my father's daughter. After all, even though Althea was promiscuous, even though she knew Dad had other wives and other children, I don't think she wanted to think about the other women in his life. She wanted to fantasize that she was his first and greatest love, something a daughter so blatantly his own would not let her do.

In any case, Judy would be fourteen before any of us knew the truth. In fact, I think that under Ohio law, by marrying Mom when she was pregnant, he became her legal father. But Frank Reed was the biological parent.

Another reason for Grandma's hostility was that she knew Dad had long played around. He may have fallen in love with Mom when she was fourteen, but Grandma knew he also was messing around.

There is a sexist joke about the man who brags that he has no children "he knows about." It was only in 1997, when I was a grown woman with a daughter of my own, that Dad discovered DNA testing revealed a previously unknown daughter who is a biochemist in Florida. Ironically, she is the exact same age as I am. While Dad has long attacked Mom for being promiscuous, Dad obviously got both Mom and the mother of my previously unknown half sister pregnant within a matter of weeks of each other. Grandma was right.

For example, there was the time when Dad, some girl he knew, Grandma, and her friend Daryl went out drinking. Everyone was in Dad's car, Grandma being the first person to feel the effect of the liquor and the lateness of the hour. She wanted to go home, which was no problem. It was just a casual evening out, though Dad had been whispering to the girl throughout the evening, as though he had other plans. However, neither he nor the girl said anything, all of them content with drinking, talking, and dancing until Grandma wanted to go home.

Dad drove them back, dropping the girl off first because she lived closest to the bar. Then Dad drove Grandma and Daryl to their homes.

Grandma would have been none the wiser for what was happening had she and Daryl not been in the backseat. Daryl's wallet fell out of his pocket and he was home before he knew it was missing. Figuring it was probably in Dad's car, he called Dad to check. But Dad wasn't home.

Daryl had his own car, but he couldn't look for Dad's car and drive at the same time. He called Grandma, who agreed to accompany him as they made the rounds of the parking lots of bars still open, figuring Dad was drinking on his own.

Dad's car was in none of the bar lots, but as they drove by some of the cheap motels, Grandma spotted the car in front of one of the units. They parked, Daryl going to the room they assumed was Dad's, knocking on the door to have Dad come out and unlock the car.

As it turned out, Dad didn't lock anything. When there was no response to the knocking, Daryl tried the door handle. This was in the days when some cheap motel doors had to be specially locked both inside and out. They did not have an automatic locking mechanism when you closed them. The door opened when Daryl tried it, and Dad was in the room, in bed with his date from earlier that evening. Too much drinking, presumably combined with sex, had left them both so exhausted, they were out cold.

On the chance that Dad was equally careless with his car, Daryl shut the motel door and tried the car door. It also opened and his wallet was on the backseat, right where it had fallen out of his pocket. Daryl told Grandma what happened, something they both found rather humorous, I suppose. The trouble was that Dad soon was stepping out on Grandma's daughter, and I guess that, for her, put his promiscuity in a different light.

Dad's marital problems were overwhelming him. He claimed later that they had no effect on him, but this was still when he was a loving, gentle man with Mom, filled with ambitions she supported because, through marriage, she had achieved her only dream in life. I have no idea if he realized the changes he was starting to undergo. Certainly he did not mention them in his autobiography. However, the changes were noted in his Navy record.

∽

U.S. Naval Hospital, Portsmouth, Virginia. Report dated January 5, 1964:

> This 23-year-old RD2 has had reoccurring difficulties for one year. His symptoms have at various times included light headedness, spells of pain and numbness of neck and arms and face, insomnia, arrested breathing while asleep, hyperventilation, hysteria (whole body shaking) etc. He has had a great deal of psychic trauma centered around his sex and marital life. But even with insight and extensive support and superficial psychotherapy by several medical officers, he has been unable to cope. Diagnosed with "Anxiety Reaction."

Dad requested a transfer to the USS *Randolph* because the ship was closer to Dayton. His Navy record indicates he was having some serious domestic difficulties, but there was no reason for the transfer. As a result, Dad wrote a letter that seemingly was meant to get him discharged from the Navy, though it was later found that most of the phrases were copied from Henry Miller's *Tropic of Cancer* and *Tropic of Capricorn*:

> I am the evil product of an evil soul. . . . To some this may seem like an invention, but whatever I imagined to have happened did actually happen, at least to me. History may deny it since I never have nor probably never will play a part in the history of my people. But even if everything I say is wrong, prejudice, spite-

ful, malevolent; even if I am a liar and a poisoner, it is never the less the truth, and it will have to be swallowed. . . . I imagined that somewhere outside in life, as they say, allay the solution to all things, and you just have to reach out for them, in the right manner, of course, so I did. I really thought I was seizing hold of life, seizing hold of something I could bite into; instead I lost hold of completely. I reached out for something to hold on to and found nothing. But in the reaching out in the effort to grasp, to attach myself to, I never the less found something I had not looked for—myself. Sometimes I think it would have been better had I been a man like Oswald and shot some good man like President Kennedy, some gentle insignificant soul like that who never had done anyone the least bit of harm. I would have wanted to see this happen out of pure vengeance, atonement for the crimes committed against me and others who have never been able to express their hatred or raise their voices, their rebellion, their legitimate blood lust. I was deceived into serving my country in the U.S. Navy. I was told that I lived in a free country where freedom is upheld by a true democratic way of life, and that I should be willing to preserve it. I did not know what democracy was but it sounded good. Now that I know, I think it stinks: neither do I advocate communism, but rather the esteemed integrity of my own individuality. I have no desire to be a leader or to contribute any good in any way to my country. I realize that because of my rebellious and destructive attitude I will be punished according to rules and regulations. That is why I am making it easy for the people concerned. I know what the Navy expects of a petty officer and a man. I did not meet these expectations.

Dad was recommended for an administrative discharge by his commanding officer based on the June 10, 1964, neuropsychiatric report. As quoted in the January 5 statement, Dad was suffering from past emotional instability. On July 2, 1964, Radarman Second Class was discharged from the Navy by reason of unsuitability. His achievements had been the high point of his life until then.

Dad returned to a life that he never quite wanted. He was exhibiting signs of manic-depressive illness, a diagnosis that was still years in the making. And in his more manic stages, he was becoming increasingly impressed with himself, his potential, and his future even though he lacked any direction other than fame and fortune.

While still in the Navy, he had read Harold Robbins's novel *The Carpetbaggers* and was so impressed that he decided that he wanted Robbins to one day write the story of his own life. This might be a novel. It might be nonfiction. But Dad would be the larger-than-life, hustling, world-conquering success adored by women and admired by men. He even went so far as to learn the name of the hotel on the French Riviera where Robbins lived while in France. Each time he was on shore leave in the area he would walk back and forth in front of the hotel, hoping to somehow be in Robbins's presence.

Upon returning to the United States, Dad returned to Dayton and a job at The Inland like seemingly every other male with his background. Mom was pregnant with me and the income was such that the family would be fine—just like everyone else who had entry-level jobs with General Motors. He would not be different. He would not be special.

Dad began working part-time in bars, including the one owned by his mother and aunt. He well understood the importance of the bars in the social fabric of working-class Dayton. And as he mastered the business, he decided to make a move into bar ownership. He called his first bar Larry's Hillbilly Heaven, and he deliberately sought out the Appalachian whites who had migrated to the area to escape the grinding poverty of their youth. The business was an immediate success and Dad quickly left The Inland behind.

During this same period Dad and Grandma got into a fight. The tension began when Grandma had Mom and Judy at her apartment. Unknown to Mom, Grandma arranged for Frank Reed to visit, knowing that Dad would be stopping by for Mom.

Dad arrived, saw Frank, and freaked out, yelling, screaming, and ready to tear someone apart. He first turned his wrath toward Mom, who convinced him that she was as surprised by Frank's visit as he was. Then he turned to Grandma, taking out a handgun and firing it into the air.

Grandma called the police, telling them that Dad was trying to kill her. They raced to the scene, but Dad had fled, going over to his mother's, where the officers found him and arrested him, planning to charge him with attempted murder. He was taken to jail, at which time everyone realized that no one had the gun.

Dad was not holding it when they arrived for the arrest. It was not found when they frisked him. They did not find it in his car when they searched that. There was an allegation of shooting, yet the weapon had disappeared.

The police returned to Grandma's and told her they couldn't find the gun. She said they should strip-search him if necessary because he had a gun and had been shooting.

The police did as Grandma suggested and found a gun—small, loaded, and recently fired. Between the time Dad fled Grandma's apartment and the time the police arrived at his mother's, Dad had taped the weapon next to his groin.

There was no question of Dad's guilt so far as the shooting was concerned. There was also no way he was likely to be able to prove he had not tried to kill Grandma. As a result, his lawyer told Dad to act crazy to avoid a lengthy jail sentence, which he did. Or so the story goes.

Electric shock therapy was the dirty little secret of psychiatric wards in hospitals in the 1960s. It had been in use for many years, but the way it worked was never understood.

Originally electric shock was used solely for extremely depressed patients living in isolation in the back wards of mental hospitals. These individuals would often sit for hours, staring without seeing, not talking, not responding to others. They were not autistic. They were intelligent and capable of pursuing any job they liked. Yet no amount of counseling would help them as they never gave any indication that they were listening.

Pharmaceutical research changed all that. Tranquilizers, stimulants, and mood-altering medications made electric shock therapy unnecessary. A pill allowed a former back ward patient to leave the hospital. He or she could hold a job, attend school, and lead a normal life, receiving outpatient counseling for whatever emotional problems led to the depression.

For a while electric shock therapy went out of favor. Even the practitioners admitted that the results were temporary at best and that sometimes it did more harm than good. Yet in the 1960s electric shock was again being used, though with the same precautions in effect a generation earlier when pharmaceutical alternatives had not been developed.

Dad's "crazy" act landed him in Dartmouth Hospital (later Dayton State Hospital) for thirty days. During that time his record indicates he underwent electric shock therapy, a fact that may suggest more than anyone realizes.

Some people familiar with Dad's records feel that he was far more seriously mentally ill than just troubled by the chemical imbalance of manic-depressive illness. With such a problem, the person does not manufacture adequate lithium salts. Taking a prescribed dosage of lithium corrects the imbalance, usually with no side effects. It was not something for which electric shock would have been given, and by this reasoning, they suspect either a genetic problem or a severe trauma such as seeing the fetus of what would have been his son as the cause. Despite this none of my siblings I've discussed this with ever felt love from Dad. I just don't think he is capable.

I wonder if Dad was essentially healthy when he faked being crazy. Certainly he was manic-depressive, but other than that he was playing a role. The electric shock was a response to his pretense. He had to go along with it because he had gotten himself too deeply committed to faking mental illness in order to avoid jail. If this is true, then I suspect Dad's later genuine problems were the result of damage caused by the unneeded treatment he endured.

From what can be learned about that period, Dad would have had to have been experiencing severe depression, not responding to staff questions, and perhaps not responding to routine medication. There would have been consent, but that could have come either from Dad or someone else authorized to act on his behalf. Whatever the case, it was not routine and would almost certainly not have been administered to a man pretending to be mentally ill. Years later, when hospital records indicate Dad was suffering from bipolar disorder (more popularly known as manic-depressive illness), the answer may have been found. Just as Dad's belief that he was the key player in the Navy represented a high point of manic grandiosity, so this time in Dartmouth Hospital may have reflected the other extreme: the depressive side of the disorder.

Mom noticed a very specific change in Dad. He still lusted after her. However, she told me, after the therapy his personal desires were different. She felt that before the hospital, he genuinely wanted a relationship that would work. Maybe he would one day abandon their shared dream of the suburban cottage with white picket fence for the grandiose mansions in which he lives to this day. But the idea of having a family, of having a wife and children, of making that family the base from which all else happened, was gone.

Other information would be uncovered about Dad long after the electric shock therapy. On February 12, 1964, just before his Navy discharge, Dad's medical records indicated that he was suffering from a long-standing personality disorder and emotional instability reaction. Later, during a hospital visit in June of that year, Dad was noted to have previously been diagnosed as having a sociopathic personality. It was also noted that Dad was sometimes acting out his violent tendencies and that he had recent thoughts of suicide.

Whatever the truth of all this, what is known is that Dad was never the same after he left Dartmouth. Mom has talked about the change in him, the end to the romantic, caring, gentle man. He had become emotionally distant in ways that may have continued the rest of his life.

Dad was also extremely insecure about women as Mom increasingly showed her pregnancy at the end of 1964. Earlier he had brought his brother Jimmy to live with the family. Mom, Dad, and Judy were in a Dayton apartment that really wasn't equipped for another adult. However, Jimmy had broken his arm and Dad thought he should be around family. The fact that the break was healing and it in no way hindered Jimmy from taking care of himself did not matter. Dad was trying to bring together whatever family he could.

Jimmy took advantage of the situation, something Dad would not understand until years later when Jimmy made an effort to take control of the *Hustler* empire while Dad was in jail. He ordered Mom about, demanding that she meet his every whim. She was feeling the discomfort of her pregnancy with me, had a toddler in diapers, and needed to take care of the house for Dad.

Uncle Jimmy denied Mom's accusations and Dad decided to

believe him. Mom and Dad were increasingly estranged, Dad alternating between being loving and almost sadistically angry. When he would become irate with Mom, he would pinch her skin, then twist it to cause her pain, smiling as he watched her face.

Although he hated his alcoholic, abusive father, Dad somehow seemed to feel he could trust men and not women. Mom had already obviously cheated on him when she got pregnant with Judy, Dad never admitting he had done the same to her around the same time. Now she was implying that his brother was somehow causing her overwhelming problems. He chose to side with Uncle Jimmy. He ordered Mom to pack her bag, take Judy, and leave.

As I say, Mom would do anything for Dad, including not argue with him when he was wrong. She packed a suitcase and left, walking out into one of the winter snowstorms that were common in Dayton. She had the suitcase in one hand, a carefully bundled up Judy in the other. There was no place to go but Grandma's.

It was like an old-fashioned melodrama, both Dad and Grandma belittling Mom for having no place to go. Worse for Mom, the anger never subsided. A few weeks later, after Mom went into labor, Dad was called from the hospital. He was working his shift at The Inland and his boss immediately told him to go be with his wife. Dad actually had the nerve to refuse, not wanting to be bothered even though his boss insisted that it was the right thing for a man to do when his wife was giving birth.

The incident with Uncle Jimmy was compounded by Dad's fantasies. No matter what had happened before their marriage, Mom adored Dad. She was not only faithful to him, she could not conceive of ever wanting any other man to touch her again. Her unfaltering devotion led to many heated arguments with Grandma, neither ever willing to back down. Yet Dad never saw all this. He never really seemed to understand just what he meant to his wife.

The problem arose when Mom and Dad were living in Virginia, Dad still in the Navy, Mom just seventeen and without friends or family nearby. Dad, in one of his mood swings, announced that he was going to leave her and never come back.

Mom, not used to what would later become Dad's very familiar mood swings, was severely depressed. She was sitting outside when a neighbor, perhaps more caring than Mom had realized those around her would be, stopped by to talk. She invited Mom to go to the Jolly Roger's, a popular Virginia Beach nightclub. Mom agreed to go.

While at the nightclub, Mom met another young man who was in the Navy. She was ready to go home, the neighbor who had brought her wanting to stay at the bar. The place was in walking distance of her apartment, so Mom decided to leave. The area was a little rough, the Navy man was hoping to know Mom better, so when he offered to walk her home, she agreed.

The man stepped briefly into the entrance of Mom and Dad's second floor unit when Dad unexpectedly returned. Mom quickly closed the door, telling the man he would have to hurry out the back. At the same time, Dad was banging on the front, demanding to be let inside.

Mom was hysterical, the man even more frightened. She was determined to not let Dad enter until the other man was out the back, never realizing that when she did open up, Dad would spot the other man fleeing.

Suddenly the chase was on. The Navy man ran and so did Dad. The Navy man ran faster, and Dad was no match. Livid, he returned to the apartment.

Dad grabbed Mom, slapped her, and threw her down. Then, determined to prove he was in charge, he informed her they were going to have sex. To him it was his rightful payoff, the dominant male having vanquished a rival who existed only in his fantasy.

She was battered, bruised, hurting, barely able to stand, yet he seemed to see none of this or to not care about the reality of what he had done. The battle was over, and the victorious warrior was going to gain the spoils he saw as his due.

Mom lay on the floor, staring at him. She was a teenager whose self-esteem had been almost nonexistent before she met Dad. She knew little about what many people would consider a normal childhood, nothing about marriage, about relations between a man and a woman. She thought she was guilty of a horrendous act. She thought my father must be right to some degree to be so angry, so violent. After all, he loved her. He was her husband, she was his wife. If he could do this terrible thing, then she must be even worse than she thought.

There was anger, too, of course. But even this underlying rage was not the rage that fueled courage. Instead, because of the way she was raised, the way she saw herself, the rage only triggered more guilt. She let my father sate himself with her body, weeping bitterly from the pain, the humiliation, and the fact that she must have done something to deserve all that had happened.

The story, which Mom told me hesitantly and tearfully, was chilling. It was something she hid from me, from all us kids, until I was writing this book. And when I heard it, when I realized the horror of it, I began to understand that the hostility toward women displayed in *Hustler* was nothing less than the window into the dark side of my father's soul. It was a dark side I would experience myself.

Years later, Mom realized that Dad had not hidden this evil side during their early courtship. Instead, no matter what problems he may have had prior to going into the hospital for the electric shock, the period after his release marked a steady decline in his words, his actions, even his moral judgment. He had never been a saint. He had never been faithful prior to marriage. But he had never been so sick, so violent, so totally focused inward, misreading even the most obvious, most intimate of his relationships.

When Dad wrote his autobiography, he talked of spitting in Mom's eye, then walking away, never to return. Once again the truth was quite different—though he did initiate the divorce proceedings.

Dad's bitterness was deep. He took Mom over the state line to Kentucky to file for their divorce so he could avoid paying child support for Judy. He was far from rich then, but his income did not matter. He was determined to pay not one dime more for child support than he had to, something he angrily told Mom.

All I know is that in the early days of their relationship, Dad loved Mom. I don't know if he was obsessed with her as she seemed to be with him. All I know is that he would periodically return to her life after their divorce, wanting her to make love with him, asking her to marry him again.

Sometimes Dad's return would be romantic—or as romantic as he could have been after Mom slashed her wrists when Dad threatened to divorce her and dump her in Ohio with her mother.

The romance was not a reaction to Mom's short-term self-destructive behavior, though he certainly knew it had happened. Instead, he just wanted sex with Mom, so one night, months after the divorce, he climbed into the second-floor window of her apartment bedroom. She heard him coming, was amused and also delighted.

At that time, Mom was on her own, living in the apartment with Judy and me. She could not go to work then, much as she was desperate to earn her own way. There were no sitters available, no day care she could afford. She had two children and received $15 a week in child support from Dad. Dad's climbing into the window was like the romantic return of a knight who has been roaming the countryside in search of dragons to slay and cities to conquer, only to realize that home is where his heart has always been. I think she suspected he would carry her off in the same manner I believed would happen to me when growing up. The difference was that he would be my protector, while Mom would again have a lover and life partner. However, when he had enjoyed what he came for, he left. It was not the ending she expected.

There are questions a daughter does not ask, dares not ask. Not as a child. Not as a teenager. Not even now as an adult with a daughter of my own. That is why I have long known almost nothing of Mom and Dad's intimate relations with each other. I didn't know if the gentle romantic who courted Mom by writing her poetry, sending her French perfume and Angora sweaters while on active duty, remained gentle after their marriage. I didn't and do not know if he loved her so much that Judy truly did not matter, for it was many years later that she discovered she was not his natural daughter. I did not know if sex was a joyous celebration of their love or brutal and perverted.

Only now, as Mom and I have talked during the writing of this book, have I begun to see another side to the man I have so deeply loved for so long. Only now have I come to understand the relationship through her eyes.

What I do know is that Mom loved Dad beyond reason, that she would do almost anything for him that he asked.

Even after they were getting divorced and Mom was staying with Grandma, Grandma believed that the two periodically sneaked around together. "She said she loved him and couldn't help it, which burned me up," Grandma later told me. "Her over there [Grandma's home] living with me free of charge." Mom had a newborn infant and a toddler. Dad paid her $15 a week. There was nothing left after necessities, as Grandma knew.

Then Grandma added bitterly, "They sneaked around so much that I didn't know what she was doing." I did not realize how much reason Grandma had to be angry with Dad, at least when it came to child support. And to be honest, Grandma may not have known all the facts. However, in 1975, Dad pleaded guilty to tax evasion. According to his guilty plea, Dad had deliberately not filed tax returns for the $16,000 he earned when I was three years old, and the $21,673 he earned the following year (1969). The conviction received only minor newspaper attention because the judge was lenient, demanding payment of a $5,000 fine within thirty days so he would be given probation, not the two-year jail sentence that was almost imposed. Dad also had to pay back taxes and penalties.

There was reason for Mom taking every opportunity to be with Dad. Despite Dad's paranoid fantasies, Mom was a one-man woman, her love for him lasting through the divorce and remarriages of them both. I also know that either during Dad's marriage to Mom or immediately afterward, he began to be emotionally and, occasionally, physically brutal to women. The sadism and objectification of women that would become the defining characteristics of *Hustler* magazine were creeping into his interpersonal relationships by the end of the 1960s.

Dad met his third wife in 1967. She was a drug abuser who cared more about drugs than either her husband or the children they produced. They married in 1968, divorced in 1970, and had a roller-coaster relationship in between. She was promiscuous, though whether she simply liked men or was so desperate for drugs that she sold her body I don't know. Ultimately she made and lost a fortune on her own, dying of an overdose.

Dad's track record with drug-abusing women is not pretty. Althea, his fourth wife, regularly snorted, smoked, ingested, and shot up everything imaginable. And Dad, so far as I have been able to learn, never tried to help her, never tried to get her into counseling or a residential treatment program.

Dad would later say that he didn't mind a man having sex with his wife, daughter, or grandmother, provided the man asked his permission first. More telling, though, he made the frequently repeated comment, "The man who controls p——y controls the world. I couldn't control her [his third wife] so I didn't want anything to do with her."[6]

2

Bachelor's Beat
and the Start of Hustler

In the 1960s, the entertainment world was just beginning to be taken seriously by newspapers. Typically a city newspaper would run movie listings, television listings, and advertisements for concerts, nightclubs, and restaurants. Some newspapers restricted certain types of entertainment advertising, excluding places where there were go-go dancers, strippers, or other activities perceived as potentially offensive to the readers. Advertising copy had to be conservative in tone, and photographs, if any, could never hint of sex or heavy drinking.

In Phoenix, Arizona, Boye De Mente and a partner created *Bachelor's Beat*, a tabloid weekly covering the local entertainment industry. The publication primarily circulated in the various clubs, combining advertising with stories about the performers, the showgirls, and anything else of interest to a youthful audience. Years later many large metropolitan dailies would introduce magazine inserts for the Friday paper containing the same type of stories as well as reviews of plays, movies, and concerts. But tabloids like *Bachelor's Beat* were in the forefront of the change.

Bachelor's Beat, despite the title, was a publication that could be taken into the home. The clubs may have been seen as somewhat disreputable, and certainly many of them catered to men seeking a vicarious sexual experience, but the paper was a serious effort to promote people who, today, might routinely be covered by the mainstream press. Boye was a respected journalist who had spent a decade working in occupied Japan after World War II. He would later become a book publisher and author, many of his books providing insight into Japan and other parts of Asia. He enjoyed the nightclub world, yet he was neither corrupted by it nor did he exploit the women who hoped to be the subjects of some of his articles.

Boye also had a track record in the field which gave him credibility both with his partner and with others in the industry. He had written a book titled *Bachelor's Japan*, meant for the many young American males anxious to see the country where their fathers once had fought. He had also developed the Bachelor's Weekly News Service, a series of articles sent to the eight franchised *Bachelor's Beat* papers. This allowed some of the inside copy to be handled locally. The rest of the inside copy was material of general interest to young men. It resembled the service fillers in magazines such as the still young *Playboy*, though on a much smaller scale.

Larry Flynt discovered *Bachelor's Beat* by chance during a visit to Phoenix and was impressed. Here was an approach to advertising that would work perfectly for his small chain of bars, now known as the *Hustler* Clubs. He stopped by the publication's office in order to obtain a subscription and convince the publishers to let him spend some time with them, discussing what they had created.

"Larry laid down a $100 bill for a subscription that, at the time, probably was no more than $15 or $20," Boye later explained. "He was probably trying to impress us because $100 was a lot of money in those days. He was right. We were impressed."

Dad and the owners of *Bachelor's Beat* went to lunch, where Boye was again surprised. As he remembered the afternoon, Dad astonished the two men with the depth and breadth of his readings. "He wasn't one of those people who reads the books on the New York Times Best Seller List," Boye explained. "He had read literary novels, Spanish authors, European authors. You could talk about anything with him—politics, taxes. He was the most brilliant young man I had ever met."

Dad also had no illusions about the bar businesses he ran. Boye remembered Dad saying, "I sell sex by the glass."

The bar business was fun for Dad, and apparently he ran a fairly clean establishment—so far as the official record was concerned. When I researched Dad's early years for this book, I interviewed a number of people who knew him and the club business back then. His Columbus, Ohio, location was the most notorious among his clubs because Columbus, the state capital, was politically conservative. In the heartland, Columbus was the perfect test market for new products and services before they were introduced to the rest of the nation. Everything from convenience foods to one of the earliest forms of cable television made its first appearance, and sometimes its last, in the Columbus area.

While the "good people" of Columbus might hold their noses and look away each time they passed the *Hustler* Club, the city could not close it down. Years later there would be many stories about what took place during that period. I have heard on television that at least some of the girls were pimped by Dad, Uncle Jimmy, or someone else working there. I have been told that drugs were available. But in talking with detectives who worked the area, I learned that there were no arrests and convictions directly related to the club's activities. Whether this means that the stories weren't true, bribes were successfully paid, or the action was discreet enough to go unreported to the authorities, I do not know. Certainly the clubs walked the fine line of legality. But Dad quickly had a six-figure income.

My father wanted to promote his business. He saw a *Hustler* Club newsletter as a way of selling the clubs he was also opening in other Ohio cities. Like *Bachelor's Beat* it would combine news, features, and advertising. But unlike *Bachelor's Beat*, he wanted to focus on his own business.

There were three types of features in the original newsletter Boye De Mente helped Dad create. (De Mente was a consultant on the publishing business, not a partner in any of the club activities.) The first was the introduction of new acts. The sex business was in transition when Dad was running his clubs. The burlesque circuit had finally died. No longer were there places where you could see strippers, baggy pants comics, and similar entertainment in a theater setting where the audience was kept at a distance from the performers.

At the same time, go-go dancing was not yet so popular a form of bar entertainment as it would soon become in Ohio. Many of the clubs would place attractive girls in microskirts, tight-fitting tops, and high-heeled boots, then have them dance in cages suspended over the floor.

But the *Hustler* Clubs were modeled after the Playboy Clubs, where girls wore tight-fitting bunny costumes carefully padded to assure maximum cleavage. They were taught to do the "bunny dip" when bringing drinks and food, yet men could not touch them. The headquarters club in Chicago even had a dormitory where many of the girls lived, working shifts planned around college; classes in acting, singing, and/or dancing; and auditions for theatrical jobs. No men were allowed in the dormitories, and all the males who acted as stewards, bringing the residents food and other necessities around the clock, were gay. It was as though Hugh Hefner had hired eunuchs to guard the harem.

Sex was thus in the fantasy of the mind. As a result, girls who wanted better pay than average had to come up with a gimmick that would make them stand out. Dad's *Hustler* Clubs' newsletter featured these girls when they were planning an appearance.

For example, one girl's gimmick was that she danced on the ceiling. Ropes were rigged so she could brace herself against the ceiling, her head down. Then she would dance for the men below.

The dancer was extremely skilled. Strong, athletic, and an excellent performer who possibly could have made a career in more traditional forms of theater, her unique act earned her top dollar as she traveled the country.

The acts had to be either enjoyable novelties or of high quality while still being focused, at least in part, on the erotic. Each one warranted a story and a photo to assure that men would both come to see them and, ideally, bring their friends.

There were also general stories along the lines of what *Bachelor's Beat* provided their readers. This was again in line with one of the men whose success Dad envied, Hugh Hefner, whose *Playboy* was as much a lifestyle magazine as one catering to sex.

Finally there was something that set Dad apart. It was a thoughtful, well-reasoned, often carefully researched publisher's column on any topic that interested him. He would discuss state politics, federal laws, constitutional rights, and numerous other subjects.

As the magazine grew into the *Hustler* that is so controversial today, Dad tried to follow the same unlikely mix, adding graphic and offensive cartoons and fiction. He hired a research department that was one of the best in the country. Writers for the magazine had their facts cross-checked, and woe to the writer who produced inaccurate nonfiction. Dad wanted the material lively and readable, but he wanted the topics to be ones of serious concern.

Some of the top nonfiction writers in the country produced work for Dad in the first few years of *Hustler's* existence. His pay was competitive with the major magazines, and the writers experienced limited editing and no requests to use foul language, graphic scenes, or anything of a similar nature. Every fact was checked, and writers were expected to provide all necessary documentation, including names of interview subjects.

In one instance, an article Dad published on the subject of child abuse was considered so thorough and objective that a number of groups dealing with the issue arranged to have reprints made without the surrounding cartoons, photos, and advertisements. Then they passed it out at various gatherings.

As *Hustler* evolved, it included more and more excellent nonfiction writing. It also included more and more cartoons and photographs meant to shock, horrify, and demean. The magazine was supposed to be humorous, a visual selection of what might otherwise be dirty jokes told by macho laborers trying to prove their manliness through rough sex and bathroom jokes. Body parts and body functions were highlighted.

As shocking as it was in those early days, *Hustler* was still tame enough to be stocked alongside *Playboy* and its older rival *Penthouse*. All three publications were often sold on large newsstands, not hidden behind counters for restricted sale.

Despite this mainstream acceptance, there was a subtly disturbing element to *Hustler* even then, one that would impact my life and raise serious issues for society. Pedophilia—a desire to have sex with children—and violence toward women were expanding themes.

∽

Despite the free-love movement of the 1960s, when Dad was in the Navy, women were increasingly objectified in men's magazines. Further, rock music lyrics by both mainstream and counterculture musicians frequently had a sadomasochistic theme. (Later, in the

1970s, The Rolling Stones advertised their Black And Blue album with a billboard that showed a battered and bruised woman, her wrists and ankles restricted by chains, wearing tattered clothing and saying, "I'm Black And Blue from the Rolling Stones and loving it.")

Advertisers used children and teenagers carefully dressed, their hair styled, their faces made-up to look more mature than their years. The mixed messages of such efforts sold not only the clothing or other product but also the idea that it was somehow all right for adults to lust after children. Children, at least little girls, were presented as inherently sexual beings capable of giving and receiving physical enjoyment well beyond their years.

Some men's magazine publishers incorporated themes of popular culture with material that walked a fine line of offensiveness. *Playboy* was especially aware that the majority of its newsstand sales were to women trying to learn what men wanted. As a result, it tried to show women enjoying whatever was depicted. If a cartoon showed a woman tied up or in chains, she was having fun. As long as the act involved consent, it was OK.

Dad's publication gradually turned vicious. Eventually he would run illustrations depicting prominent women arranged as sex objects and being deliberately hurt as punishment they "deserved" but did not want. Bondage images were designed so that the man shown was getting revenge or using the woman as a receptacle for sex. And pedophilia became "fun," especially with the introduction of an ongoing character named Chester the Molester, created by a man who himself had been arrested for child molestation.

Chester the Molester was always shown tricking small children or adolescents into giving him sexual pleasure. In one example, a little girl in a hiked-up dress was sliding down a playground slide with Chester beneath it, his head at the bottom of the slide with his tongue out. The creator, Dwaine Tinsley, was considered a major satirist of our times by Dad, who used his work every month. This stopped in 1989, when Tinsley was arrested on charges of child sexual abuse. Tinsley was convicted, then the conviction overturned because the prosecution had, in part, used his cartoons as evidence against him. The use of the drawings was in conflict with past court decisions related to First Amendment issues, according to the appeals courts, and he was freed from jail. Later the cartoons were returned to the pages of *Hustler*.

I did not know anything about this as a kid, though of course *Hustler* was lying around everywhere when I visited my father. I had yet to see Larry Flynt as anyone other than a successful businessman who loved me dearly and was working to have me with him forever. But this world Dad had created for men, a world justifying the exploitation of women, would affect my childhood in ways impossible to imagine.

3

Jacksonville

No one talked about dysfunctional families when I was young. Child abuse was an issue few schools or social work agencies were equipped to handle except in extreme cases. If people mentioned it at all, it was usually in regard to "them," whoever formed the least respected class in any community. Emotional abuse was never considered a problem, so a troubled child was ignored—even by most religious groups.

When I was born on March 5, 1965, I became a member of two different dysfunctional families. I was so much the physical image of my father that Larry Flynt would never question the fact that I was his daughter. Nor would Mom's mother, who has held this fact against me most of my life.

In my fantasies, my father's never being around was part of the proof I needed of his love. He was obviously working hard to earn enough money to take me away from Mom and Grandma. When his work was finished, he would return to me and never leave again.

Years later, when Judy and I discovered that Dad was not her biological father, I was pleased to learn that his September 19, 1963, marriage to Mom was meant to give Judy a good name. I reasoned that if this good and caring man could so love a stranger's child, then he obviously loved me, his natural born daughter, all the more.

Perhaps there had been a time when my reasoning was valid. Certainly Mom feels that the youth who courted her, who became the first meaningful love of her life, was a good and gentle man. He changed radically in her eyes, changed in ways that left him cold, hard, unable or unwilling to commit emotionally to anyone else. There might have been some inherent flaw in his personality that did not show until he was in his twenties. More likely the change was a combination of factors—Grandma's actions following Mom's abortion of what would have been Dad's first son, the manic-depressive illness, the possibly unneeded electric shock therapy. In addition, Navy records indicate Dad was preoccupied with pornography, an obsession that could have also been a contributing factor.

Dad no longer wanted the 1950s white suburban ideal portrayed on television shows and in popular magazines. He certainly had no interest in taking a wage earner's factory job. Instead, he decided to become a player in the urban white trash world of booze and sex. It was a decision that did not allow him to go home each night to a wife and children.

That first bar had an interesting family connection. It was his mother's bar, the one where he learned the business and knew the customers well. He paid $4,000 and began his rise to wealth.

From what I have learned in recent years, I do not believe that the sex addiction and molestation had anything to do with some form of mental illness. I believe that the seeds for that were planted during Dad's childhood. He was raised without intimacy. Sex was separated from commitment—his parents separated, his mother was involved with many men. His father was abusive to both his wife and kids. Yet Dad, like all children, craved a consistent family life. He needed the stability of a loving father and mother, which I doubt he ever experienced.

The one strong relationship he had, ironically, was with a woman. Dad's mother, the woman I was told to call "Little

Mommy," doted on him. She loved Dad with the devotion that comes from surviving a struggle together against seemingly overwhelming odds. And Dad ultimately returned the favor, caring for her when she was dying of cancer.

In hindsight, Dad's entering the booze and sex business was a logical way for him to make a living. His mother ran a bar that sold both legal liquor and moonshine. My grandma was a heavy drinking, verbally abusive, hardworking laborer who had had her daughter too young to be an effective mother. Her husbands were destructive, never providing real stability. And Mom had been running wild for the previous six years. Her idea of home life was to escape each night.

There was also another aspect to Dad, something I only began to see as an adult. The serious relationships in his life, including at least three of his four wives, have always been with extremely intelligent, highly troubled women. They all came from abusive backgrounds. They all had low self-esteem when they married him. And they all occasionally engaged in self-destructive behavior, or the drug use and heavy drinking of his last two wives. He gained pleasure from putting them down, building himself up at their expense in whatever way he could. Given that attitude, no relationship could last.

Mom has always been a woman of great contrasts, and that fact affected all our lives. She, like Dad, has a strong work ethic. His seems to be motivated by a desire to show people his power. He likes being in control of others. He likes being shown the difference money can bring. He likes humiliating intelligent, hardworking individuals and undermining their sense of self-worth. A master manipulator, Dad is capable of selecting advisers whose ideas he can appropriate or incorporate into his business.

Mom is different. She has always been determined to be self-sufficient, to meet her financial responsibilities, to prove she can be independent of Grandma.

At the same time, Mom has a desperate need to be loved by people who are seemingly incapable of providing her with the emotional support she needs. That is why I feel she was long willing to stay involved with Grandma, even when she knew she or her children might be yelled at and ridiculed. She did not want to walk away from her mother's seeming abuse because she still wanted love in a way Grandma was probably incapable of giving. Only lately, as Grandma has become much older, have I felt a mellowing that perhaps can give Mom what she needs.

Likewise Mom has let herself be manipulated by Dad long after their divorce, ever hopeful he will change, yet always knowing she is setting herself up for pain.

I was too young to know the pressures on Mom when Dad left her. We were still in Dayton, and I had the pleasure of spending time with aunts and uncles who loved me and probably would have raised me had Mom allowed it. For example, I remember when I was two and a half and suddenly came down with the mumps while being cared for by my Aunt Ruth. That dear woman held me and comforted me as the disease progressed rapidly and I began crying uncontrollably from the pain.

Years later, Aunt Ruth told me that she felt my parents were needed at once, that I might have to go to the hospital. She knew the mumps were more painful than serious for many children, but that complications could turn the routine illness into a life-threatening one.

It was Aunt Ruth's understanding that Mom had gone to Dad's bar to be with him, either to help or, more likely, with Aunt Ruth taking care of me, for a chance to be intimate. She was certain they would want to know what was wrong, certain they would want to get me and decide if I needed immediate professional care. She immediately called the bar, talking to some woman whose job it was to run interference for Dad that day.

Aunt Ruth explained who she was, what was happening, and why she needed to talk with Dad. The woman excused herself and then covered the mouthpiece of the phone to muffle her side of the conversation. There were voices of the woman and a man, presumably my father, then instead of the woman saying anything, she hung up the telephone. It was one of my earliest rejections by my father, and while I did not know it at the time, hearing the story as an adult and the mother of a daughter of my own, I was emotionally devastated by his callousness. I was also hurt by the idea that Mom might have been present and gone along with Dad's wishes.

Perhaps the high point of my time in Ohio was my third birthday party, an event that was filmed by my uncle. It looks like one of those ads for Kodak where they showed a happy middle-American family enjoying life and each other.

The party was a backyard picnic in the home of Aunt Ruth and Uncle Elmo. Mom was there, along with cousins, aunts, and uncles. It was a gourmet treat for kids—barbecue, baked beans, and coleslaw along with a big birthday cake. We played and laughed. We ate and made a mess, the reason we were outside with such sticky finger food. Dad came in the middle of the party, bringing me a gold tricycle which I cherished. It was my first set of wheels from Dad, and meant as much to me as the Mustang convertible he would buy for me fifteen years later.

It was a happy time, and in the perspective of a child, it proved Ohio was perfect. I had no sense of Mom's economic and emotional plight. I had no sense of the tensions within the family. I was small and loved, protected and perceived as an object of joy by the people who mattered most in my life. The idea that such feelings could be taken from me was beyond my comprehension. In fact, even today, whenever I see the video made from the home movie, the memories of my lost roots return and I cry bitterly.

Dayton was important in many ways. And though I didn't realize it, I needed that extended family to give me the love and nurturing others seemed to fail to provide. Leaving that extended family would be more costly for me than anyone understood, perhaps even those who seemed to love me most.

However, Mom had lost too much over too short a life. The idea of not keeping her children was one she could not contemplate. It was also one of the reasons why she decided to follow Grandma and Grandma's husband, Carl, to Jacksonville, Florida.

It is hard for me, even now, to be objective about Jacksonville, Florida. It was a strange city where I knew no one and lacked the extended family to watch over me. Mom was working as many hours as she could, a single mother with two small children to raise. She knew no one, so she willingly let any new acquaintance serve as our baby-sitter. There was no professional child care available that Mom could afford, and many women in Mom's predicament chose to try to go on welfare.

Mom wasn't like that. Our family was poor, but Mom never stopped working. One of her first jobs was as a cocktail waitress, the ideal position for someone with great looks, a beautiful voice, high intelligence, but very limited education. Men delighted in her just being around, and she made good tips.

Although my mother's family was more sophisticated than Dad's, they had their own dirty little secrets. My grandmother told me her father molested her, though I never knew the details. Mom also later told me that she had been molested as a child, and like my grandmother, this became a dirty little family secret. It was not something they knew how to complain about, not something for which they knew how to seek help.

Like many abuse victims, though, Grandma in turn often married abusive men, including Carl, a man who liked to touch little girls. I don't know if Grandma was aware of this when they first married. I doubt it. Yet over the years I have seen that all the women in my family, including me, experienced a certain amount of denial about the traumas we endured from men whose love we desperately wanted.

For example, there was the time when my older sister Judy and I were taking a bath together. I was no more than three, and she had not yet turned five. We were just two little kids capable of washing ourselves with a little help, and happy to play together in the water while the adults had a break.

We were visiting Grandma and her then husband, Carl. She was out of the house, probably running some errands, and he was making certain we were safe. Or so Grandma thought.

Suddenly Carl appeared in the door of the bathroom. I wasn't scared by his presence, even though, from the perspective of a little kid sitting in the bathtub, he appeared to be an overwhelming giant. The bathroom was very small, with barely room for two adults.

Carl had never hurt me, never shown me special attention one way or another. I don't think he had ever been alone with me before; Mom or Grandma had always been present, though this was not always the case with Judy. Carl was holding, menacingly, what I remember to have been a hammer. (Grandma later said she remembered the incident involving a screwdriver, though whatever it was, it was meant to be perceived as a weapon to be avoided.) I was not concerned, but Judy was. She was instantly terrified.

Over the years Judy and I have talked little about that day. I remember her looking at him with such fear that now I think his presence was a reminder of past experiences. So many years have passed and I was so young, and not everything is clear. I understood that my big sister was afraid, while I felt strangely empowered.

Judy and I fought like all siblings, and we were close enough in age that I did not see why she should be allowed to do things I could not. The fact that she was older, her motor skills more developed, her language skills superior, and that she simply was more mature never mattered. We were sisters. We were close in size, close in age, and I wanted to prove I was at least as good at everything as she was. The idea that she was scared gave me courage.

Then my stepgrandfather, Carl, unzipped his pants.

I remember little of those next few minutes. Carl closed the bathroom door behind him, looming over us in the tiny room.

"Get out of the bathtub!" he said.

Judy immediately pushed herself as far to the back of the bathtub as she could, as though an extra inch or two of space might keep her safe. I heard screaming, crying, but I did not look at her. I was focused on Carl, on the object in his hand, on what he was doing with his clothes.

"Get out of the bathtub!" he repeated. He demanded that we open our mouths.

Judy, screaming, crying, did not move. I got out of the tub, closed my eyes, and let whatever was going to happen, happen.

I don't remember the feelings. I don't remember exactly what he did to me. I think the good Lord protects us from some memories so that we can get on with our lives. But I do remember saying to myself, "I'm going to be strong. I'm going to get it over with. It will be over with. I will be strong. I'm just going to do it and get it over with."

Most of the details are gone from my memory. Whatever I had to do was over and we all heard Grandma return. Carl warned us he would kill us if we told. We had already seen his violence. He would beat Grandma. He was even so sadistic that whenever he could get away with it, he would steal a roaming cat or dog, place it alive in a plastic bag, then dump it from a bridge, where it would suffocate from lack of air, be crushed by passing traffic, or drown in the water below. One time he even strangled a dog that Grandma loved. He claimed it had run away, but the body was discovered buried in the backyard.

Grandma and Carl fought constantly. The city police saw a man's wife as his property, a man's home as a place where violence, if not appropriate, was certainly no one else's business. Nothing could be done short of divorce, and Grandma had too much to lose financially to be rid of Carl. Or so she seemed to believe.

We knew the worst of Carl. We knew he did not make idle threats.

And so we said nothing. Years later, when Judy and I were adolescents, we finally felt angry enough, trusting enough, and safe enough to tell. There was no question that Mom and Grandma believed us, and from their reaction, I would not be surprised if they had learned of other perversions prior to his becoming a helpless, sick old man.

A few years later, a male relative of Mom's[1] came to visit. With Grandma remarried and Mom in no position to give him a room in which to stay during his visit, the man registered in a motel. We children were anxious to see him, and since we were very young, no one saw any problem with our spending the night with him. He seemed the type of man who would show us a good time, keep us safe, and give the adults in the family a respite from kids for the night.

We went swimming after dark in the illuminated pool. There were spotlights overhead, colorful lights under the water. It was as beautiful to us as one of those underwater shows at Marineland.

Everything we wanted was given to us. We used the vending machines to buy exciting gifts—travel-size toothbrushes, miniature tubes of Pepsodent toothpaste, little fingernail files, candy, bags of snacks, and numerous other items that delighted us. The man had been drinking, but I don't remember what or where. I must have considered that part of the night completely normal or I probably would have remembered. Whatever the case, the liquor eliminated any inhibitions that might have held him back from the action he eventually took.

The motel bed was large, and Judy and I were little. We decided that one of us would sleep on the bed with the man, and the other would sleep on the floor on blankets. It sounds uncomfortable— but to us it was like camping out, with a bathroom and color television.

Judy and I were asleep when my the man, an obviously trusted relative, drunk, awakened me. His hand was under my nightclothes, and his breath was sour. He was talking softly, saying, "Did anyone ever tell you what a pretty little ——— you have?"

I was terrified. His fingers were probing my vagina, hurting me. He said words I did not understand, but I knew something was wrong.

It was not that family members did not commit incestuous acts back then. Of course they did. Dad came from a tiny community where such experiences were considered normal. But almost no one talked about it. Most men either did not believe it, blaming the child for being somehow overwhelmingly seductive, or did not want to face the truth about a trusted, often beloved family member. Women were far more aware of such matters, yet often unwilling to confront the issue. Most didn't want to scare their daughters. They didn't want to seem to be accusing a member of their own family of such a heinous act. And in some cases, they did not want to admit that an experience they had had when young was now one taking place with their own daughters, whom they had once thought they could protect.

I did not know what to do. Judy was asleep. Mom had left us with this relative thinking he was safe. I had no idea if anyone would hear me if I screamed.

I told the man that I needed to go to the bathroom, and he did not argue or try to keep me with him. I washed myself, my heart pounding, wanting to cry, wanting to run, not knowing what to do. Finally I came out and announced that I was calling my mother. Then I went to the telephone and, to my surprise, was allowed to call her.

I told Mom that she needed to come for Judy and me. She had to come right then. We needed to go home. I did not tell her what the man had done to me.

Mom came quickly, though she stopped for Grandma and the delay made it seem like forever. I kept my voice calm, and to my regret I said nothing when Judy asked to spend the next night with the man. We had both enjoyed ourselves prior to going to sleep. She had no idea what had happened to me and was delighted to get his undivided attention when I refused the chance to spend a second night with him.

When Mom, Grandma, and I went to pick up Judy the next day, Judy came running out to the car. Mom said she and Grandma were going to Jax Liquors to buy some beer. We should stay at the motel with the man, she said, until they came back.

Judy and I were already in the car. The minute we heard that we were to stay, we became near hysterical. We began kicking the backs of the front seats, crying, shouting, "No! No! No!" over and over again.

Grandma did not understand what was happening, why we were having what looked like a temper tantrum. She and Mom insisted we get out of the car. We refused.

Our refusal to obey was so intense and so out of character that Mom and Grandma knew something was wrong. They looked at each other, then looked back at us, insisting we tell them what had happened. Finally, we told what had occurred.

The man was still in the motel room as this went on. Mom and Grandma said nothing. They took us back to the house, leaving us with George. Then they went back to handle the man.

For many years I thought Mom and Grandma not only confronted the man but also called the police, sending him to prison.

Certainly we did not see him or hear about him for almost three decades. Later I learned that they raised hell with him, banishing him from their lives until he became sick and enfeebled in his old age.

Either because of compassion, sense of duty to the man who had once helped raise her, or because of an inheritance she felt he owed the family, Mom agreed to help care for him when his wife died. His house, investments, and possessions were transferred to her name. She feels justified, and maybe she is. I remain so deeply hurt by what happened to Judy and me, that I feel no price is worth having him back in any of our lives.

As for Carl, many years later, when I was an adult, he began having a series of strokes. They affected his mind as much as his body. He became a child again, thinking that Grandma was his own mother. His mental decline caused her great emotional pain, and I realized that the man who had attacked me ceased to exist long before his physical death. I found myself able to forgive him, laying to rest emotions that had been the foundation for the journey through darkness I had no idea I would one day make.

The impact of my dysfunctional family and my horrible sexual experiences left me feeling somehow different from others, even though I suspected that all kids went through what I had endured. Perhaps that was the reason I never mentioned my problems to other kids, their parents, or my teachers. If this was "normal," why talk about it? I was living the same childhood as everyone else, and if they weren't discussing it, why should I?

Instead, I was a sad, lonely, withdrawn little girl as I entered my elementary school years, not unlike many children whose lives have been disrupted by a divorce they do not understand. I was also falling in love with my father.

∽

As a small child I did not know Dad well. Visits when I was very young were rare, though I did see him more frequently as I approached elementary-school age. I heard about him frequently, though—he was a continuous subject of arguments between Mom and Grandma.

Grandma looked on Larry Flynt with pure contempt. She saw him as a liar and a cheat. She knew him as a philanderer who refused to be responsible for Mom and us kids. She berated Mom over child support. She also did not like the world he had created for himself with the clubs, the liquor, and the women.

Mom knew she had made a lot of mistakes and was doing the best she knew to do to correct them. She was still depressed, still torn between blaming herself for everything that happened and being angry with Dad for not keeping what Mom took as a serious commitment. She did not need her mother constantly reminding her what a rotten individual Dad was. Yet that was exactly what Grandma did. They argued frequently in front of us kids.

I was caught in the middle of all this. I didn't understand the fights. I didn't understand the very adult problems with which Mom and Grandma were wrestling. All I knew was that I was miserable, relatively friendless, and wanting to be somewhere else. Since I did not know that Dad was a philanderer subject to often violent mood swings, I made him a savior in my mind. I was unhappy with Mom and Grandma, so rather than considering that they might be right, a situation that would mean being with Dad would be worse than being in Jacksonville, I mentally nominated him for sainthood. He had left us kids because he was being held back by the angry, often harping women with whom Judy and I lived. Dad really wanted to have full custody of me, yet he could not quite afford us. Fortunately he was rectifying that fact.

Larry Flynt, as I began to create him in my young mind, was like a knight forced to temporarily abandon all he loved in order to go on a mission he could not avoid. Dad's mission was to stay in Columbus and anywhere else he expanded his business in order to make a lot of money. He was working night and day, not because he loved the world of alcohol, beautiful women, and casual sex, but because he wanted to impress me. He was going to get his house, fill it with clothes and toys and games, then mount his white horse and ride to Jacksonville.

I would not know he was coming, of course. Dad would want his arrival to be a surprise. One minute I would be playing. The next minute I would be swept away, Dad's strong arm lifting me onto the armor-clad horse. I would be placed between his shield and his heart, simultaneously protected and loved. Then we would gallop back to Columbus, the shop girl who discovers she is a princess, Cinderella rescued from the drudgery of her evil family, Tonya Flynt carried off by her dad. It was a fantasy that helped me get from day to day.

Mom was also desperately lonely while in Jacksonville. She is a woman who is unhappy when there isn't someone special in her life. Yet she had been hurt so badly, she did not use her best judgment when it came to dating. She sought any man whose seeming desire for her would reassure her that she was capable of being loved. One of those men was George.

There was much about George that was good. He was kind, had a steady job, and made our lives seem stable. He accepted us kids even when Mom got pregnant with their son, Shawn. And he had a unique understanding of children that enabled Mom and him to occasionally leave Judy and me alone in the four-bedroom apartment we all shared in a run-down section of Jacksonville.

The tragic part about George was something I did not understand at the time. He was addicted to pornography. He looked at pornographic magazines and photographs the way chain-smokers go through cigarette after cigarette. There would be pornography in the master bathroom, and in his locked study. Mom was against it, and though we kids saw a little of it, he did not deliberately allow that to happen. In fact, he never tried to touch me in an improper way, never said anything wrong, never tried to show me any of the pictures.

Years later, when I was a woman and felt more comfortable talking with Mom about such matters, she said that George was "kinky." I assume that means he liked to act out some of what he looked at, but I never had the nerve to ask. George seemed to care, was a good father and an honest man. If Mom did not particularly care for George's sexual variations during their lovemaking, she was willing to tolerate them for the sake of our family. I was happier than I had been in years.

Judy seemed to hate him for reasons I do not fully know. I remember her putting sugar in his gas tank, knowing it would make him mad when he couldn't start his car. It was her idea of revenge, though she did not realize it would destroy the engine. But George never showed me whatever it was that created such anger in Judy, and I suspect in hindsight the reason was that he knew I was Larry Flynt's daughter. He was an extremely insecure man, jealous of anyone he saw displacing his position no matter how foolish that might have been. He was jealous of Dad for his having been involved with Mom. He destroyed every photograph that showed Dad, whether alone, with Mom, or with us kids.

At the same time, George had great respect for what Dad had accomplished in the counterculture business. I think it was because of this that George treated me with respect. However, he allegedly was not the man I thought. My sister's memories are of repeated sexual abuse, which I knew nothing about until we were both adults.

I was furious, and I suspect Mom was hurt as well. She never stopped loving Dad during those years, making George's being an avid reader of Dad's magazine all the more odd. He apparently was able to separate the product from the purveyor, enjoying one while hating the other.

George was even jealous when he took Mom and us kids to see Elvis. Mom was so excited, she refused to stop looking through her binoculars.

∞

This was also the time when I first discovered the church. There was a Baptist church in the area that was actively involved with evangelism. The church bus would go to housing projects, low-income areas, and other places where the people were too poor to have a way to travel to church. Sometimes just children got on. Sometimes just adults. Sometimes entire families.

We met one of the members of the church before we decided to take advantage of the opportunity. He was married with a couple of sons, a man seemingly filled with faith who believed in sharing the Word. As it turned out, the man was what I have learned is often called the "unlikely vessel"—the wrong person to carry an important message so that you know God's hand is in the communication. Years later I learned of his arrest and conviction for molesting his sons. I was horrified and outraged. Yet at the time, he helped me in a way I could never have imagined possible.

Not that I instantly developed an adult faith. I attended Sunday school, where we learned stories about Jesus. I was taught about his selfless love, his constant presence in our lives, and the way in which we only had to reach out to him to feel his comforting arms. I understood Jesus when I heard those stories. He was just like how I believed Dad to be. However, when crises in my life arose, it would be Jesus, not my father, on whom I could rely without fear.

Mom stayed married to George approximately four years, giving birth to Shawn. Mom tried to make the relationship work, hoping that at last she could have something long-term. Instead, they divorced, and sometime later, George called me to say goodbye. He treated me as a real daughter, asking nothing, giving what he could, and he wanted to speak to me once more. Then, not long after that, he took his life. Sadly, he was as close to a real father as I would ever know in my young life.

4

Looking for My Knight

Florida meant a new beginning for Mom. She found work as a cocktail waitress, enjoying the admiring looks of men from all walks of life. Her income was good enough for us to get by on our own with a minimum of support from Grandma. Mom had to use Grandma's washer and dryer—the Laundromat was too expensive. And what truly enjoyable meals we had were supplied by the occasional bags of groceries Grandma brought. Yet Mom was essentially independent and doing well enough to begin pursuing her dreams.

Mom never saw herself through our eyes. She never realized that no matter what other problems we may have experienced as a family, her work ethic made a strong, positive impression on me and probably the rest of us kids. Through her we understood that we could pursue our own dreams, we could gain an education, we could achieve our goals no matter how limited our resources.

Mom eventually became a hairdresser with the business skills to run her own shop, went into sales, and has spent her life moving among fields of interest and economic necessity. She has mastered anything she has set her mind to learning, though her continued low self-esteem has prevented her recognizing this aspect of her personality.

At the same time, Mom was at a constant loss when it came to being a mother. She was ill prepared for children because she was ill prepared for independent adulthood. From the time she was barely into adolescence, her idea of being "big" was to run with older teens and young adults whose lifestyles focused on bars, music, and sex. Her dreams of suburbia with Dad were the dreams of television shows, not ones formed from knowing people enjoying such a lifestyle.

Work provided Mom's home, refuge, and safe harbor when we first moved to Jacksonville. Our various apartments were the enemy, places to be endured. She was always tired, always trying to sleep or rest, avoiding dealing with her mother's frequent criticism and the wants of us kids. We had food, clothing, and shelter. She rarely could bring herself to sit and hold us while reading a book, take us to play on the beach, or just let us know that despite the hard times, we held a special place in her heart and thoughts.

This emotional neglect, which I think reflected her own unmet needs, not deliberate abuse, led to even more trouble. Judy and I began fighting with each other, desperate to get her attention. Each of us wanted to be more special than the other, and ultimately that meant we wanted to hurt each other.

This extreme sibling rivalry was further fueled by my grandmother. She knew the truth, that Judy was not Dad's biological daughter. Thus Judy was the acceptable granddaughter, the one whose genes had not been sullied by Larry Flynt's lust. By contrast, I was a constant reminder of the man Grandma hated with all the passion of a spurned lover. I doubt Grandma ever tried to know me as a unique individual. Instead she reacted to whatever was happening between Judy and me as though it was my fault. If I was on the floor with a bloody nose and Judy was standing smugly, her knuckles bloodstained from hitting me, Grandma was likely to punish me for pushing my face into Judy's fist.

Not that I was an innocent. I am certain I initiated half our fights. But like all kids, I could be righteously indignant over any injustice I endured without considering the time my sibling also suffered from such injustice. My social conscience was limited to a world of one, myself, as I'm sure was Judy's. Unfortunately Grandma's attitude was so biased, I was able to feel sorry for myself rather than trying to learn to get along.

At the same time, I avoided making many friends. After all, I was going to be swept away by my father as soon as he could manage it. I did not understand that he loved us less than Mom, and he had come to desire Mom only for sex and humiliation.

By the time Mom was set to marry George, Dad's business had expanded to several cities. He was not yet rich, but he could afford an expensive car while Mom never owned a car until after divorcing George, when a boyfriend gave her a 1957 Chevrolet sedan—which we knew as the Green Bomb. We never went out to eat. By contrast, Dad ate regularly in restaurants. Price was no object.

While I didn't fully understand all this, any more than I understood the issue of child support, I just knew Dad had money and Mom did not. I just knew Dad never yelled at us and Mom yelled all the time. (Never mind that I wasn't with Dad during any of this time. My world was black and white.) I was certain Dad loved me, and certain Mom did not. When Dad asked Mom, Judy, and me to come to Dayton to visit him, I was elated.

Judy and I were put up in Little Mommy's house, eating there and spending little time with Dad. But I was in Daddy's city, a part of his world, and I was happy. He was not physically affectionate, but he smiled a lot and he bought us white go-go boots and matching dresses. And then, on the way back to the airport, he turned to Judy and me and said, "What do you girls think your mom would say if I asked her to marry me?"

Mom was shocked. Her mouth opened and she turned to stare

at Judy and me in the backseat. Then she turned to Dad. Finally, the shock worn off, she quietly commented, "I can't. I'm already engaged to George."

Judy and I started crying. We began begging Mom to marry Dad. We knew nothing of their past, nothing of the commitment Mom felt she had made, nothing of her integrity and faithfulness. Dad wanted us to be a family again. That's all I knew. And Judy and I both wanted what we were certain would be a Walt Disney movie happy ending.

"He's a lucky man," was all Dad said.

Dad was deeply involved with Althea by this time. I don't know if she considered herself engaged, but I think she felt a commitment from Dad just as Mom felt she had committed to George. Dad apparently made up his mind to marry Althea immediately after all this.

Mom refused to get involved with Dad again. George would never be the success Dad had become, but George wanted her and she had agreed to the marriage. Remarrying Mom would make our lives easier financially, but in hindsight I can see that he was the right man at the wrong time.

George's relationship with me was so positive, I know now I was better off. But at the time losing Dad was deeply troubling and added to my hostility toward Mom.

Dad began visiting us after George and Mom got divorced. I don't know why. I just know that these were special events.

The first time I remember, Dad gave all of us the impression he would be staying in our apartment. Mom was to pick him up at the airport and bring him to where we were living.

It is hard to imagine the esteem in which I held Dad in those days, well before the nightmares began. Dad coming to see us was like the President sneaking out of the White House, renting a car, driving himself to the airport, putting on a disguise, then flying in for a private visit. No living person could surpass my father. Not in my fantasies.

We were in HUD housing, an apartment complex with four units upstairs and four units down on each end of the two-part building. There were two bedrooms and one bath for four people.

My sister Judy, being the oldest child, was given her own bedroom when Mom realized we could not get along together, and I agreed to move out of the room we originally were going to share. Despite that fact, Judy's winning the room was something I resented for years. I had always been jealous of her, so desirous of being my father's only daughter that I began praying to God for a miracle. I would get on my knees and ask the Lord to make me Dad's oldest child. I asked God to let Judy be the child of some other man. She was around thirteen at the time I became obsessed with prayerfully removing her from so close a connection to the man I adored, and it was shortly after this that we all learned the truth. Judy had Dad's name, but another man's genetics had created her. She was my half sister, not my sister, and I was almost as shocked as she was.

I did not think that my prayers had nothing to do with the reality of the situation. I did not think that the adults had secrets from us kids. I just knew that one day I was on my knees, praying fervently, and the next I was Dad's oldest daughter.

The idea that Dad would be staying in such quarters was ridiculous. Other than sticking a stuffed chicken in the recreation room of the Bexley Manor, he had no intention of remembering his own humble roots. Yet we thought he would be staying with us, and we felt deep shame concerning our surroundings.

Years later I came to understand many of the feelings Mom, Judy, and I shared. I have learned that dysfunctional families filled with emotional and physical abuse quickly learn to say, "I'm sorry. I failed you. I'm worthless" even before anyone so much as hints they are going to make a hostile remark. It is as though someone is accosted on the highway, robbed, beaten, and has his clothing slashed. Then along comes a well-dressed businessman who notices the battered and bloodied figure groaning by the side of the road. Instead of the victim feeling hopeful for the compassion of Jesus revealed by the stranger, he says, "I'm sorry I am so disgustingly unattractive lying here in this gutter, making my groaning sounds. Perhaps you should kick me as well for that must be all I deserve."

It was Dad's failure to help his family that led to our being in such poverty. It was Dad's efforts to keep Mom from getting her rightful child support, a figure routinely changed based on the noncustodial parent's income fluctuations, that led us to this misery. Yet instead of feeling righteous anger or relief that he might finally understand our plight in the midst of his wealth, we were embarrassed and ashamed by the bad impression our circumstances would make. We decided to do the best we could, staying up all night to clean. We had to do the right thing for Dad when he walked among us instead of recognizing that he was the one who should have been doing right by us.

So we went to work. Scrub brushes, detergents, sponges, soap. . . . We filled wastebaskets, drawers, and shelves. We were on our knees scrubbing. We were on our tiptoes, holding brooms, making certain there were no hidden cobwebs or other surprises on the ceilings. We made the bathtub sparkle more than usual, the sink shine. We scrubbed the baseboards. We cleaned dark corners of the closets so hidden that, even with a light on, we could not see them clearly. Our arms ached. Our backs ached. We grew exhausted as the hours passed and we moved relentlessly through that already clean apartment, inch by inch, spotting anything that we thought might displease my father. And when we were done, we were too exhausted to move, too wired with anticipation to sleep.

This was also one of those rare occasions when the Green Bomb worked well enough for Mom to drive to the airport to get Dad. However, the interior of the car was such a wreck, it was always a wonder that one of us wasn't stabbed by a loose spring. We suspected that Dad would need to have his suit cleaned after riding in it, yet it was all we had.

It was Christmastime. Certainly we would be getting gifts, and Dad could well afford a new car for Mom. Perhaps the Green Bomb would be like one of the ghosts in *A Christmas Carol*, showing Dad the true tragedy of our existence compared with the joy we could have if he would share just a little more of what he had achieved.

Mom was extremely reluctant to pick him up, knowing he could afford a cab. We encouraged her, though, equally convinced that Dad would be so upset by the car that he would change our lives. In the end, none of this happened. Instead, Dad stayed at the Hilton, overlooking the St. John's River from his suite on the top floor. He never saw our car or our apartment.

The truth which I neither wanted to face nor possibly was old enough to face was that Dad did understand where and how we were living. He wasn't coming to Jacksonville to look at poverty. He had been there, done that, and "shaken the dust from his Guccis" when he made it big. Dad did not want to face the apartment, the car, or the way we were living. He wanted only to have us look at him like a big success.

Dad wanted us to see how much Mom had missed out on by not being with him. He wanted us to see his wealth in action.

And so we visited the luxurious suite. We went to a nice restaurant. And when Dad left, I had the treasure he gave me—a pink, vinyl-covered jewelry box on which a ballerina rested until the lid was open and she began dancing to the tune of "London Bridge Is Falling Down."

�❧

Many years have passed since that Christmas of hope and dis-
appointment. But there was something more important about
that time, something I have only recently come to understand.
Children who survive childhoods filled with abuse and perceived
neglect do so in a variety of ways. Those of us who are classed as
"incorrigible" and treated in one or another facilities, as I would
be, sometimes become institutionalized. These children make the
abnormal world of the youth authority or psychiatric ward their
homes. For some it is familiar, and if not nurturing, at least safe.
For me, it was terrifying and left me with a sense of being totally
alone and abandoned. They get three meals a day and a structure
they were often lacking. If they let themselves keep acting in ways
that return them to institutions, and eventually this often means
our nation's prisons, they feel safe. They never have to deal with
the pain of relationships with a spouse, a child, an employer, or the
other people with whom the rest of us must interact each day. At
the same time, they will never know the love of another human
being, the joy of nurturing an infant into adulthood, the delight
that comes from walking in the woods on a crisp autumn day. They
give up the chance to know the pleasures God has allowed every
human to experience in order to feel none of the pain that is also
a part of life.

Others of us use drugs of one sort or another. Cocaine and related
stimulants are substitutes for the euphoria of human existence.
Tranquilizers and other depressants replace normal forms of relax-
ation. And alcohol lowers inhibitions, combining a numbness to
life with the fantasy that we are having a good time in the bar, the
nightclub, or the privacy of our own homes.

Still others bounce among spouses and lovers. We are so afraid
of being abandoned as we feel we were in childhood, even if that
abandonment was emotional rather than physical, that we never

fully commit to anyone. In the back of our minds is the idea that one day the person is going to leave us, so we try to have a new relationship before the current one is over. So long as we do the "dumping," we are all right. We cannot stand the idea of being the one who is left alone. And we have too little self-esteem to believe that anyone could ever commit to us for life, even though the person we abandon may very well have made that commitment.

In my case, I coped by creating a fantasy life that has taken almost thirty years to acknowledge, and by simultaneously turning to God, whom I now know to be the only constant in life. I never realized this until recently, when I was devastated by two tragedies. The first was the news of the death of John Denver in a lightplane crash near his home. The second was a report from friends in Cincinnati that Dad was possibly seriously ill. He had lost what they said was sixty pounds in weight and his face was oddly colored. Since he is in his fifties, disabled from a gunshot wound, long abusive of drugs, alcohol, and sex, and never physically active in constructive ways, the idea that he might also die is very real.

Suddenly I went into deep mourning over John Denver and felt a desperate need to see my father. My friends could not understand my reaction. I never knew John Denver, a troubled man who battled drug addiction and alcoholism. And the times I was with my Dad included many instances of emotional brutality, psychological torture, and physical violation. It was not real men who sustained me.

For me, home life was always hell. Perpetually lonely, convinced I was unattractive, certain no one would ever love me, I felt ignored by Mom, berated by Grandma. I rarely had my own room in the many apartments in which we lived. I felt constantly under attack by Judy. And even my achievements in school seemed inadequate for anyone.

Instead of being broken by what was taking place, I learned to retreat into my mind in the walk-in closet that frequently defined my world. John Denver's voice brought me peace and my first safe "love affair." He was the man I was going to marry, and it was a bonus that his music took me along country roads.

I would put a record on my little player, close my eyes, and be transported to a place where the sun was always shining. I felt the dirt of the paths we were taking as it was kicked in the air by our footsteps. I basked in the beauty of the wildflowers. I listened to the rustle of the leaves, the songs of the birds, and the warmth of the sun as it enveloped me like a down comforter on a frozen winter's night. Sometimes we sang together. Sometimes he sang alone while I listened.

The rural world I fantasized held none of the multigenerational incest, the alcoholism, and the hardscrabble poverty many in Dad's family endured. For that matter, I did not know my father's country background at that time. If I had, it would have been in harshly glaring contrast to the world in which John Denver enveloped me, his voice a loving blanket to warm me through cold nights.

In my fantasy, country people were happy, everyone loving one another. They all valued their health and the beauty of God's world more than the riches found in the city. They had enough to eat, enough to drink, and the clothing they needed to be warm. It was a world of poverty as told through one of those 1930s musicals where even the ravages of the Depression could be erased by singing, dancing, and falling in love.

As for Dad, I viewed him as the consummate protector, provider, and savior. I was separated from him in the manner of some mythological woman who had to find the formula for getting away from her captivity in an evil, uncaring world so she could join the man who was awaiting her. Dad would comfort me. Dad would end my loneliness. Dad would take me in his arms and show me that I was loved.

John Denver had shown me the joy of Dad's past. The Hilton suite showed me the riches possible being a part of his life. This was the father who would never hurt me and John Denver was the "uncle" who was nurtured by the gentleness of life, never hurting himself or others. And one day I would be with Dad, my life at peace.

Dad is an incestuous abuser who tries to dominate anyone he respects. But in the world I created in my closet, reinforced by seeing Dad in his hotel suite, looking out over the city in which we lived so miserably, Dad became a symbol of all that was good. I could always put aside the terrible things he has done with his empire built on pornography. This allowed me to see the "other" father, the idealized fantasy who kept me emotionally strong in my lowest moments.

The world in which I would soon be living was one built from what I now know to be an insidious evil affecting far more than just the person who is obsessed with pornography. But the father I love, the father whose eventual passing I will one day mourn with a sadness that may last my lifetime, is the father I created in my closet room, in that Hilton Hotel suite, and during all those other too brief visits—before I experienced his abuse.

∽

When I was five or six, I began having what I now call night terrors. It is hard to explain what those were like. They began when George was still married to Mom and they don't seem to be related to anything I was allowed to watch on television. Certainly they didn't come from the stories I was reading. Yet they were so vivid that I remember many of them to this day.

Some of the terrors involved being dismembered or eaten by monsters. One night I dreamed that there was something green on my leg. It was slowly devouring me and I could not shake it off. I partially awakened, alert enough to leap from bed and run down the hall screaming, yet not so fully awake that I knew I had been dreaming.

George came rushing from his room, bumping into me. I was still screaming and crying, clinging to him for help, knowing I would soon be completely devoured. He calmed me down, then started laughing at my hysteria. Mom also found the situation amusing. However, I was still young enough to know that what happened must have been real, that if I hadn't awakened, I would have been destroyed before the night was over.

In Sunday school I had been learning about Jesus in the manner of most small children. He was portrayed as my special friend, someone who was always present, always comforting. I could not see him, but children have a naive trust they later lose through adult cynicism. If my Sunday school teacher said Jesus was real today, long after the death he suffered at Easter time, then he was real. I needed no other confirmation, none of the reinforcing experiences that come through the Holy Spirit as we move through adulthood.

The night after the green monster almost devoured me, I knelt by my bed in prayer. I prayed to Jesus that he would keep me from having any more bad dreams. I prayed that the night terrors would be over, that I would be kept in peace.

That night I went to sleep, certain I would be safe. And the next morning, when I awakened, I realized I had slept peacefully through the night. That was a long time ago and I have never had another nightmare again.

I had found my other Father, the one who truly would not forsake me, who didn't lead a double life. Over the years I have stumbled. I have made serious mistakes. I have sinned in ways all too human. Yet my faith has continued to deepen, and it has helped me through my most troubled times—times that ultimately were far worse than those early night terrors.

5

In My Father's House

There are those who tell me I publish a "dirty book." They argue that *Hustler* is "dirty" because of the candid manner in which we deal with sex and, most specifically, with sexual taboos. The taboo most frequently cited by my critics is incest. But other printed works deal with the same perversion and are not reviled. One of these is the Bible.

This quote, from an early *Hustler* magazine publisher's note, continues: "An aberration such as incest is a consequence of a sexually repressed society."

Child molesting has always been the dirty little secret of American society. Studies of immigrant families in overcrowded New York tenements at the start of the twentieth century indicated a serious problem with incest. Similar problems existed in rural America on large family farms where children came frequently and neighbors were often some distance away.

It was the Polaroid camera that changed societal attitudes toward child pornography. Before that time, photographs of naked children standing alone, touching each other's genitals, simulating sex, or actually having sex with an adult were not very common. American porn producers were usually connected with a photo lab and studio, often working after-hours or as part of a large-scale pornography production center. These were relatively rare, because most of the material was imported from Europe. Often it was the same children in different poses year after year, the faces and bodies never maturing. This was proof to some experts that the pictures had been taken in large quantities, then parceled out to the market over time.

The advent of instant picture technology changed all that. Pedophiles did not need a processing lab. There was no risk that a quality control inspector would see the negatives or prints and call police.

How widespread the issue of child molestation and child pornography actually might have been by the 1960s is not known. What was known were several factors of great importance. First, a child who was molested repeatedly was likely to in turn molest others as an adult. With an estimated one in four girls and perhaps one in eight or ten boys being molested each year, the potential for an ongoing pattern of abuse was large. Not that this problem was inevitable. However, during the period when Dad founded *Hustler*, therapy was rarely an option. Most therapists could not deal with the issue, and most victims were uncomfortable talking about what happened. There was still a stigma to having been molested, raped, or abused as a child. There was still the belief that the child must have somehow seduced the adult because it was such an abnormal act.

But advertising and the underground world of the live sex business changed. By the time I was nine, many advertisers were taking prepubescent girls, hiring makeup artists and hairstylists to make them look like seductive young women, and using them for fashion and cosmetics ads. Publishers of sexually oriented material skirted the law by hiring flat-chested girls who were at least twenty-one, and baby-faced boys the same age who had little pubic or facial hair.

Then they would have the photographers make certain that all body hair was shaved or retouched in the final images of the adults having sex in a way the reader would assume involved children. Or they would team each adult "child" with a mature-looking adult for sex. The law was never broken, but the images were only of interest to those whose sex lives were perverted.

The live sex business changed in a horrifying way. First, the 1960s and early 1970s saw a large number of runaways moving to cities such as Los Angeles, New York, Boston, San Francisco, and other large metropolises. Some of the teenagers were rebellious in ways that went too far, separating them from all they once held dear only because they were too scared to call home and admit they wanted to return. Others were the victims of abuse and/or neglect, fleeing a life they had no idea how to handle. Shelters and counseling centers filled with professionals who would act as advocates for the kids when necessary were just beginning to come about. Most of the kids ended up hustling any way they could. Some shoplifted. Some panhandled. And some sold their bodies.

The market for ever younger prostitutes, both male and female, grew to such a quantity that many of the old-time madams running traditional houses of prostitution closed down their enterprises. They could not stay in business "renting" the bodies of the adult women who worked from their brothels, no matter how beautiful and willing they might be. The requests from men and some women were increasingly for children, a commodity they would not provide. At the same time, organized criminals began setting up rings of these children, and their appearances in areas such as Boston's "combat zone" and Los Angeles' Sunset Strip were carefully controlled.

Eventually foreign sex junkets came to America. These were mostly Asian men looking for a different type of thrill than they got at home, where, ironically, pornography was very much a part of the "normal" culture.

The abuse of children was a low priority among police departments throughout the United States. Abused children live with fear, convincing themselves that what they have experienced is what every other child their age is experiencing. The fear of future violence and the hope that their silence will prevent further attacks helps them keep their stories to themselves.

The signs of abuse are also the signs of shyness and normal adolescent withdrawal from adults. Many mothers did not complain about the molestation of their children because they were in denial. Either they did not want to face that fact or they were relieved that their often drunken husbands were not bothering them.

This was a period when such movies as *Behind the Green Door* and *Deep Throat* drew a mainstream audience. Marilyn Chambers, one of the pornography stars of the era, had the distinction of both having sex in an X-rated movie and being one of the models on Ivory Snow boxes. She was the epitome of feminine, motherly purity—and of hard-core sex.

Linda Lovelace, another porn star, was portrayed as the quintessential liberated woman, truly enjoying her successful film career. Only later would she reveal that she was forced into a pornography "career" through physical violence, including rape, and the use of drugs. She was an unwilling victim, a participant from fear and forced addiction.

But the most outrageous attitude, in hindsight, was the reaction to *Deep Throat*. Some observers had the audacity to call it a "feminist" film. A number of supposedly respectable sociologists lauded the movie for being concerned solely with the sexual pleasure of a woman. No longer were porn flicks about what a man could do to a willing or unwilling sex partner. No longer was the man's pleasure of ultimate importance. Now the happy ending occurred only when the woman said there was a happy ending. She was a modern woman who would not be deterred from her quest.

With such cultural approval, the movie was frequently shown during early hours at movie houses that were previously either not booking it or keeping it to a near midnight hour when only adults would come. It became a popular part of a date among college students who had to pretend to be sophisticated enough to appreciate the depth of value to the picture.

And no one wanted to be ridiculed for saying it was nothing more than a hard-core porn movie demeaning everyone involved, but better publicized than most. You didn't have to enjoy perversion in whatever form it took, but you had to be cool enough to pretend you at least respected it all.

That was why a magazine like *Hustler* grew so rapidly. Valid objections that might have been raised in the mainstream press, objections that might have given potential buyers second thoughts, were deemed inappropriate. *Hustler* was hailed, for the most part, even if it was a bit extreme.

But that did not excuse the child molester "humor" and allusions.

Child pornography flourished at that time partly due to society's naiveté, and partly due to the fact that other, more publicized social problems received primary attention from law enforcement officials. Political protests were at an all-time high, especially over the war in Vietnam. The free-love movement led to serious drug problems, involving everything from heroin to LSD. Groups such as the Weatherman faction of the Students for a Democratic Society (SDS) had turned violent, bombing buildings and committing robberies to finance their cause. In this context, child pornography and child molestation were almost invisible.

Psychologists and psychiatrists were also just beginning to understand such concerns as pedophilia, at the same time that the free-love movement enabled some people who practiced perversion to be more open. For example, there was the National Man/Boy Love Association whose motto was "Sex before eight or else it's too late." Eventually some of these men were found to have entered professions and avocations where they could involve themselves with boys—youth work, coaching, Scouting, even the ministry. Their spokesmen were interviewed on television and radio, claiming that they had never "seduced" young boys; rather, they had the desire to have a loving relationship with boys. They felt that the experience could be healthy for everyone, that adult males could serve as role models. But in no way had they actually done it.

That was a lie, of course. It was a sick, dirty world in which they practiced, yet the media gave them attention as though they had a legitimate issue, not a compelling reason to be locked away for long-term therapy.

There were also men and women who enjoyed sex with children but were not true pedophiles, though they often were given that label. For some it was just another "interesting" sexual experience. For some it was wrapped in pagan religious beliefs, the power inherent in taking the essence of a virgin child. And for some it was a way of striking back against an estranged spouse, hurting him or her by hurting the children.

"Nice" men's magazines dealt with child pornography through humor. Young girls were sexually aware, sexually seductive, or well-endowed. One *Playboy* cartoon showed a little girl, with silicone-enhanced breasts, on a movie set. As I remember the image, she may have been smoking a cigarette as well. The director was saying to her, "Let's face it. Your days as a child star are over."

Funny? Perhaps. Harmless? Maybe. But even this simple twist of humor could not have been printed a few years earlier. My father took advantage of the spirit of the times by featuring Chester the Molester in the pages of *Hustler*.

One question that has long existed in the study of pornography is whether people are psychologically changed by the words they read and the images they see, or whether the pornography reflects what they would do anyway. Does a normal, healthy man rape women after viewing photographs and movies of men committing rape? Or does a rapist look at such images in order to tell himself that he is normal, that real men like to rape women?

I certainly did not think about such matters when, at age nine, Judy and I were invited to visit my father in Columbus, Ohio. His *Hustler* empire was headquartered there prior to his relocating to Los Angeles.

Dad's business was thriving, and though he at first had to combine his home and office, he eventually moved into the Bexley Manor in one of the better areas of Columbus. He was married to his fourth wife, Althea, and seemingly happy, probably another difficult reality for Mom. And his support payments were less than Mom had a right to expect given his large and growing income. As a result, Mom felt anger, jealousy, love, and sadness—emotions my grandmother knew how to manipulate. Althea was the most beautiful, perhaps most brilliant, and certainly the most troubled woman in Dad's life.

There are many "official" stories about Althea's past—the nicest being that she came from a troubled, abusive childhood, got a job as a dancer in one of Dad's clubs when she was seventeen, and he fell in love with her beauty and brains.

She had endured the horror of her father's murdering her mother.

Althea was also brilliant. Boye De Mente remains convinced that without Althea, *Hustler* would have had a slower start with far less success. Although she had never seemed to aspire to more than being a dancer in Dad's club, she had a mind that would rival the skills of a top MBA.

Dad was smart. He was willing to learn. And he ran a highly profitable operation. However, Flynt consultants such as Boye De Mente considered Althea to be the natural. She understood the business of magazines, the business of publishing, and how to achieve the maximum profits while expanding beyond a pornography base.

Althea was one of the most naturally beautiful women I have ever seen. Her face, her figure, the way she walked made both men and women look. She could have been a model or a movie star or the CEO of a legitimate corporation. Instead she was a self-educated hooker, a drug addict, a sex addict, and an emotional marionette who turned over her strings to Dad.

I did not understand all that at the time. I did not realize that there was a sadistic side to her, an angry response to the pain she had endured. All I knew was that she was beautiful, her voice softly comforting, enveloping both children and adults with a warmth that instantly brought peace. She seemed to be someone who had one foot in heaven, the other in hell, and she would spend her too short life trying to decide which way she wanted to go. In his book *Larry and the Lord*, Larry Jones quotes Althea as saying her greatest fear was of going to hell.

Dad and Althea used the Columbus *Hustler* Club as their base. The club was downstairs in a large building, and the entire second floor was devoted to their offices and living space.

Judy and I were met at the airport in a white Lincoln Town Car with emerald green interior. The car had air conditioning, FM stereo, a cassette player, and every other accessory offered. The wood finish on each door panel was engraved with his initials, L.C.F. The car ran silently, smoothly, with no foul smoke coming from the exhaust. It was like a billboard for success and I was overwhelmed with the luxury of it all. What I did not anticipate was the pain that lay ahead.

Dad and Althea were working in at least three cities at all times—Columbus, Dayton, and Cincinnati, moving among the *Hustler* Clubs and developing their magazine. But the Columbus club would be the first one I would encounter.

Though the building was in a commercial district, the apartment was spacious and beautifully decorated. You entered the living room, turned to the right wall, and on your left would be the door which led to Dad and Althea's bedroom. As I remembered it, there was a dark-blue carpet and matching bedspread on the big king-size bed centered against the far wall. There was a table in the room and a nightstand. Unlike the bedrooms they would have when they began leasing or buying mansions around the country, this was more functional than anything else. The only unusual decorations, at least to me, were framed posters of women in the magazine, all of them naked, hanging on the walls of the offices.

One other bedroom served as combined offices for Dad and Althea, though Dad had a personal office farther down the hall in the portion of the building used for business. Dad's office had a massive desk and a big chair large enough that I could sit on his lap and pretend I was a part of his world.

Althea was extremely insecure around me back then. I think she saw me as a threat, like a big sister reacting to a younger sister who is getting what is perceived as too much parental attention. Althea knew her place in Dad's life was very different from mine. At the same time, she was little more than an insecure kid herself, a young woman trying to get the attention of a rapidly rising businessman who had been married three other times. Having been a prostitute, she was also accustomed to the insincerity of males, at least among those who paid for her services. She had no way of knowing if Dad would commit to anyone, so any attention he paid to me was seen as a threat.

It was only later that I realized she was jealous. At the time I thought her to be mean, yet another vicious female from whom Dad was my only protector.

When Judy and I first arrived, everything seemed wonderful. During the day we were to be with Dad, who would take us over to the club. At night we stayed in his apartment.

Judy and I have slightly different memories of this, each of us certain we are right. She recalls the club where we played being Little Mommy's, but as I recall, Dad's mother had a bar that also had dancing. However, I am certain the club was the one he owned.

We both agree that it was an off-hour, a time when he would be doing the ordering, working on the books, and generally preparing for business later that day. None of the employees were around, so we had the run of the place. There was the dance floor, the changing area, an antique jukebox, and an area filled with the costumes the girls wore while dancing.

Dad told Judy and me to go in the other room and put on whatever we liked. There were white go-go boots, a fashion craze both on and off the dance floor in all types of establishments. There were silver G-strings, fringed tops meant to show the maximum cleavage of the dancers, little pasties, and tassels.

As we looked for things to wear, Dad put coins in the jukebox. I still remember the music—classic country western cheatin' songs or happier tunes such as "Just an Old-Fashioned Love Song." Some were about men who cheated on their women. Some were about women who cheated on their men. And some were about the men and women who led the singer astray. It was the kind of music conducive to either dancing or drowning your sorrows in beer, one of the bar's high-profit items.

Judy and I were delighted to see all the costumes because we had never experienced anything quite like it. The dressing table loaded with brushes and makeup was exciting, but both of us had experimented with Mom's cosmetics when we were at home and she wasn't around. Instead we went over to the racks of clothing and boots. We found pieces of fur which we wrapped around our necks and threw across our shoulders. We covered ourselves with long, white furry things—probably part of a striptease number—then held hands and shook them to watch the effect in the mirror.

We found clip-on earrings, silver lamé material, and, of course, the boots. Finally we added lipstick, mascara, powder, and I don't know what else. We must have looked like clowns trying to be sexy and failing miserably, but when we came out, Dad pretended not to notice.

He was smiling, watching us out of the corner of his eye. We found a microphone and began dancing to the music playing in the background, proudly announcing each other as we performed. We danced. We sang. And we obviously pleased our father.

I was euphoric when it was time to leave the bar and go upstairs to the apartment. My dad loved me. He didn't yell or tell me I was in trouble for playing with the clothes and equipment in the club. He didn't put me down. He seemed to delight in my life since he, at least, was proud that I looked like him.

Althea was increasingly jealous of Dad's pleasure in us, especially me. Althea knew that Dad had given Judy his name, but that I was his biological child.

Althea's drop-dead gorgeous figure was the result of both a physically active life and drugs. She used recreational stimulants at least since she had been a prostitute, and Dad shared her enjoyment of them after their marriage. She also had a junk-food diet.

Dad's weight fluctuated greatly, the drugs also influencing him at times. Ironically, their world was one of physical appearances, of girls whose bodies had to be lean and supple to impress the men.

Judy and I were kids. We loved burgers and fries. We delighted in pizzas and soft drinks. To most people we probably looked like normal, growing kids. Althea seemed to think differently. She said I was too fat. Later she would try to "help" me reach the weight she and Dad decided was desirable. Unfortunately their idea of "helping" me was to engage in endless ridicule that increased over the years.

The most painful incident during the trip was when Althea gathered some old clothes, presumably hers, in boxes from which we were going to be allowed to choose what we wanted. We sat on the floor and excitedly started going through what, to us, were beautiful, priceless treasures.

Judy and I chose blouses, skirts, and other clothes, made certain they fit us, and began dreaming how we would look when we were dressed.

Suddenly Althea announced that I could not have any of the clothes. I was too fat. Nothing would fit me. Judy was the right size and her choices were perfect. My choices might have been good for a thinner girl. However, since I wasn't, I would have to leave everything for Judy.

I began to cry. I was no more than nine years old, a child who had lived with the least expensive clothing Mom could buy because that was all she could afford. I had experienced the normal teasing of elementary school kids who were just beginning to be influenced by television commercials. The kids who came from families with money enough to buy the latest thing frequently ridiculed those of us who had to make do with the generosity of others.

Suddenly I was faced with clothes that were at once beautiful, nicer than anything Mom could ever afford to buy us, and because they came from Althea who lived with Dad, they seemed a love offering from him. Yet I was told no. Judy was told yes. I was told I was too fat, that I would ruin them. Yet I also knew that many of the clothes would fit me perfectly.

As I cried uncontrollably, Judy looked at me and grinned. Our rivalry was so intense that the pain of one caused pleasure for the other.

Althea, who could behave like a jealous sibling herself, seemed more amused than compassionate. She was typical of any adolescent with a younger sibling she sees as a threat for a father's attention. It seemed as though she felt that if anyone could change Dad's life, it was me. If anyone could be brought into the empire he was creating, eventually usurping her role, it was Dad's firstborn. After all, she already knew what I did not—that Dad was modeling his efforts on Hefner's success though taking the business to a sick extreme.

But there was no reason for such rivalry or jealousy. Not then. Not ever. And it was all impossible for me to comprehend. All I knew was that I had been treated unjustly and the shock was overwhelming.

∞

Tonya, keep your friends close and your enemies closer. No one can hurt you more than your family and friends.

—*a quote my Dad used to tell me frequently when I spent*
several months living with him after I turned eighteen

∞

I couldn't stop crying. I wailed. I whined. I bawled. I whimpered. My face was covered with tears. My nose was running. And my voice undoubtedly rose to the pitch every parent has to endure more times than any of us wish as we are raising our kids.

Suddenly Dad came in, livid. He didn't know anything about clothing. He didn't know anything about the pressures we kids were under in Jacksonville's schools. And he certainly didn't see what, to him, were a bunch of old clothes being important enough for the noise I was making.

Althea told Dad I was upset because I was too fat to wear the clothes. Dad agreed with Althea. I was too fat. I should lose weight if I wanted clothes like that. Besides, Althea had a gift for me, a red leather notebook. The folder was a trifold. On the vinyl center section, Althea had carefully taped a copy of the advertisement requesting young, beautiful women to work as dancers and waitresses. It had a line drawing of a woman with hair flowing over the ad, her hands up around her face. It was similar to a publicity head shot or a cameo on a piece of jewelry. The effect was one of glamour, not depravity and condescension. Judy wouldn't get one. She'd just get the clothes.

I cried some more, staring at the boxes, watching Judy try on first one outfit and then another. If I tried to touch one of the garments, she'd grab it from my hand. "No, you can't have that," she'd say. "It's mine."

Finally Dad could take no more. He started screaming at me, then grabbed me, hauled me into his bedroom, threw me on the bed, grabbed his belt, and began whipping me. He was angry and he wanted to hurt me, and he did. By the time he stopped, there were welts on my back, butt, and legs.

I stopped crying. The pain, the fear, the shock were all too great. I desperately wanted comforting. I desperately wanted someone to hold me, to love me, to tell me I was special, not just a vehicle for ridicule and wrath. I curled into a fetal position, then began reflexively kissing the inside of my arm near the elbow, trying to comfort myself.

Sometime after that Althea looked in on me. I don't know if she wanted to gloat or if she felt a little guilty for what had taken place. All I know is that she saw me, then started to laugh, announcing to the others that I was French-kissing my arm.

More time passed. I lay too sore to move, too sad to want to live. Althea came in again, this time with Judy. They saw the welts, realized that the beating was extreme. They also quietly told me that Dad was in the living room, sitting on a chair, crying. He, too, realized he had gone too far. I don't know if he understood what caused my grief in the first place. In hindsight, I wanted him to know his reaction had been too extreme. I wanted him to hate himself for the pain he had caused me, for the loss of control, the loss of compassion.

Their words were meant to comfort me, though they were just words. I think I fell asleep. I think Judy and Althea went out somewhere, perhaps to eat. All I know was that I was in that room for what may have been minutes or hours before the door opened again and Dad came in holding a copy of *Hustler* like a repentant lover bearing roses and candy to his beloved.

I don't remember exactly how it happened. I know Dad touched my back in the gentle, loving way of any parent comforting a hurt child. His voice was soft, caring. He began to rub my shoulders and neck.

Nothing hurt as Dad touched me, telling me he was sorry, asking my forgiveness, telling me he loved me. I had been spanked, sometimes harshly, by Mom, who even had a cat-o'-nine-tails to use as a threat. I had been yelled at. I had been ignored when in pain. But no one had ever come back later to say they were sorry, that they overreacted, that they loved me. No one had ever tried to reconcile what took place, to show me love when I was in the depths of despair. No one until Dad.

He loves me! My Dad loves me! Judy's jealousy didn't matter. Althea's hostility didn't matter. I was safe, loved, in a place where neither Mom nor Grandma, Judy nor Althea were present. My knight had found me.

Until he removed his armor.

Dad started talking about his magazine. I had no interest in his business, but if Dad wanted to talk, I was willing to listen a bit.

Dad told me what a great responsibility he had as a publisher. He dared not ever print a lie. Everything he ran in his magazine had to be the truth. That was the law.

Then Dad began showing me the pictures and the cartoons, especially Chester the Molester. I would see more of those cartoons over the years and do not remember which ones he showed me that night. I recall one that may have been from that magazine where Chester was lurking in an alley, with an erection, a swastika tattooed on his shoulder. He had a piece of meat tied to a string, the meat on the sidewalk outside the alley in the path of a Seeing Eye dog leading a blind little girl.

Another one had Chester the Molester in a similar position, with his pants down and a full erection, but this time using a dollar bill tied to a string. A little girl is walking with her oblivious mother and has just dropped her mother's hand, ready to grab the dollar before her mother knows she's gone.

Dad showed me these cartoons and began to explain what little girls do with their fathers. I no longer remember the explanation, just that the cartoon character with the erection represented a good, loving father.

Dad's hands moved to my breasts.

He rubbed my stomach and worked his way down. Then he told me to take off my panties.

I remember Dad standing up, stepping back, and watching me, his voice becoming stern as he again told me to take off my panties. I was scared, almost frozen, not certain what was happening or what I should do. I wasn't thinking about sex or incest. I just knew that something was not right, yet I felt guilty for thinking that anything Dad could do might be in any way wrong.

I did as Dad asked and he returned to the bed, holding the magazine, continuing to show me the pictures. He was proud of what was in it and kept stressing it was all true, he could not publish lies.

Dad touched me again, this time slowly probing my genitals. He began kissing me, began having oral sex with me.

I lay there, not knowing what to do or where to turn. Dad said he loved me, and I wanted that love more than life itself.

I had longed for that touch night after night as I lay in the dark on my mattress, the closet door closed, my mind filled with images of Dad's childhood created by the lyrics of John Denver records. There were times in Jacksonville when I would curl into a fetal position, then imagine I was on Dad's lap, cradled in his arms.

This was different. This was everything I had ever wanted—and everything I had ever hated. What had started as a tender, loving experience with Dad had degenerated into a familiar scene—a variation of what had been done to me by others.

Then I was told it was my turn. He asked me to touch him. I was shaking, wanting to cry, to vomit, to run from the room.

No, Tonya, I told myself. You don't know what a father's love is supposed to be. That's why he was showing you his magazine. That's why he said he couldn't lie in the magazine, couldn't have something wrong. This must truly be what a father does with his daughter when he loves her. This must be why Carl did it that first time.

The love was special. Carl had come into the bathroom when both Judy and I were in the tub. Dad had come into the room when Althea and Judy were not in the apartment. This was special. This was love. This was what Chester the Molester was all about, just as Dad said. This was like those pictures.

And then it was over. Dad pulled up his pants and walked into his office. And I was left on the bed.

☙

If my father truly believed the publisher's note that he wrote and I quoted at the beginning of this chapter, then he was not ready to admit he was a product of this society. Instead, he would claim that such perversion as he showed me, as he used to justify his own horrific acts, was satire. As he explained about what he published in the same publisher's note, he was trying to "poke fun at society's hypocrisies and inconsistencies, while providing the necessary vehicle for effecting social change."

I never said anything about this to anyone. I understood that this was just what adult men do, so everything must be OK.

But I knew it wasn't. Something was wrong in ways I could not understand. All that was certain was that Dad said he loved me, Dad gave me special attention.

Don't cry. Crying is wrong. Crying will get you whipped. Crying means you think your father is a liar.

I went to bed that night, never having spoken of what happened. My father treated me no differently than before he whipped me. There was no wink and a nod, no sharing of a dirty little secret. He had hurt me and he had apologized, showing me his love in the way a good father shows his daughter he cares. It was just like a hug. It was just like kissing a skinned knee when you first try to ride a two-wheeler and scare yourself when you fall off. A dad who loves you and makes a mistake apparently shows the love the way Dad did. The way Carl did. The way Mom's relative did.

I fell asleep, then awakened drenched in sweat. At least once I was screaming, though everyone, including myself, thought it was just a nightmare, not the memory of the afternoon.

Restless, I touched myself. I thought that might be a way of giving myself comfort. I may even have fallen asleep that way.

Nine years old. I had never touched myself before, never thought about anything related to sex.

I tried to feel what it was that made Dad's actions be love. I became hot, sweaty, confused. I was suddenly terrified of what happened, what I was doing, why I was doing it.

Yet I convinced myself that what Dad had done was love. It bothered me. It was not what I wanted. It was not what I had ever wanted.

Perhaps I had misunderstood my needs. Perhaps I just had to accept it. I could not ask Judy. I could not ask Althea. I certainly could not ask Mom and Grandma.

And so I said nothing. Dad did nothing similar for the rest of the visit, and I felt a twinge of regret leaving Columbus. At the same time, there was a nagging fear in my stomach as I returned to the routine of Jacksonville. I did not know what it was. I just knew I would have to endure it.

6

The Hustler *Empire*
and My Search for Faith

I'm not sure I ever wanted to understand my childhood from some philosophical viewpoint. I was always too scared, too mad, too hurting. My father was a pornographer and incestuous child molester. My mother was like a pinball in an arcade game, bouncing from man to man, pausing here, being shoved away there, never losing sight of her goals, yet never fully overcoming the pain of her own past. No matter where I lived, no matter where I traveled, there was always a dark side. Loneliness and poverty greeted me at home. Subtle psychological torments were regular companions during the happiest of visits to Dad's. I longed to be embraced in a loving family, yet my closest relatives were so estranged from each other that there was no hope of reconciliation. And each time I tried to create a family of friends and acquaintances, I was drawn to those as disturbed as myself.

I sought a simple metaphor for life, hoping that with a definition, somehow it would be easier. Life, I decided, is like an artichoke, whose layered leaves are experiences that must be uncovered and tasted before ultimately reaching the tender heart.

Or this: Life is like a calm brook in which we drop pebble after pebble, sending out ever-widening circles that overtake and blend with the circles that have gone before. Each newborn infant is the pebble. The days of each person's life are like one of the circles.

Metaphors are helpful, yet frequently they do not answer many of the questions that overwhelm us. This was especially true in my case.

Some religious leaders speak of our lives as the great human mystery, the acting out of the will of God in a manner we cannot fathom. They openly question why bad things happen to good people. And conversely, they sometimes whisper about the even more perplexing issue of why good things can happen to bad people.

It is easy to accept the idea that God's way is not humanity's way, and that we must let God's will be done. It is harder to imprint that concept on our hearts when the life we are experiencing is filled with perversion, emotional and physical violence, and experiences that reinforce our self-doubts. It is more difficult still when our questioning revolves around extreme traumas of childhood. According to the teaching of Christian faith, I did nothing to deserve what I experienced as a child. I certainly was not suffering for some sin in a previous life. I believe with all my heart that Jesus was with me every moment of my days and nights—and yet I was molested. Men who should have been trustworthy, protecting me, violated what many of us consider the ultimate human taboo.

Perhaps this is the frustration so many people have with the issue of free will. I can choose to do good for others. Someone else can choose to do only harm. And yet a third person can choose to not get involved. Should I be attacked by the person choosing to do harm, a crime witnessed by the person who chooses to not get involved, suddenly there is a victim, a sin of commission, and a sin of omission. Yet it may not be until each of us must stand before God that we fully understand how our seemingly uniquely personal decisions have impacted the world around us.

I cannot condemn my father for his actions toward me in the years I grew to womanhood. I cannot stand in judgment of him at the time of his death. I cannot truly say I have or will gain an understanding of someone who has caused such pain at the same time that I needed him to be my rescuer, healer, nurturer, and friend.

What I know is that my father sought a life of hedonistic self-indulgence that would bring him power, money, and a clear window to the dark side of the human soul. My mother sought love with an obsession born of insecurity and, at times, self-hate. She would pursue the wrong men, periodically subverting her hopes, dreams, and values in a desperate try for adult acceptance by someone she saw as a rescuer. Each made choices that affected me deeply. And I had to make choices to decide if I wanted to endure the life we were sharing.

My father has always been someone who has frequently commanded a mixture of contempt and respect. People who despise both pornography and the impact it has had on those people who have come to rely on it for entertainment and as a guide for interpersonal relations still view Larry Flynt Publications as a remarkable achievement. The business, as well as *Hustler*, are part of a remarkable rags-to-riches success story. Dad was a barely literate hill kid who left a small community where sex, alcohol, and physical survival were the only concerns, educated himself through aggressive reading, and then utilized the expertise of others to develop a business that is worth hundreds of millions of dollars. His business structure is on a level with that of such past media greats as Henry Luce, founder of *Time*, *Life*, and *Fortune*. It is a remarkable achievement, made even more so because the product is irredeemably reprehensible.

Dad also is aware that the love of perversion and the forbidden knows no boundaries. Most women would like to think that any man addicted to pornography or seeking justification for his desires to demean and/or abuse the opposite sex is a slobbering idiot. They want him to be as recognizable as the deformed Hunchback of Notre Dame or the living dead creature reanimated by Dr. Franken-stein. They want to be able to spot him on the street, warn their daughters against him, and use such men as examples that scare their sons away from pornography. That is what they want. That is what I want. And that is what, tragically, is not and has never been the reality.

Dad is successful because his readers are a cross section of con-temporary society. At one extreme, *Hustler* is popular with prison inmates in those institutions where it is allowed. It is read by men whose crimes involve violence against women and by men who have been jailed for possession, for use of "recreational" drugs such as marijuana, cocaine, and crack. It is read by child molesters and other perverts.

Hustler is also read by manual laborers, some of whom are high school dropouts, others of whom have diplomas, GEDs, and tech-nical training. It is read by curious college students who see pornography as a way to rebel or to fantasize about the activities they might one day have with the women they are dating. And *Hustler* is read by doctors, lawyers, even members of the clergy.

Some *Hustler* readers use the magazine to make themselves and their violent urges seem normal, bringing them into a community where their actions are lauded, not despised. Others have been seduced by such material, slowly desensitized to healthy relation-ships, loving actions, and respect for the opposite sex. Shock turns to titillation. Titillation becomes acceptance. And acceptance becomes ennui requiring ever more unusual images. Sometimes it is shared openly in a relationship, in a family, and/or on the job. Sometimes it is a dirty little secret, a hidden vice that is obsessively controlling yet hidden to avoid humiliation, condemnation, and overwhelming public shame. The former can assure that the person does not know when he needs help to stop. The latter can assure that the person will not seek help because even the admission of such an interest can shatter a career, a marriage, an otherwise righteously constructed life.

This is not to say that *Hustler* has had a readership on a par with large circulation mainstream magazines. Most men and women have never picked up a copy. Certainly the vast majority of Americans have never looked inside the magazine and wonder why anyone would bother buying something so blatantly antifemale. And of those who do turn its pages, many are likely to be curious one-time readers, not the eventual long-term subscriber who supplies Dad with the bulk of his income. Yet the fact is that the men who do let the *Hustler*/Larry Flynt mind-set become a part of their personal lives come from all backgrounds and look like anyone you might see on the job, in the store, in church, or in your own family. The average consumers of pornography are adolescent boys between the ages of 12 and 17, a time when they are trying to form their ideas about interpersonal relationships, sex, and sexuality.

Dad has long been both angered and amused by the hypocrisy among some of his critics. If someone's secret life is no better than his own, he wants to ridicule and hurt them. Sometimes I have had the impression that he sees himself no differently than many of the great social satirists throughout history. The difference is that social satirists use their words and drawings as mirrors to effect positive change. Dad's "satirical" material is vicious, obscene, and so hurtful that it will destroy its target long before it will encourage change. And in Dad's mind, any change should involve the greater toleration and acting out of pornography. He does not want to see the improvement of the moral character of his critics.

Dad's actions are not just meant for a national audience. Within his own organization, he seems to attack many of the people whom he respects. He seems to want to crush their spirit as a way of making himself feel more important. In fact, in hindsight, I feel he often acts like a lonely, scared, insecure man, a predator with just enough morality to feel uncomfortable with himself. He is a flamboyant purveyor of behavior he knows is often inappropriate, yet he lacks the courage to change.

I did not understand all this in the summer of 1976 on the first day I saw Dad in action in his newly leased Palm Beach residence. Judy and I were invited onto a chartered yacht where Dad was taking some employees and associates deep-sea fishing. Dad made certain Judy and I were properly equipped, though he had no interest in the sport. He stayed comfortably cool and relaxed in his terry-cloth bathrobe in the air-conditioned cabin while the rest of us were fishing. Althea spent her time on board leaning over the side of the boat, vomiting from seasickness.

I was determined to catch a fish that would make Dad proud. I did whatever any of the experienced fishermen told us to do, but nothing took the bait from my hook. I didn't even get a nibble.

Judy, on the other hand, caught both a tuna and a barracuda. I don't know if Dad was really impressed with the feat as he really wasn't that interested in fishing. But I do know I was intensely jealous and deeply saddened when he praised her. Once again I had been bested by my older sister. Once again I felt that I looked like a failure in my father's eyes.

Suddenly one of the men hooked a blue marlin. The fish was large, strong, and difficult to control. Few men had the strength to land such a fish by themselves. In fact, on most chartered fishing boats there was at least one person designated to help land such a trophy. And when there wasn't, the other men and women who were fishing would work together.

The man strapped himself to a special chair to keep him from being pulled into the water by the powerful marlin. He worked the fish, reeling in at times, letting line out as the fish sought an escape, then reeling in again, trying to force it to exhaustion so it could be lifted into the boat.

The man was not a laborer. He was a business associate of Dad's, and though he was in good physical shape, he did not have unusual upper body strength. His hands were soft, not calloused. Working the rod and reel was draining his energy and blistering his hands.

His face grew red. The sun was hot and he was sweating profusely. Minutes passed, the man fighting in silence. Finally he realized that he was rapidly becoming exhausted. He asked for one of the other fishermen to help him.

I watched the scene, expecting to see one or two of the others reach over, grab the pole, and work with him to land the fish. Instead, no one moved without first looking over at Dad to get his approval. Dad told them no.

The man continued fighting that marlin. His skin was burned from the sun. He was obviously in great pain, and soon his hands were bloody from breaking blisters.

Again the man asked for help. Again the others looked to Dad. It was like being in the Coliseum with the Romans watching two gladiators. The crowd had turned to the Emperor to see if he would give thumbs up or thumbs down.

"No one goes near him," I remember Dad shouting. He looked at the man, then said, "Let's see what kind of man you are."

I was appalled, and from the looks on the faces of the other fishermen, they were shocked as well. They had tremendous compassion, knowing that the catching of the fish had become some sort of a test of the fisherman, a test he did not want. I was astonished that despite their obvious sympathies, none of them had the courage to do anything. Had the seat harness broken and the man been pulled into the Atlantic Ocean, I doubt that any of them would have thrown him a life preserver without first getting Dad's OK. It was a frightening demonstration of the abuse of power.

The man understood that he had to land the marlin. There was no stopping except for a broken line, a heart attack, or a stroke. Yet he fought that fish in a way that made it obvious he was willing to die rather than let go of the rod.

Dad watched through the open cabin door, an amused look on his face as the man fought the fish. He was sipping some dark whiskey drink from an ice-filled crystal glass in that air-conditioned cabin, and from time to time, when the man with the marlin glanced over, Dad acted as though he was ignoring him.

Finally the battle was over. The marlin gave in before Dad's employee, and it was hoisted onto the ship. The man's hands were a sea of red.

Neither Dad nor the other men said anything. Dad was satisfied that he had forced the man to endure great suffering just to rise to a ridiculous challenge. The other men were seemingly embarrassed by their fear to intervene.

The man understood what had happened, understood the pain he had endured to keep my father's approval, understood, I suspect, that the greatest strength would have been in abandoning the fish despite the ridicule that would have followed.

I may have been a kid but I understood instinctively the dynamics. The action was vicious, and while I was too young to put what I had seen into context, I was still chilled by this previously unfamiliar side of my father.

∞

These concerns were way in the back of my mind as we enjoyed the life at the mansion. There were two swimming pools on the grounds, not just one. You could swim in fresh water or salt water— one pool was used by day and the other by night by everyone except Judy and me. We fancied ourselves princesses as we jumped from pool to pool, delighting in hedonistic luxury.

There were other amenities, including a maid and a private cook. It felt a little like Dad had purchased an entire restaurant just so he could dine alone. It was exciting, a luxury I had never imagined possible.

We passed the time swimming, walking on Dad's private beach, enjoying the luxury of the place. Dad had business associates working there and spent little time with us, but he did spend part of each day in our company. Once again I felt loved, safe, and strong in his presence.

Prior to this time I had sent letters to his office, letters to which he never responded. Instead I would hear from a secretary who explained how busy Dad was. She would tell me I was loved, tell me how hard he was working. And though I kept my fantasy image, the truth was that I was hurt. I felt separated from him, rejected, yet proud of what he was doing, whatever that meant.

Now there was no rejection. I was in his new home. I was sharing his world. I was with him at least part of each day.

I don't remember how long Judy and I had been staying in Palm Beach on the day when I grew tired early. I had been swimming a long time and was overexposed to the sun. I needed to go inside, to take a nap.

My room was a beautiful one. The king-size bed was white. The walls were yellow. There was a bamboo breezeway leading out, as well as a regular bedroom door.

I was still in my bathing suit when I lay down. Judy was outside by the pool. I didn't know where Althea was, though she wasn't in the house. And the staff of the mansion were either off duty or busy elsewhere.

I fell asleep, then was disturbed by the sounds of heavy footsteps. I roused myself as I realized that Dad was coming. I could tell by the walk. Judy's steps were light and rapid. Althea moved with the grace of a gazelle. This was the gait of a big man moving purposefully: my father's walk.

I opened my eyes, staring at the door which he was approaching. Then I heard him stop, heard his hand on the doorknob. I immediately closed my eyes, pretending to be asleep.

There seemed no reason to be afraid.

He touched me. A father's touch. Neither loving nor angry, just a touch to rouse me from slumber.

Dad had copies of *Hustler* with him again. He wanted to show me something he was working on. He wanted to show me some pictures.

There have been times when I have awakened in the middle of a nightmare, throwing open my eyes, seeing a mix of reality and the end of the dream that had terrorized me. The effect lasts only a moment, but during that time I cannot tell what is real and what is from the dream. I prayed I was in such a state. I prayed Chester the Molester and all the sexually implicit pictures I had seen before would disappear as I came to full consciousness. But I was awake.

Dad explained how important and successful the magazine was. It was the magazine that paid for the luxuries I was enjoying. It was the magazine that was the reason his friends were present and "enjoying" such activities as the fishing trip. It was the magazine that was giving people pleasure in ways they had not previously experienced.

Dad showed me pictures again. He explained that the images were different ways people give and get pleasure from each other. As I looked, not really seeing, not really caring anymore what was happening, Dad began touching me. Then he had me take off my bathing suit.

It began like that first time. Dad had oral sex with me. Then he dropped his pants, showed his erection, and tried to penetrate me.

I did not fight, could not fight. I was emotionally defeated, devastated by what was happening. This was not my father, the beloved knight I had created with my mind while alone in the closet, listening to John Denver records.

The pain was intense. I think I screamed. I know I was hurt.

Dad had not penetrated. There was no actual intercourse. It was the attempt and my tenseness that had caused the pain.

Judy was coming inside. Dad dressed quickly, grabbed the magazines, and left. I was nauseated, my head spinning. I tried to see and could not. Then I lost consciousness completely, gradually repressing the memories over time.

Later Dad took us for ice cream. Nothing was said about what had happened. Again there were no private signals, no comments about the sex. He did what he did, heard Judy, and left. It was all a part of an afternoon's activities.

I never blamed God for what happened to me with my father, Mom's relative and Carl. I never thought that God should magically save me from what I endured. I never felt abandoned by the Lord. At the same time, I was sinking deeper and deeper into depression, filled with self-hate, anxious to be done with life as I knew it, even if death was the only way out.

∞

Church had become a mixed blessing. Sunday school classes and the minister's sermons at the South Side Assemblies of God gave me a degree of hope. I learned about Jesus' life, death, and resurrection. I learned of his presence in my life, in all our lives, and of the choices we can make concerning his way. I also learned about Bryan Wilkes.

Bryan Wilkes entered my life as my father was leaving it. After the visit where he molested me, he turned viciously against me. It was as though he felt guilt for what he had done, and instead of taking personal responsibility, he chose to blame the victim of his actions. After Judy and I returned from Florida, Dad told Mom that I wasn't worth a "shit." Later he would refer to me as "the cunt." The language was vicious and inexcusable under the best of circumstances. To use it in regard to his own child was more than inexcusable—it was destructive beyond anything anyone in the family understood.

I needed Dad's approval. I needed his love. It was as though he was the fourth essential for my life. I craved food, clothing, shelter, and my father's getting pleasure from my existence. Anything less seemed to leave me with an ache so intense there seemed no chance for healing. I would suppress the knowledge of the potential for ferocity in his heart, the memory of the indecencies to which he had subjected me. I had to believe in my knight, had to keep his tarnished armor polished so I would not look at the real man hidden inside.

Somehow in the midst of all this and the onset of puberty, I focused on Bryan Wilkes. He was one of the most popular kids in church. Short, yet, good-looking, and with a beautiful voice. He played the drums and was an alto in the choir, where he would continue to sing as an adult. He was also a little older than me.

The crush I had on Bryan was both excessive and obsessive. I somehow decided that if I could gain Bryan Wilkes's adoration, then I would be OK. Where before I was looking to my father to justify my self-worth, now I was looking to Bryan Wilkes.

I suppose my actions might have been humorous had they not been so pathetically connected with the molestation I had endured. I tried to follow Bryan everywhere, including into the choir.

There is something you have to understand. I am a singer of enthusiasm, a lover of music who delights in the vast variety of praise songs sung in many churches. I can sing in the shower. I can sing in the car. What I cannot do is sing well enough for anyone to want to hear me. The idea that I could become part of a choir was even more ridiculous than the idea that my self-worth depended on whether or not Bryan Wilkes wanted to play Prince Charming to my imagined Cinderella. I attended a couple of rehearsals, then was gently and lovingly told that, in effect, I should not consider returning until I could sing with someone else's voice.

Having failed to gain the type of attention I sought through the choir, I began seeking every opportunity to be near my unrequited love. I tried to talk with him in church. I tried to find ways to intrude myself in whatever he was doing. Had we lived closer to his home (he was one of the rich kids, or at least he was living far more of a middle-class existence), I would have walked up and down his street, staring at every lighted window for a glimpse of my beloved.

I thought my opportunity had arrived when there was a youth group skating party. I did not ice-skate, and I also did not have a strong sense of my body that would enable me to keep my balance. In fact, if someone had to choose between using me in the choir and having me show my ice-skating technique, they would have preferred to endure my singing.

Not Bryan Wilkes, of course. And not the girlfriend. They might as well have been born to skate. Arm in arm they moved about the ice as gracefully, in my mind, as Olympic athletes part-nering in the figure skating competition.

I don't know if Bryan and his girlfriend were really that good. I just remember my feet slipping out from under me, then sliding along the ice, and the two of them skating past, laughing at my helplessness. I was humiliated and wanted to die.

My mother, Bryan's parents, and the minister were all con-cerned about my obsession. Finally the decision was made to switch churches. We began going to a Pentecostal church, which did not diminish my desire for the attentions of Bryan Wilkes but did open me to a more flamboyant religious experience.

The Pentecostal movement was not even a hundred years old when I was introduced to it. The emotional exuberance of some of the members was taken as a slap in the face by many members of mainstream religions. So many mainstream religious practices involved solemnity, a dour demeanor, and constant awareness of the sinfulness of humans.

The Pentecostals saw life differently. To be one with Jesus, one with God, was to be filled with the joy of the Holy Spirit. Sin was a reality. And Jesus' death for our sins was preached from the pulpit. But more important, we were children of God, who wanted us to succeed, to be healthy, vibrant, loving.

The church believed that when you are baptized with the Holy Spirit, you will be able to speak in tongues. This conviction, church members claim, can be traced back to the experience of the disciples on the day of Pentecost.

Sometimes someone else in church was also touched by the Holy Spirit, and was instantly able to translate what was said. At other times the speaking in tongues occurred for a variety of reasons and without human translation. It might be during fervent praise or deep prayer, or for many other reasons. Some do it frequently. Others only occasionally. And always, I believe, it is connected with the Holy Spirit's acting directly in our lives.

Today I belong to a nondenominational church that accepts the Pentecostal experience. There is the same excitement to the services, the same joy in the music and the praise during sermons, much like some of the Baptist churches I have attended. Thus, as an adult, I have found a blending of what I consider the best of all the approaches to the worship of Jesus and our Father in heaven. But this particular church, my first such experience and the one in which I was baptized, was extremely conservative. The structure was excellent for a child, and the nurturing congregation did not allow those who slipped on their path to be condemned. Thus it was the ideal mix for that time in my life.

The Pentecostal experience was good for me. My father's importance was relegated to the back of my mind. Bryan Wilkes's importance stopped being my focus. Instead, I realized that there was love, hope, a chance for us all. Although I rarely go to a Pentecostal church today, it was the Pentecostal experience that began to break my bondage to pain and to open me up to the joy of life.

This is not to say I was instantly healed. I have never had the immediate type of pain-to-pleasure experience of some who are born again. I still had to go through the depths of despair in the years ahead, enduring pain in order to be free from it. In hindsight, however, I know that the changes that took place and were about to take place one fateful night formed the lifeline I needed. In hindsight, I know that when I again had to wade through the quagmire of perversion, abuse, and evil, instead of being at the bottom of a pit, as I fancied myself, I was actually on a narrow bridge, holding firm to the rope of life.

I was about twelve years old when life seemed to overwhelm me. I had been to the Paxton Revival Center, the Pentecostal church to which we belonged, and was planning to go back for another family worship service that evening. The service had been joyous, yet I somehow reflected on why we had come there. It was Bryan Wilkes, or more precisely my obsession with him, that had led us to this new place. And then I realized that I might never be with him again. As much as I loved the Lord, as much as I loved where I was going to services, I still felt overwhelmed by Bryan's rejection. In my heart I had decided that it would be Bryan's attention, or lack of it, I would use to gauge whether or not I was worth anything as a human being. And now that we were deliberately separated, I was seemingly relegated to an emptiness nothing could fill.

My head hurt that afternoon. I felt nauseated. I wasn't sick so much as having physical symptoms that matched my emotional pain. I cried inconsolably, filled with despair.

I was alone, unable to be comforted by anyone I might have approached. If anyone in the apartment was aware of what was taking place, it was either ignored or dismissed as the intense emotionalism of the young adolescent female. But this was serious, a low point I had never before experienced.

There was a lump in my throat. Speaking without weeping was impossible. I knew that I would never find love, never know the happiness of another person caring, truly caring if I lived, died, or even existed on the face of the earth.

I began praying in the spirit. I was speaking in tongues. I told God that only he knew what was wrong with me. I wanted healing, was desperate for healing. I had to share the pain with God because I could no longer handle it alone.

I dropped to my hands and knees, laying my face on the floor. I was prostrate before him, knowing I needed his strength even to rise. "Okay, Lord, my pain is yours. I've held it too long. I have to let go to you."

That was when I heard the familiar words from the Bible: "Come. My yoke is easy, and my burden is light. Give it to me."

Weeping, my head buried against my arms, I whispered, "Lord, let your will be done."

And slowly the tears stopped, the strength being recovered. I felt as though I had been given the privilege of carrying my troubles to God. My cares had become his cares, and through his Son, my burden had been eased. I felt a relief I previously had not thought possible.

The afternoon went easily, and I was pleased to reinforce the day by being in church that night.

The pastor was alive with the Spirit that night. He was praying and singing, speaking the word as though he was a vehicle for something higher. It was a rare experience and one that seemed to reinforce all that had taken place earlier in the afternoon.

I was sitting in the back of the church, outside the line of sight of the pastor until he suddenly jumped onto a pew and, from that unusual vantage, pointed straight at me. "Sister," he shouted. "Since you said, 'Lord, let your will be done and not mine,' the Lord said he is going to give you the desire of your heart."

I was shocked. The pastor could not have known what went on in the apartment. My family did not know. I had spoken to no one. Yet here was a man of God in whom I had confided nothing that day yet who knew what was said. He had to be a vehicle for the Lord at that moment. He had to be.

That night I went to bed still shaken. I felt relief, yet I also knew that nothing had changed. I still had a broken heart. I was still tormented and depressed. I still saw no reason for life as I knew it. My parents didn't seem to love me and I certainly didn't love myself. I even went so far as to avoid looking at myself in the mirror. I might focus on my hair in order to brush and comb it, but I would not look at my full face or figure. I did not want to see what I was certain was an abomination. I appreciated God's having eased my burden that day, but I could see no reason why I existed in the first place.

And it was with this mind-set that I fell asleep that night.

The dream, if that was what it was, began in a hospital where I lay dying on a bed. There were doctors and nurses gathered all around me, desperately trying to save me.

My body was weak. I had no will to live. My eyes were closed and I might have been going into a deep sleep even as they all tried to revive me. I heard someone say that I was dying of a broken heart, and though I knew the diagnosis was correct, I felt no reason to keep from drifting to nothingness.

Suddenly I was lifted from the bed by the strong arms of a robed figure I knew at once was Jesus. I thought I was being carried bodily, yet when I looked down at the hospital bed, nothing had changed. My body was still on the hospital bed. The monitors hooked to my flesh were still reading my vital signs. It was my soul that was in his arms.

Trying to fully describe the experience would make it seem like a superhero movie filled with special effects. We flew three times around the earth, then approached the most beautiful tree I have ever seen. It was tall, thick, stately, obviously healthy yet without leaves. It was a tree undamaged by weather or insects.

We approached the tree, and as it seemed as though we would crash, I was filled with peace. This was the tree of life, and when Jesus and I passed through it, we were in heaven.

God was enormous as he sat on his throne. There was a brightness greater than any light I had ever known, yet I did not have to look away. I was home, truly at home. I was accepted just for me, with nothing desired from me, nothing expected of me, nothing I had to do or prove or endure. This was a love beyond human experience, a love so complete that to doubt my worth seemed a sacrilege. I was a child of the Father and in that I had value regardless of my achievements, my failings, or any other precondition we humans too often require of one another.

I looked at the face of Jesus. He was wearing a robe and had brown hair, but other details escape my memory. What struck me, what I found so compelling that only the appearance of God could tear me from studying them, were the eyes of Jesus. The only way I know to describe them is that they seemed like bottomless pools of love. And I knew when I looked into them that everything I longed for would be fulfilled.

I remember Jesus saying, "Father, give her the ability to understand the things of heaven that I will show her because with her carnal mind she cannot."

And then my eyes were opened. It was as though the sight I had known on earth was no different in heaven than if my lids had been sealed my entire lifetime. I did not see God again, but I was taken through the streets of heaven. I remember that the streets were golden and that there was a crystal-clear, totally placid body of water next to which a little girl was playing in the field. As I looked at her I realized that the girl was my sister, a child Mom had aborted. And as I studied the water, I saw that whatever was beneath the surface had colors more vibrant than all the blooms of all the flowers in all the fields of earth.

There were trees as beautiful as the tree of life. There was grass as lush and thick as the finest carpet. I can't recall it all, yet I imagine that it was how Eden must have looked during the first days of creation. There was no death, no erosion of even the tiniest patch of land.

Eventually we came to another tree where a lion was resting on one side, a lamb on the other. The Lord Jesus told me to lie down between them and go to sleep so I could go back from where I came.

I did not want to leave. I clung to Jesus' arm and begged him to let me stay. I looked down toward earth and remembered all the people I had left behind, who did not know what wonders awaited them. Yet I did not grieve for them. Their existence, their actions were not important, not in any way that could affect my emotions.

I may have been crying. I know I was pleading to stay, to not have to go back.

There was no choice. I was given a vision of myself speaking before the multitudes. I was told that this was something I was supposed to do in my life, though when, how, to whom, and for what reasons I did not know. All I was told was that it was important, that I had to go back.

Then I lay down between the lion and the lamb. I entered the deepest, most restful slumber I had ever known. And when I awakened, I remembered the vision and was convinced that I would be called to give witness to what I called a "dream" but truly believed, and still believe, was a time of going to heaven. I imagined that I would one day travel from church to church, telling people I was taken by Jesus for healing and renewed strength to endure the future.

It would be wonderful to say that what I experienced was my equivalent of Paul's being struck blind on the road to Damascus. I want to say that my heart was forever filled with joy, that my burdens were as feathers floating on the wind. I want to say that I had the wisdom and the courage to do only that which was right with God and a living witness to his holy name.

Perhaps if I had been older, this might have been the case. Certainly there was a change. My obsession with Bryan Wilkes was over. I no longer saw my mother as an enemy but as a troubled individual whose life was as much in need of healing as my own. I felt an easing in the tension that had been so much a part of me. Yet my journey through lands I did not wish to travel was not over. In the small amount of healing I let myself acknowledge, I realized that one reason for being back on earth was so that I could show others I was not a failure. Close relatives had long told me I would never amount to anything. Yet after this experience, I knew they were wrong. I was not allowed to continue through the muck and mire of my life.

Instinctively I thought I must become rich, important, as famous for good as my father was for his empire of perversion. I did not understand that when we are truly with the Lord, the ways in which we are altered, the ways in which we influence the lives of others, often have nothing to do with our status as defined by humans. Where I would go, where I seem to be traveling as I write this, is not toward the boardroom of a major corporation. Instead, it is to let my life, my choices both good and bad, my understanding born of a family whose actions now frequently seem so wrong, be a guide for helping others with the questions that weigh heavily on their hearts.

But I did not know this then, could not have imagined where I had to go and which paths I would ultimately have to take.

All I know now about that night was that my faith was strengthened, my love for God sealed in my heart forever. Yet I still sought my father on earth. I still made choices that would force me into his world of degradation. I would still have to experience the wanderings of the prodigal son before he understood the errors of his ways and returned to beg for the opportunity to be but one of his father's servants.

7

Spiraling out of Control

Looking back I can see that I went home from my Dad's house with an understanding of life as tragically perverted as the act committed against me. First, I had learned that fathers show their love for their daughters by having sex with them. My own father had done that to me before I was ten years old. I needed no further proof.

Second, I understood that relationships do not involve long-term commitments. Mom, Dad, and Grandma all showed me that marriage was a wonderful institution in which a person should indulge over and over again. There were side issues of sex and security, but the main message was that commitment was for the short term. Equally important, that commitment did not include meaningful involvement with any children who were the product of those unions.

Third, I had learned that money was more important than integrity. If you couldn't have affection, then wealth would buy comfort. The way in which it was accumulated was of little concern if, in spending it, you found pleasure.

And finally, the most humiliating lesson of all. Sexual ability was a key to being loved and valued by others, especially those who counted most in your life. Where before I would touch my genitals as a way of relaxing when alone, I found myself going to private areas where no one could see, then masturbating frequently. Often I would take one of the copies of *Hustler*, find pictures similar to the ones Dad had shown me, and masturbate while looking at them. It was my dirty little secret, an act so horrible in my mind, so unique to my filthy, damnable self, that God would never forgive me.

In recent months I have learned how typical I was as a victim of incestuous molestation. Many young women confessed their secret to me, telling me that they had something horrible they had to share. They stressed that they had never told anyone else. They stressed that they knew no one else had ever reacted as they had. They said that they were coming to me to unburden themselves because they felt that I would at least have compassion. I would not condemn them even if I was repulsed by what they had to say.

Then they told me about the compulsive masturbation, something I know now is yet another symptom of a sexually abused child crying out for help. Unfortunately, because of the extreme guilt we all felt, we also suffered severe depression. Thoughts of suicide and even an occasional attempt were common. This was not some secret pleasure or part of a punch line concerning a joke about nymphomania. This was the cry for help by a terribly mistreated child.

I have learned about other symptoms. Some molested girls become promiscuous with boys and men. Some become rigidly antisex. Many take drugs or alcohol to deal with stress. As adults, it is often easier to get a tranquilizer or an antidepression drug such as Prozac, both socially acceptable, than to risk scorn by telling the doctor the root cause of one's emotional problems.

There are also any number of reasons why some of us choose to come forward and tell what happened years after the fact. This dirty little family secret is often a crime covered up by other family members, either deliberately or through denial that the incest ever took place. In some instances the statute of limitations has run out. In other instances, the adult is within an acceptable time frame for prosecution. Whatever the case, the act of coming forward and filing, of announcing to the police that the woman knows she is innocent of wrongdoing, is healing in itself.

There are other times when the woman feels so full of self-loathing that she remains convinced she was the seductress—even at age four, or five, or six, or whenever she had her first experience. She stays in contact with her father. She marries and perhaps he is at the wedding. Then she has a child, and suddenly she sees her father beginning to act inappropriately toward her own daughter. She sees that her own child is an innocent. She sees that there is nothing seductive about her daughter, no reason why any normal, healthy adult would behave as her father is acting. And then she realizes that she was no different from her own child, delighting in the special attention which will ultimately lead to inappropriate touching or worse. That is when she takes her stand.

In my case, it was when a movie was made about my father, portraying him as a humorous eccentric dedicated to the First Amendment, that the memories came flooding back. *The People vs. Larry Flynt* showed him as a rogue, a brilliant clown tweaking the nose of the pompous and the hypocritical. Even worse, the movie was produced by Oliver Stone, a man known for creating film myth, then using brilliant public relations to imply that his fantasies are truth.

As I read the screenplay, then saw the movie, I flashed back to the real Larry Flynt. All the incidents I did not want to think about came vividly to the front of my mind. I looked at my daughter, a child of innocence the same age I was when Dad first sexually molested me. Finally, I stopped the self-loathing that had been such a powerful force in my life.

Yet it took me almost a quarter of a century to do it, and that is not uncommon. Research for this book led me to incestuous molestation victims who were in their seventies, their fathers long dead, before they felt safe in talking about it. That is why so few little girls ever talk about what happened when it occurs. That is why so many little girls assume that all their girlfriends are experiencing the same home life as themselves. And that is also why many children of both sexes suppress the memory until something forces them to confront the pain of their past.

And so I returned to Jacksonville, and to Mom, Grandma, Judy, and Shawn. There was hostility toward Dad, and I had defended him at every opportunity. I was in total denial about what had happened. I again focused on the John Denver country fantasy father, a man of pure nobility who remained my imagined savior from HUD housing, cheap food, and secondhand clothes.

The kids in my neighborhood came from a variety of backgrounds, all of them poor. Some had parents who worked two jobs or who were going to school and working full-time. Their goal was to provide their families with a better future than the past had given them. Sometimes the children were well cared for, often by relatives or by women who shared responsibilities with their neighbors. The latter would work out their job shifts so they would be able to look after both their children and those of friends working different shifts. The adults would change with the hours of the day, but there was always a familiar face, a loving hand, an adult who cared about where they were and what they did.

Some of the kids were latchkey children, running the streets from the time school was out until their parents got home from work. During the summers they were often outside from dawn to dusk. Some got into trouble. Others survived relatively unscathed, though lonely and desperate for adult presence at times.

The school represented a mix of kids from the HUD housing and kids from neighborhoods where there was more money. I never felt a part of any of them. I had been a good student, especially in English. I frequently lost myself in the writing of poetry and stories. But I had experienced too much to relate to most of the kids.

In Florida I lived in subsidized housing. Our food was sometimes enhanced by gift bags from our church. Our chauffeured limousine was a bus. When we had access to a car, it was as likely to stall as to run, as likely to be belching smoke and violating noise laws from a faulty exhaust as it was to be running smoothly down the highway. It was a life shared by my friends, shared to a degree by most of the kids I knew.

Then, as if by fairy godfather, I would be flown first-class across the country to a mansion that was a monument to new money. The drugs consumed by Althea every few weeks probably cost more than Mom earned working two jobs all year. My father had more people working in his home than most of the small neighborhood businesses had employees. I was chauffeured in a limousine owned by Dad, not rented to impress someone. And no matter how rich he was when I arrived, his enterprises were growing at such a rate that he was even wealthier when I left. It was as though he could not spend money fast enough.

There were television shows purporting to show the lifestyles of the newly rich. There were soap operas and prime-time programs revealing the opulence of their lives, the secrets of their bedrooms. But instead of fantasizing about some program with friends, I was periodically living it all.

And I felt like an unwelcome guest in both places.

In hindsight, I know my mother tried to love me. When Grandma was making nasty remarks about Dad and bringing me into the fights because I looked like him, Mom would invariably defend me. She would not allow Grandma to attack me.

Yet Mom was also overwhelmed by life. She could not sustain a relationship with a man because she could not seem to look objectively at him before she committed herself. She constantly tried to better herself with the jobs she held, yet she was almost always in positions where she would earn a low, set wage. She would never be an entrepreneur. She would never be in management except for the dream of opening her own beauty shop. She would always be beholden to others for a paycheck, an extra discount, or whatever would help her family get through the day. There was no thought of a better tomorrow because she knew there was nothing to hope for.

The tension and fights between Judy and me became worse. During one of our moves I was finally able to have a bedroom of my own. It was the first time I had such luxury, such privacy. I would not have cared if it was the same size as my walk-in closet so long as it was not part of someone else's living quarters. But one time I became so outraged at Judy that I grabbed a two-pronged roasting fork and jabbed at her thigh, breaking the skin, drawing blood. I didn't want to kill her. I wanted to hurt her. I wanted her to have physical pain as intense as the psychological abuse her taunting had inflicted upon me for so long.

The one break during sixth grade, an experience with my father, was not as much help as it could have been. Either because of feelings of guilt, because he was in a mood to help his daughters, or because he again wanted to seduce Mom, Dad decided to pay for us to go to a private school. I assumed it would be for the rest of my education, and I think Mom did, too. After all, it was so out of character that it was hard to conceive of him doing it for only one year, though as it turned out, that was all he did pay for.

The school was a Christian school, but the kids were as petty as they had been in public school. Some of the parents were struggling, barely able to pay the tuition yet determined that their children would experience positive values. Others were wealthy. The parking lot was a mix of battered cars and luxury sedans.

Money made a difference among the students. I was frequently ridiculed for not being part of the in-group. And when I fought back, I was forced to do the standard school punishment—push-ups. I felt frequently humiliated and hated the discipline. I was also reaching puberty ahead of many of the other girls, and that was an added burden. In any school the girl or boy who is among the first to show signs of moving into adulthood is the object of painful teasing. One classmate wrote a note about my breasts saying that I was "making a mountain out of a molehill."

I began running with the misfits in school, the girls whom others scorned. Some were loners. Some were latchkey kids who never adjusted to the time alone and sought any attention they could get, even if it was for inappropriate behavior. I was emotionally withdrawn and had come to so dislike Mom that I deliberately made her life difficult. There was constant tension between us which Judy liked to aggravate.

Oddly, I was not that different from Mom when she first turned thirteen. I didn't try to pass as a young adult, though my face lacked the maturity hers had held back then. However, I did sneak out of the house at night, often with Judy. She began experimenting with marijuana and alcohol as most of us did. We saw it as a rite of passage, as being cool, as being grown-up and independent. We'd meet in a friend's house to talk and relax, Mom never knowing we had left the apartment.

I was also less interested in school. My emotions were in turmoil and I was confused about sex and sexuality. I went to church, and

I prayed for forgiveness, yet I was also convinced God could not want me. There were times I remembered my positive feelings for Jesus, turning myself over to him in prayer, feeling the loving warmth of his embrace as I lay in bed or sneaked back into the house. There were other times when I felt completely alone, help-less, miserable, choosing to not reach out to the comfort that was always available just because I had come to loathe myself too much to believe for certain what I was learning in church.

While all this was taking place, Dad was becoming notorious in ways I did not realize. He delighted in openly flaunting obscenity laws wherever he could. The issue was not free speech, though Dad usually said it was. Instead, the issue was making money. He would do anything that would bring him more income without limiting his ability to distribute the magazine.

The city of Cincinnati decided that *Hustler* magazine violated the community's standards for decency. They brought him to court on obscenity charges in 1976; Dad was convicted and given seven to twenty-five years in jail. That decision was overturned on appeal, though the people of Cincinnati remain firm to this day in their desire to keep the magazine from being distributed there. In fact, when he opened a store selling his magazines and a variety of sex-related paraphernalia twenty-one years later, peo-ple of all religions, political beliefs, and economic backgrounds rallied. Some felt the store should be ignored. Others wanted it removed through enforcement of one or another zoning, building, or related city codes. The store remains open at this writing, though the ongoing confrontations reveal the intensity of public opinion regarding pornography.

�❧

Most Americans no longer remember Ruth Carter Stapleton, the late sister of former president Jimmy Carter. The family business was peanut growing. The family religion was Baptist. And the family itself was a mixed bag of characters.

First there was Jimmy Carter, a man of high morals, stable marriage, and a firm belief in the teachings of his faith, which he shared with others in his church as a Sunday school teacher. The teaching was not a photo opportunity. He had been involved with the church since before he was governor of Georgia, continued while in the White House, and continues at this writing. He was pragmatic enough to let himself be interviewed by *Playboy* when running for President, yet honest enough to admit that he had committed adultery "in his heart." President Carter took literally the teachings of Jesus, which say that if you lust for someone in your heart, you are committing adultery—even if you never act on it. Jimmy Carter had looked at other women and occasionally found them desirable. He said nothing. He did nothing. Yet his admission that he had committed adultery in his heart became a joke. At the same time, his honesty also helped him win the 1976 presidential election.

Billy Carter was an alcoholic. A beer-drinking good old boy in and out of trouble with the law, he was an embarrassment and a reminder that even the rich and powerful have an uncle no one likes to talk about. At the high point of Billy's efforts to make a few dollars from his brother's stay in the White House, Billy allowed his name to be used in connection with Billy Beer—a brief success that Jimmy Carter could do nothing about.

Jimmy's mother, Miss Lillian, was a woman of independence, caring, and an adventuresome spirit. She joined the Peace Corps in her seventies, was outspoken, and accepted the idiosyncrasies of all her children. She was closer to the character Auntie Mame than she was to the white-haired grandmother sitting rocking on the front porch of a Georgia plantation.

And then there was the evangelist sister, Ruth Carter Stapleton. She was a woman of deep faith who felt the need to reach out to others she felt needed desperately to know the Lord. My father was becoming prominent, and in her eyes, he was a man needing help. She wanted to talk with him, show him that his actions were as much from pain as from anything positive, and help him turn his life around.

There are any number of stories about what happened. One story is that Dad was in his manic phase when he met with Mrs. Stapleton. Certainly he was disturbed at this time. As Christina Echols, Ph.D., would later write: "The majority of evidence suggests that Mr. Flynt is likely suffering from a bipolar affective disorder, manic type, which includes frenetic activity, restlessness, grandiosity, flight-of-ideas, irritability, and distractibility. Moreover, Mr. Flynt has likely been suffering from a personality disorder of longstanding duration. Specifically, this personality disorder consists of narcissistic, histrionic, and antisocial features. Briefly, some major features which show up in Mr. Flynt include inflated self-worth, preoccupations with fantasies of unlimited success, interpersonal exploitativeness, intense need for control, self-dramatization, insatiable need for attention and irrational angry outbursts."[1]

But it is simplistic to talk of my father as mentally ill or to say that his actions at this time reflect mental illness. The manic side of Dad's personality had nothing to do with what took place. At least since Dad left the small community where he was raised, he has been searching for something greater than himself. He may frequently quote the Bible out of context, including in some of his publisher's columns in *Hustler*, but he is aware of the Word, its impact, and its potential for changing people.

There is also the reality that when people have no spiritual stability in their lives, they often have to hit bottom before they will seek the Lord. Dad's emotional problems may have led him to the point where he was open to change, open to God. The fact that we have the choice to change after being shown a better way, to go with the Lord or again move away from him, is not the point. Dad was in a period where, if it was possible for anyone to reach him and change him, this would be the opportunity. And Ruth Carter Stapleton seemed to sense that fact.

I think Ruth Carter Stapleton touched Dad with the Word at a time when he was searching. Tragically he refused to move beyond the destructive people surrounding him. They wanted the money *Hustler* generated. I still remember Althea's quote when she thought Dad's conversion would not change: "Jesus may have just walked into your life, but $20 million a year just walked out."

There had to be a change in Dad to some degree for Althea to make the comment she did, but was he truly touched by the Word? I do not think so. Christians, especially those new to the faith, are not perfect. Jesus spent his time with the outcasts of society and held the rich in disdain whenever they seemed to feel that maintenance of their wealth was more important than being right with God.

I think that for the first time in his life Dad felt nurtured and loved unconditionally by this Christian evangelist who walked with him, talked with him, and cared more about his future than his past. She did not want his money. There was no offering made or requested at the end of their conversation. She genuinely loved him as a child of God in a way no one else ever had.

But Dad was not ready to turn away from the god of money he had worshiped for so long. As tempted as he was to change, and Althea's comment reinforces my belief that there was such a temptation, he could not bring himself to leave the world of pornography from which he gained his wealth. Instead, he chose to mock what he may have come close to embracing, as though by publicly ridiculing what he almost welcomed in his heart, he could distance himself from God's love.

The magazine reflected this sudden hostile reaction. For example, there was the illustration of Jesus "coming" with the word implying a sexual act. And there was the picture of a blond woman being crucified on a glass cross, as well as a picture of women upside down with their legs spread around a glass table. The latter was meant to satirize the last supper, the men who would be arriving obviously planning to engage in oral sex.

Not being grounded in the Word of God is the downfall of many new Christians. They have come from what is often a hedonistic lifestyle. They have found that lifestyle shallow and wanting, but it has still been the lifestyle they have known. There are times when they will backslide. If the noncelebrity experiences this, most church members will understand. But celebrity Christian converts rarely get that type of love. They are often used by others, vultures preying on the weak, the hungry, the seeking.

The celebrity Christian is quickly condemned if he has any human failings. The support on which he relied, usually high-profile individuals who don't want to be tainted by "failure," disappears. He becomes embittered in most cases, declaring Christianity to be a false faith or certainly a destructive one. And unless he has unusual strength, he remains hostile.

At first Dad did what he always did. He threw himself into change. He became obsessed with religion, though not with the quiet, serious study needed to become grounded in the Word. He also decided to start having a healthy diet with natural food, according to those around him. He talked of changing *Hustler* into a religious magazine, an idea Althea and Uncle Jimmy rejected. And he briefly made himself available to anyone seemingly Christian who had a scheme that required his money.

For example, the late senator and former vice president Hubert Humphrey was greatly admired by many people around Dad.

Humphrey was a man of strong moral principles. He was a man who had been a leader in what were considered liberal causes, especially writing and helping pass extensive civil rights legislation. And he was a man for whom a group of people wanted to hold a three-day fast and prayer vigil. They asked Dad for the money to advertise the fast in the *New York Times*, whose readers were the only ones they wanted to reach. Dad, determined to prove how changed he was, ignored their request and instead spent $200,000 placing the ad in numerous newspapers throughout the United States. It read, in part: "I'll be praying for you for world peace, for an end to hunger, and for you, Hubert Humphrey, and all the good and decent things you represent."

Dad's actions were viewed as erratic by those around him, and in December of 1977 the *Hustler* corporate counsel, Howard Spies, became so concerned about him that he attempted to have him evaluated by the C. F. Menninger Hospital in Topeka, Kansas. Among the charges were two that both reflected Dad's manic condition and related at least some of his plans. The first, the one that was pure mania, was Dad's belief that he would be reborn at Christmastime as the new Messiah. The second, which may have been a serious plan even then, was that he would become president, replacing Jimmy Carter in the White House. It would not be too many years later that Dad actually did run for President.

Dad did allow himself to be evaluated by Dr. George Harding on behalf of the Menninger Foundation. At that time Dad was cautious about what he said, seemingly delusional in his thinking (at least about being the new Messiah), grandiose in his attitude toward life.

Althea was also evaluated with Dad during a December 19, 1977, hour-long session with Dr. Renate Falck. She related that Dad felt his brother was conspiring against him to take over the business. He also felt that he needed to take time off to rest, to review the Christian experience he had had, and to try to understand how to begin involving himself in doing good for others.

Uncle Jimmy supplied additional information for that evaluation. He said that Dad was no longer sleeping long or well. He said that for the two weeks before Dad was hospitalized, he had eaten very little. He talked of converting Larry Flynt Publications into a nonprofit corporation, and tried to borrow $20 million to buy a $5 million airplane. Dad had also become a conspiracy theorist, worrying that there was a "Rockefeller-Rothschild" plot to take over the world. Uncle Jimmy also said that Dad believed he could foretell the future and was all-powerful.

Ultimately during this period there was a recommendation for emergency hospitalization, treatment with lithium, and forced commitment if Dad refused to cooperate. Dad was seemingly out of control, his religious conversion seeming to justify his grandiose ideas about himself, and Uncle Jimmy's efforts to hospitalize him reinforcing his paranoia. In other words, Dad was a mess.

In March of 1978, with Dad's personal and business life still in turmoil, he was again in court to defend himself against obscenity charges, this time in Lawrenceville, Georgia. What he did not know was that a man named Joseph Paul Franklin was waiting for him.

Franklin, whose real name was Vaughan, was a teenager when he found some pamphlets on Nazism. He liked what he read and believed that Hitler's "Final Solution," the murder of all Jews and others whom he hated, was a blueprint for action. He immediately sought out like-minded groups, eventually joining the American Nazi Party, the Ku Klux Klan, and the National States Rights Party. He got into trouble with the law, later regretting actions that prevented him from joining the Rhodesian Army as a mercenary who could then legally kill South African blacks. He changed his name to Joseph Paul (for Joseph Paul Goebbels, Hitler's propaganda minister and an avowed anti-Semite) Franklin (for Benjamin Franklin), which enabled him to lie his way to Rhodesia. However, instead of traveling to South Africa, he decided to stay in the United States to do his killing.

Franklin later said that his first effort at murder was the bombing of an Israeli lobbyist's home in Bethesda, Maryland. "I blew most of that house to smithereens. But I put the bomb on the wrong side, away from where people were sleeping."[2]

He made other attacks at random. Franklin was in Chattanooga, Tennessee, in July 1977, when he looked in a telephone book to find a synagogue. Selecting one at random, he bombed it, though the explosion was mistimed for his purposes. The blast tore apart the building one hour after services had ended, so no one was hurt.

Franklin killed an interracial couple in Wisconsin in 1977 and two black men jogging with two white women in Salt Lake City in 1980. But the crime that touched my life was the one where he decided he hated the fact that *Hustler* had a photo spread called "Georgia Sweet Peach and Butch." This depicted a white woman sexually involved with a black man. Hearing about Dad's obscenity trial, Franklin traveled to Georgia to kill him. He took a rifle and fired at least three rounds, keeping himself so well hidden that he escaped without being identified.

Half of Dad's stomach and his spleen had to be removed. In addition, because of a bullet that struck the cauda equina area of the spine, Dad lost the use of his legs. He was permanently confined to a wheelchair, and had to rely on a surgical implant to continue his sex life.

I had little awareness of any of the obscenity trials Dad was involved in, and I did not then realize the intensity of feeling Dad's work could generate among both the readers and those who hated his work. He was not the primary topic of conversation at home. His troubles with the law were not ones Mom would bring up to me. So far as I knew, Dad was busy being Dad, and whatever troubles he had were ones he was taking care of.

The day of the shooting, the day after my thirteenth birthday, Judy and I boarded the school bus and I suddenly saw two black cars approach. They were dark, late-model sedans with tinted windows. I might have not given them a second thought had they not stopped across from the bus. The front doors opened and two men emerged from each car. They were almost identical in height, trim, and wearing dark suits and dark sunglasses. Years later I learned that they were probably FBI agents since Dad's would-be killer was not caught, the issue was probably interstate, and their role was likely to have been as armed observers. The suits and the cars were holdovers from the days of J. Edgar Hoover, when he ordered even undercover agents to dress conservatively and drive only similar sedans. To my thirteen-year-old mind they looked like something out of a movie.

I didn't say anything to Judy. Suddenly Mom drove up in front of the bus, ran to the door, climbed on board, and looked around frantically. Her body was shaking and her voice was hysterical. "I've got to get my kids!" she shouted, pushing past the driver who had no idea who this woman might be. "I've got to get my kids!" She spotted us and ordered us to come.

I looked at Mom, trying to read in her face whatever had happened that she was not telling us. Her face was hard, her mouth set, her teeth clenched. Her eyes seemed to be moving back and forth, back and forth, frantically checking every seat of every row until she spotted us.

She took us off in silence. Then, inside the car, she told us, "Your dad's been shot," and Judy burst into tears.

I lost all awareness of the moment. I did not really understand what had happened or why. I just knew that Dad was in real danger and I had to be with him. I had to see him right then. There could be no waiting. As soon as I got home, I called his office in California. They told me nothing.

There was so much I did not understand back then, so much pain and so little knowledge. Dad, my real Dad, not the John

Denver creation of my closet "bedroom," almost certainly did not love me, did not see me as important to his daily life. There was little if any chance that Dad would consider having me come to the hospital important when he recovered enough from the surgery to have visitors. He was unlikely to think of me and he certainly would not consider my feelings.

Althea was everything Dad lusted after in a woman—and everything he hated. She was beautiful when she wasn't using drugs heavily. She was the type of woman who could arise from bed after a rough night's sleep, not bother with makeup, use her hand to comb her hair, put on jeans and a T-shirt, then walk outside and look great. When she took the time to care for herself, she dominated any room she entered.

Dad lusted after Althea. Dad relied on Althea. Dad admired Althea. So, of course, Dad had to verbally and physically abuse her, make certain she knew he was not faithful, and do nothing to stop her drug abuse. Six years later, when Dad was having a psychological profile during his jailing for contempt of court, he was quoted as saying of Althea that she was "the only perfect woman I ever met." He further explained that this meant that she "idolized and worshiped me." He said, "she runs around like a little puppy dog over everything I tell her and more." She was a "robot but independent." Then he added, "I don't trust nobody but myself, not even Althea. Eventually she will meet somebody who can offer her more than me."

And so Dad was brought low, shot by a would-be assassin, still in physical and mental turmoil, only a wife with whom he had his usual love/hate relationship by his side. I was told I could not see him, could not talk with him. Although eventually Mrs. Stapleton would speak with him, two points had been made perfectly clear to Dad. First, he was not the new Messiah. Second, loving God did not keep you from becoming a paraplegic in constant pain. What good was faith? The hostility Althea had shown him was apparently justified in Dad's mind.

At the same time, Dad, in his manic state, felt that he must have some sort of special mission. He believed that during the height of his suffering in the hospital, he had frequent out-of-body experiences. He also frequently said, "If I'm not the second coming, then tell me who I am."

There was also severe depression. He contemplated suicide. Later he would tell a reporter for the *Chicago Tribune*, "As far as I'm concerned, I've already lived my life. There is no life in a wheelchair. You've got to be paralyzed to appreciate that. You have to have wallowed in your own urine and excrement for years to know what it's like. My life has been lived."

But all I wanted was to be near my dad, especially when he was transferred to a Columbus hospital for rehabilitation. The horror of his condition, his mental state, the actions of those around him were of no concern to me. My knight in shining armor had fallen in battle and I had to minister to his needs.

I began acting out at home. I was inattentive in school and paid no attention to Mom. All I talked about was Dad and my need to be with him. Finally, on June 12, 1978, Mom, Dad, and Althea's sister and brother-in-law, Marsha and Bill Rider, worked out a custody arrangement in which I would go to Columbus to live with them. I would be close to Dad, and though I never got to see him at least we would be in the same city.

As I recall the arrangement, it involved a payment of $30,000 for one year's caring for me. Bill was working in distribution for Dad's Flynt Distribution Company and being well paid for his efforts.

That year was a strange one for me. When I left Mom, the apartment complex had developed a personality as odd as my family. There was one section for the elderly, a quiet place where the residents were a mix of native Floridians and former snowbirds. Another section was younger, with more children, and backgrounds typical of Jacksonville, Florida, ghetto regions. There were a handful of Hispanics but mostly low-income blacks and whites.

Many of the people were working poor like Mom. Others were on welfare, either making no effort to work or unable to get a job because of disabilities or a lack of day care.

There was a soap-opera element to some of the families. One single-parent neighbor was being kept by an older man. There was also someone we just called the "dirty old man" because he lived with his son and a daughter who had gotten pregnant by him. The abnormal was normal in that environment, so everyone fit in and everyone was a misfit in the greater world beyond.

The Riders were upper-middle-class in a family-oriented suburb of the city. The Rider home was extremely large, and while it wasn't as dramatically ostentatious as Dad's, I was still impressed. The kitchen alone must have been 600 square feet. It was obviously meant for such purposes as preparing food for large parties.

Bill Rider was nice to me, though I spent relatively little time with him because of his work and the pressures that were being put on the publishing company with Dad laid up. Althea was placed in full charge of *Hustler* and all related businesses at a base salary of $800,000 a year. This was more money than the base pay of all but the highest paid officer at General Motors that year. One study of executive positions found that she was the highest-paid woman in America. She was also one of the most powerful women in publishing, rivaling such women as Katharine Graham of the *Washington Post* and *Newsweek*. She was also becoming a hard-core abuser of drugs with Dad.

Bill was working in distribution, then would later be promoted to head of security in California. At that time he naturally felt the need to heighten security. Eventually Dad's home would have electronic monitoring everywhere, guards with Uzi machine pistols identical to the ones used by the Presidential Protection division of the Secret Service, and a mammoth bank-vault type of door on his bedroom. But the office was also a potential target of a crazy person. Everything was tense.

When he could be with me, Bill was delightful. He would sing many of my favorite songs, and was sensitive to the deep hurt I was feeling. He knew Dad did not want to see me, even though I was so close. He saw Dad and Althea in drug-induced stupors. He understood my pain.

Bill would sing such songs as "You are so beautiful to me . . ." and "I'm being followed by a moon shadow . . ." The words were meant to be soothing, flirtatious. He wanted me to think of myself as pretty, as someone a man would one day care about. His actions were almost romantic, though unlike so many other men in my life, he never tried to seduce me, never tried to rape me, never crossed over the boundaries that should exist between an adult male and a child young enough to be his daughter. For me, it was a rare experience.

Marsha was overly strict. She was sometimes hurtful, and her words—she called me an ugly duckling—destroying what little ego Bill was trying to elevate.

There were even times when I experienced the reverse of the movie cliché where the man looks at his secretary, removes her glasses, lets down her hair, and sees her beauty for the first time. Instead of changing my look, then admiring my beauty, Marsha made suggestions such as pulling my hair in front of my face to try to cover my cowlick. She looked at me critically, and I thought she was going to be pleased. Instead she dismissed the effort saying, "No, that doesn't help." Although she probably did not mean to depress me, I felt that nothing could be done to make me attractive.

Marsha made certain that staying with her was no vacation. Judy had run away. I was going to work for my keep, even though it was prepaid. I had to scrub the kitchen floor and handle numerous other chores. I reached a point where I knew Dad would live and I also knew that I would not get to see my father. I wanted to leave.

I called Mom, begging to return. HUD housing had never looked better than when I was living elsewhere. I promised Mom she would be surprised by how I had changed. I would clean and paint the apartment, cook all the meals, care for Shawn, do the laundry. I was going to be Saint Tonya, servant to the family.

I hope Mom did not believe me. I was willing to do exactly what I told her, but I was also a teenager. "Forever" can be a very short period of time under those circumstances.

Finally I was given approval with conditions. I still remember my joy on returning to Jacksonville. But there was no joyous reunion. I remained in turmoil. My relationship with Mom hadn't changed, and with distance from Dad and Althea, I returned to my old fantasies about him.

∞

Dad has had problems with his stomach all his life. Long before the shooting, he would get severe cramps and often have to take medication to control the pain. Once I returned from Ohio, I began suffering in a similar way. Finally it became so bad that I had to go to the hospital, where I was examined, then given a strong tranquilizer of some sort and sent to the psychiatric unit.

At last the doctors recognized that my problems were emotional, not physical. I told myself I was proud to have stomach pains, severe gas, and other discomfort because then I was a Flynt. Each cramp connected me with Dad. It was silly, childish, and disturbed thinking, which the staff recognized.

The problem with the hospital was that they really did not know what to do with me. Even in the psychiatric unit, adolescents were limited in the help they received. There was little investigation into the dynamics of the family.

The hospital environment was rigidly structured. Everyone had to get out of bed at the same time or the nursing staff literally rolled you out of bed. Teens were tutored and had to endure occupational therapy. I'm not certain if occupational therapy was meant to keep us from getting into mischief or if it was to prepare us for career opportunities when we were discharged. If it was the latter, I'm now able to earn my living making clay ashtrays.

I don't remember how long I was in the hospital that first time. Nothing was resolved. Nothing changed. I went home and life was still difficult.

Once again I obsessed about my father. Years later I realized that I had been coping in the same manner as many children who are victims of sexual abuse. I repressed the memory of traumatic events because it was the only way I could be safe.

I was living with a mother who could not cope with parenting. I was constantly harassed by a grandmother, who hated me solely because Larry Flynt was my father. I had few friends, and those who were closest to me came from families as unstable as my own. The apartment complex in which I lived was terrible. I lacked the right look to be part of my school's elite—I wore my mother's work clothes, or secondhand. Absolutely nothing was right. Without my fantasy of Dad, I would have had nothing. Life would not have been worth living. I needed the fantasy for survival.

Repressing the horror of Dad's molesting me, going into conscious denial, was how I could get from day to day. What I never realized, nor did anyone else, was that I was crying for help, crying for intervention, crying for love.

Judy was seventeen when she and her boyfriend returned to Jacksonville. She decided to get her GED, then go on to a community college. She had grown up in many ways, but the pain of her life and the knowledge that she wasn't a legitimate Flynt daughter kept her hatred and jealousy festering.

At the same time that Mom was welcoming Judy home, I was running wild. On one hand, I was determined to be the first person in my family to graduate from high school. On the other, I was not making an effort to do my best. I just wanted to get by, from day to day.

I caused Mom the most problems at night. I began doing to her what she had done to her mother—sneaking out. I occasionally went to bars. More frequently I went to friends' homes to drink alcohol. We talked, danced, listened to music, and actually got into very little trouble relative to what Judy had done.

There were also boys during this period, a lot of boys. I had little interest in anyone, but I also didn't want to be unpopular. Many of my girlfriends were experimenting with sex. Even those who weren't could not stop talking about boys and the idea of going to bed with them. The feminist movement had not reached my world, and my friends and I were content to compete for the cool boys.

I remember one older teen who was self-centered and tried to dress like Gene Simmons, the rock star who led the demonic group Kiss. He wore black-and-white makeup and lipstick, and he frequently stuck out his tongue to imitate Simmons's stage manner.

I had enough maturity to find such boys disgusting. I had enough insecurity to find myself in competition with my friends. And I had enough of a desire to be wanted by anyone that one time I actually said "yes" when I became his special girl of the moment. I regretted it immediately, but I was hurting too much to take the moral stand I wanted to take.

Mom, age 27.

Mother, age 18, with my sister Judy (4 months) at Grandma Jackson's house.

Me and sister Judy, 1967.

Judy, me, and Grandma. The only affectionate moment I remember with her (1968).

Judy, me, and Mom at Marineland.

Judy and me (3 1/2 years old). Christmas at Grandma's.

Judy and me. I was 6, she was 7 (1971).

Judy (age 12) and Althea in Columbus, Ohio.

Christmas 1982. From left to right: Debbie and Marsha (Althea's sisters), and Althea (seated).

Christmas present for Dad, 1982. From left to right: Me, my half-brother Larry Jr., and my half-sister Theresa.

Dad and me, Christmas 1982.

Dad and Althea with her hand bandaged from shooting up drugs.
December 1982.

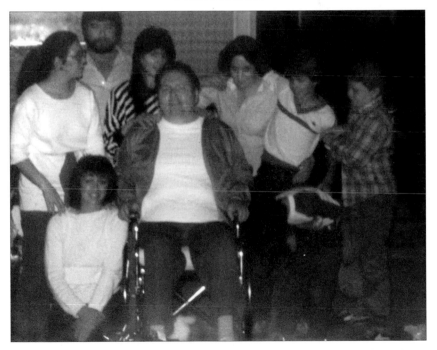

Back row left to right: Marsha Rider (Althea's sister), Bill Rider (Marsha's
husband), Althea, my sister Theresa, my brother Larry Flynt Jr., and
Debbie's son. Front row: Debbie and Dad. Christmas 1982.

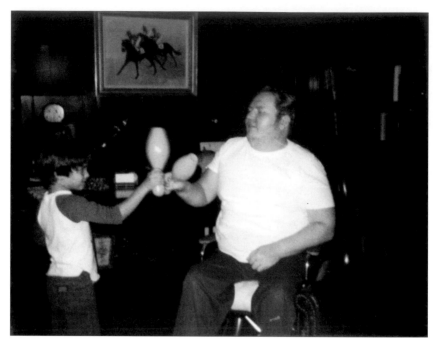

Damien (Althea's sister's son) and Dad. December 1982.

My sister Theresa and me, 1983.

The exit gate of Dad's mansion at 364 St. Cloud Road. The entrance looks the same except with a call box. Rebecca and I begged for food from that gate.

Dad and Larry Jr., 1983.

High school graduation photo,
June 3, 1983.

One of Dad's bodyguards and me, 1983.

Me and Dad at Butner Federal Correctional Facility, 1984.

Me making a mistake in 1984—being interviewed by *Georgia Monthly*. The reporter lied to me and sold a version of this to *Star Magazine*.

March 29, 1987: Me and Lawrence Vega after our wedding.

Marilyn's 2nd birthday party at our apartment, 1989.

With Pat Robertson after the *700 Club*, 1997.

My daughter Marilyn, my husband Larry, and me, 1996.

Stacey, me, and Marilyn, at the Beverly Hills Hilton, 1996.

Left to right: Stacey, Anton (Althea's old body guard), Tony (manager of The Rainbow, where Althea spent a lot of time), Mike (also a manager), me, and Steady (doorman for as long as I can remember), 1996.

Me and Michael Coren after *The Michael Coren Show* in Canada, 1997.

Left to right: Gloria Steinem, Charlie Rose, and me after taping
The Charlie Rose Show, 1997.

Eventually Mom realized that I was what juvenile authorities like to call "incorrigible"—in other words, I ignored authority figures. My grades were much lower than my intelligence warranted. I engaged in self-destructive behavior. The only answer for Mom was to send me to another psychiatric ward, one whose adolescent unit gave kids the best treatment their parents' insurance could buy.

CO

21 August, 1981 Psychological Services Evaluation

FLYNT, TONYA

DATE OF EVALUATION: July 14, 1981

REASON FOR REFERRAL AND BACKGROUND INFORMATION:

Tonya was referred for psychological services by her mother due to Tonya's unhappiness and low self-esteem. In a parent interview conducted during services to Tonya, it was learned that Tonya is desirous of a great deal of affection and approval, as she was not provided this emotional comfort substantially when she was younger. Tonya is reported to fluctuate in her emotional mood from being depressed to being elated and she feels some rejection from her father, Larry Flynt, who is publisher and owner of Flynt Publications in California. Furthermore, Tonya and her mother have some difficulty getting along as she has a tendency to manipulate her mother, at times. [The report mentioned chest pains I had been having, and the fact that a previous doctor felt they were of psychological origin.]

Tonya is reported to have other difficulties, such as her psychosexual development, her blaming herself and putting herself down about negative events which happen to her, and her lack of satisfaction with what she has or is. . . . There appears to be some insecurity in this 16-year-old girl.

PSYCHOLOGICAL INTERVIEW AND FEAR SURVEY:

. . . . The conflict she experiences with her father is one of rejection, while the conflict with her mother appears to be one of occasional acceptance and occasional frustration. Tonya is a girl who enjoys writing and listening to music, as well as her interest in boys. She is concerned about her father and her weight and in living a good lifestyle as she grows. There are some classical fears and a lack of motivation sufficient to doing well in school or on a job and Tonya appears to have little internal control of what she sees her problems are. She has a habit of putting herself down frequently.

Ultimately the therapy focused on the symptoms for treatment, not the underlying cause. I had all the classic symptoms of a child who had been sexually molested, but in 1981, even the professionals did not look very closely at such matters. The therapy approach mentioned in the evaluation included five points: improve my self-concept; become desensitized to various anxieties; lose weight; receive family counseling with Mom and Judy; receive guidance in managing myself to achieve goals. There was never an effort suggested to find the root cause of my problems. Back then, it just wasn't done. No one seemed to want to think too deeply about how a teenager could come to the problems I manifested. It was better to treat the symptoms.

It was in the hospital that I took my first critical look at my father's world. The kids there were eccentrics and crazies, amoral individuals, and truly good people who had been victims of physical or psychological abuse. All were experienced beyond their years.

My admission had been arranged in advance by Mom. She could not handle me anymore. She did not want me at home, yet she had no place to send me where I might get help. The arrangement with the Riders had failed. Dad certainly didn't want me then, and Mom would never turn me over to juvenile court so I could go to some foster home type of facility. That would be too personally humiliating. Instead she plotted with the hospital, with Judy and her boyfriend to surprise me with the trip.

The day of the admission, I was taken out to the car and forced into the backseat between Judy and her boyfriend. I was near hysteria as I learned what was being done, filled with outrage, wanting to attack them. They restrained me, and Judy laughed at my helplessness.

This time I did not have to make ashtrays. Instead, we involved ourselves in gluing beads to construction paper and calling it art. This time there were enough "crazy" kids for us to be among those who were close to our own age, but we were also mixed with adults. We also experienced a naked older woman, slithering on the floor in close imitation to a snake, raising her hand and begging, "Help me. Help me."

The kids I met were a fascinating mix. There was Rebecca, a girl whose school record showed she was involved with drugs and needed to be rehabilitated. As it turned out, though Rebecca was a lot of things, a drug abuser she wasn't at the time. Instead that was the false paper trail the school administrator created to have her placed in the hospital for the duration of her insurance. It was better to lock up your daughter than to risk having her a wrecked addict.

Though I was admitted legitimately, not all the kids were so lucky. The dean of girls of one of the high schools from which teens like my friend Rebecca were sent made an arrangement with the adolescent care wing of the hospital. She would learn which students had insurance that would cover at least several days of inpatient psychiatric care. Then she would "document" inappropriate classroom behavior in records no one ever checked. A student could be doing well in classes, liked by his or her teacher, yet have a record in the dean's office that showed the teen to be an unruly troublemaker. Parents were called, and if anyone ever challenged what was taking place, usually they would stop with the paperwork instead of going to the teachers who interacted with their sons or daughters on a daily basis. Horrified by the findings, determined to help their children, they agreed to their going to the hospital. Then the administrator would receive a "commission" for the "referral."

I don't know if the hospital was aware that teens were being falsely sent for admission. I do know that there was a mix of legitimately troubled youth and those who were rebellious because they were there, not because they should have been sent there.

For example, there was Little Bobby, an eleven-year-old who had molested his sister. And there was a girl named Rainbow who was the type of girl Uncle Jimmy would have hired for Dad's club. Rainbow was a topless dancer in biker bars, where the size of your breasts was far more important than your birthday. If you were underage but overdeveloped, you could have a job, a drink, or the sex act of your choice.

Rainbow was tattooed. Rainbow was experienced in ways we girls could not imagine. Rainbow also decided that we should break out of the adolescent psychiatric ward and go party with the Hell's Angels.

The idea of running off to join the Hell's Angels was like a kid running off to join the circus. We would break out. We would party. And then I'd be tooling down the highway on the back of a Harley hog, a bandanna around my head because only sissies wore helmets, holding on to my old man, feeling the wind, and showing our colors. In my mind I saw it all—it looked like a B movie from the 1950s.

The original breakout involved Rebecca, Rainbow, and me. Our first attempt involved breaking a first-floor window so we could jump out. When no one was looking, the three of us took a chair, pointed the legs toward the window, ran as fast as we could, and smashed into the glass. The window bent slightly but did not break.

Little Bobby came running into the room, told us he was going to tell, then rushed out to the nurse.

We tried again while Little Bobby was squealing on us, this time moving faster and striking so hard that we felt the shock in our arms and shoulders. This time the glass broke, but the staff caught us before we could escape. We were placed in a higher security area, the dreaded East Wing, for three days' punishment.

Undaunted, we planned our next escape from the outdoor recreation area. There was a big open field, an area with a volley-ball net, and places where it was possible to sneak off the grounds when the staff wasn't watching. Since this was not jail, and since those patients who might be dangerous were locked away, no one paid much attention to the kids. Everyone relaxed, assuring us that we could sneak off.

The great escape involved Rebecca, a girl named Ashleigh, me, and Little Bobby, who was made a part of the plan to ensure his silence. We had no place to go, so Rebecca suggested we go to my mother's apartment complex. Her boyfriend would be waiting for us with a car.

It was early evening, and all we could think to do was party once we had our freedom. Rebecca's boyfriend brought a bottle of rum and a jar of orange juice, mixed the two together, and began drinking.

We drank, talked, laughed, and wandered, eventually ending up on a seemingly deserted beach. We never thought that a bunch of drunk, noisy kids on an otherwise empty beach would be instantly spotted by the police. We were, though, and two cars drove up as we sat near a dark house on a cliff overlooking the water, delighting in our freedom.

"What are you kids doing?" I was asked.

I was offended by the officer's tone, so I responded, "You can't talk to us like that."

Suddenly the car doors opened and the two officers stepped from their cars. The one nearest to me was so tall that I'm sure my head only reached his belt buckle. We decided not to argue further as we were placed in the backs of the cars and transported back to the hospital.

Rebecca was a belligerent drunk. She sat in the hall of East Wing where we were taken for punishment, begging everyone for a cigarette. Then she tried to fight the staff, kicking, crying, and occasionally being reinforced by Rainbow, who was already in the East Wing for some other punishment.

If there was anything positive that took place in that hospital, it was one of the therapist's allowing me to truly immerse myself in painting. Instead of keeping me involved with the make-work type of crafts whose purpose I never could understand, he let me nurture a talent I had. Soon I was painting with a seriousness of purpose, trying to bring myself closer to Dad through re-creating the shack in which he was raised.

The painting I made of the shack was a technique painting. It was a learning exercise, much the way perspective can be taught through the drawing of a cityscape that looks dramatic yet is actually so simple it is meant as a beginner's lesson.

I had never been to Dad's childhood home. What I had done was listen intently whenever he described the place. For a while I interwove John Denver lyrics, but by the time I was hospitalized, I no longer needed his singing to help define my life or shape my fantasies. The painting was a combination of those well-established thoughts about the place and the technique I was being taught. I mailed it to Dad as a peace offering.

Later, during one of the most impoverished times in my life, when Dad was already wealthy beyond his earliest dreams, I learned he decided to get rid of the painting. I have never been quite certain how I feel about that decision. If he loved it, why didn't he keep it? Yet if he hated it, why did he take it to a gallery to try and sell it? He must have respected the work far more than he respected his daughter, and he certainly had the background to appreciate it.

One of Dad's secrets is that he is a connoisseur of high culture. He loves fine art and antiques, having enough knowledge to quietly own his own gallery. The manager handles the daily chores, but Dad is well aware of quality and fair pricing. When he placed my painting, never identifying it as being connected with Larry Flynt, the pornographer, or his daughter, the gallery manager sold it for $1,000.

Actually I never would have found out about this had it not been for my half-sister, Lisa. She worked at the gallery and told me about both the placement and the sale.

Eventually we all went home, none of us particularly changed by the experience, at least not in ways our families had hoped. I was still wild. I was still lonely. I still had no self-esteem, and I continued to repress memories of my father's abusive behavior so I could plan on being with him once again. It was not a good time for anyone in the family. I fixated on graduating from high school, then moving out to see him.

8

California or Bust

I must be the loneliest person to ever live. . . . I feel as if I'm the
only person on earth. The kind word, "depression," would not
exactly fit the way I feel. All the emotions of this world are gone
from me. All I feel is emptiness.

> —*from a letter I wrote to my doctor*
> *during my last stay in the*
> *adolescent unit of the psychiatric hospital*

The Los Angeles of the late 1970s and early 1980s was about excess
and access. It was about power and privilege. It was about manipu-
lation and mind games.

Not for everyone, of course. There were good people in Los
Angeles, hardworking family people whose values, goals, and spiritual beliefs would fit nicely into what the television world likes to
call Heartland America. But such people were rarely power play-
ers. They seldom held meaningful positions in government or the
entertainment world which dominated the region. Instead, they
were the often anonymous workers who spent their time behind
the scenes, caring for others, trying to live their faith.

I did not know I longed for the world of the often anonymous
faithful when I began a journey that would take me to some of the

wealthiest areas of Los Angeles. I did not yet realize that I was becoming the prodigal daughter, led by the basest of desires until I would return to my real Father, the Father of us all. All I knew was that I was a miserable, lonely teenager whose last couple of years of high school seemed an interminable, intolerable hell. And Dad was a rich business success living the good life in a Bel Air mansion, a man whose hurtful actions had been suppressed in my mind, a man who could offer me the loving family I did not have at home.

It is in hindsight that I have come to understand how Dad could be effectively run out of Cincinnati, Ohio, and embraced in the Los Angeles area. Cincinnati was and is a family town. There are liberals and conservatives, Christians, Jews, atheists, and members of other religions. People may disagree with each other about lots of things, including the appropriateness of sexually oriented businesses. However, most people want the same thing—a healthy, nurturing environment in which to raise their children and educate them to be productive citizens. The differences that can create dramatic clashes are over the means to a common end.

There are few meaningful debates in Los Angeles, and there haven't been for the past half-century. It is a city, along with the Bay Area, that has led the nation in permissiveness. It is a region that has made acquisition an idol for worship. It is a region that has defined extreme, often destructive permissiveness as "tolerance." It is a region that has come to elevate foul language and violent rhetoric in the name of First Amendment freedom.

The film industry began pushing the limits of good taste during the silent era. Religious films were often made with what, for the day, were moral excesses shown on the screen. The thinking was that the audience going to nickelodeons and other early theaters would enjoy a little titillation so long as those practicing evil were destroyed in the end. Biblical epics allowed for such efforts, and though some of it was censored, others were quite shocking in their day.

A hint of morality came to the film industry after World War II, when the casting couch was made illegal. Prior to that time, many producers, directors, and others involved with casting a film would exchange a role in a movie for sex. After the war, reformers declared that such practices were demeaning and immoral. Instead, a role in a film had to be earned. Saying "yes" to the sexual desires of the producer or director was required only after the actor got the role.

The Los Angeles Police Department diligently pursued offenders. Every day, buses from small towns across the country brought beautiful young women to the city. They came with a suitcase, money saved or donated by loving, faithful relatives and friends, and the fervent conviction that, within weeks, they would be stars. After all, they had enjoyed the leads in numerous high school and local theater productions. They had clippings from local papers that compared them favorably with the best-known actors on Broadway, none of whom the writers had ever seen perform. And when they arrived with their photographs, their perpetual smiles, and their willingness to burst into song or render a dramatic reading at the snap of a director's fingertips, they discovered that they were a dime a dozen. The studio schools were filled with them. The counter stools at Schwab's drugstore, the poor man's casting office, were constantly taken by them. And no one cared.

Some stayed with the depressing rounds of cattle calls, open auditions where dozens or hundreds would show up for two or three undemanding roles. They worked as waitresses and carhops, store clerks and models, the latter a term used rather loosely since it covered everything from walking the runways in fashion shows to prostitution. And a few gave up, seeking the security of a civil service position by joining the Los Angeles Police Department. It was the latter who were used to check on the compliance with the casting couch law.

The female police officers would go to auditions, presenting themselves as professionals since they were experienced with this type of effort. If they were invited for a second reading, usually alone, often on a yacht or in a private home, they would go with revolver, handcuffs, and hidden backup. Sometimes they would do a reading, being seriously considered for a part. Sometimes they would be told that the role was guaranteed if they would slip off their clothes and relax in bed, in which case the director or producer would be arrested. Since sex could still be legally demanded after casting, it was morality with a wink and a nod. Yet for Los Angeles, it was a major step forward.

Prostitution was an industry with different values. Paramount Pictures at least once had the LAPD close down a prostitution ring made up of starlets trying to boost their studio pay. But the action was not from moral outrage. Other starlets were being used by some studio executives as favors for visiting financiers, big-name stars, and top entertainment personnel. The freelance prostitutes were simply interfering with the "authorized" prostitutes.

Likewise there was the famous Studio Club, a safe, clean residence for women trying to break into the industry. Marilyn Monroe was a resident for a time, and she, like the others, were treated by movie fan magazines as ambitious, talented, beautiful virgins focused on their careers before any relationship. In truth, many, including Monroe, supplemented their living through prepaid "dates" with top entertainers.

Sexual violence came to Los Angeles in a headline-making manner in 1958. By that time the area was known as a source for male-oriented pulp magazine illustrations. In the early 1950s and well into the 1960s, a number of mainstream publications sought three types of images—cheesecake, fresh-faced girls next door, and bondage photos. In fact, the freelance girl market was dominated by both cheesecake images and bondage photos. And if a photographer trying to make some money while breaking into more respected areas of commercial photography lacked studio space, there were facilities for rent throughout the area.

Most of the publications involved were tame by today's standards. There were the "naughty" cartoon and joke publications such as *Laff*, each illustrated with photos of pretty girls in one-piece, form-fitting bathing suits. Often one model would be photographed in different suits and different poses, then used a half-dozen different times with different names. The late billionaire Howard Hughes enjoyed such reading and frequently had an assistant locate the model so he could "date" her.

Blue Book for Men featured stories of heroic men who became heroic by saving women who were usually bound and tortured. The stories frequently harked back to World War II, a gallant American singlehandedly saving women from Nazi torture camps. Naturally, in order to understand the heroism, the helpless women were shown partially clothed, their garments torn by the torturer's whip.

Among the larger markets were publishing companies that produced both "true" romance and "true" police magazines. The editors would have mostly freelance photographers hire male and female models, requesting that they photograph both head shots and images of obviously romantic couples for the romance magazine covers and internal illustrations. Then they were asked to use the same models for the covers and inside illustrations for the police magazines. The latter usually involved the woman being tied, gagged, and menaced, or otherwise in danger. The man would either be her attacker or her rescuer.

The pay was relatively low for such work, and the images seldom made a model's portfolio, but many Los Angeles area photographers paid their bills with such sales, and wanna-be models eagerly posed for all callers.

It was into this world that Harvey Glatman appeared. He was a freelance photographer who rented studio space throughout the area. However, he did not come to public attention until the models he was hiring began disappearing. When he was caught, he was found to have moved from photographing bound and gagged models to raping, then murdering them. The photographs were located and quickly rushed to the wire services after he was convicted (he was executed in 1958). Instead of just appearing in a limited circulation magazine, Glatman's helpless, "about-to-be-murdered" beauties made front-page news in more than a thousand newspapers. It was the first time violent pornography was made mainstream by calling it news.

Dad relocated Larry Flynt Publications to Southern California. But where other regions were trying to balance constitutionally mandated rights with local moral values, the Los Angeles area had become a region where excess was normal. Most pornographic magazines and film production companies were either based there or had a presence there. Actors found little stigma in participating in such productions while trying to succeed in mainstream film and stage productions. Models who did not have the luck and special look needed to gain top assignments were frequently willing to pose nude so long as the work was "tasteful" and the pay above average.

The police vice units avoided dealing with most mainstream pornography, concentrating instead on the extremes. Although being paid to have sex in a pornographic film is prostitution, a crime throughout Los Angeles County, such issues were ignored. They were consenting adults. They were acting in films legitimized in some legal minds by First Amendment interpretations. And besides, no one was getting hurt. Or so they told themselves.

Instead, most of the prosecution was for child pornography, the ultimate crime in the field by everyone's standard, and by pornography producers who committed crimes to get their images. This usually meant images of sexual violence and bestiality where the models, when located, bore the marks of the violence that had been recorded. Fake violence using makeup to create the bruises so inspiring to the perverted fans of such images was considered all right. Real violence was not. It was a hairsplitting of the law that seemed to match the issue of the casting couch right after World War II.

And so the mainstream and extreme in the fields established their California connections. Dad moved there. Hugh Hefner brought his Playboy empire there from Chicago, also a wild big city yet with far more limits to its tolerance. And the Christmas before I graduated from high school, I decided to move there.

∞

My main problem is I don't like ME! That is the worst thing anyone can say or think. When I think about me I just want to get sick because of the things I say, do, the way I act.

—*from the letter I wrote in the hospital*

∞

I did not understand the notorious nature of Los Angeles. I was not familiar with the nightclubs whose upstairs rooms Althea frequently visited with rock star friends out for a night of getting high. Los Angeles represented only one thing to me—home. In my mind, wherever Dad was living was the home I had been denied, the home I felt I could deny myself no longer. I had to do whatever it took to be in his presence.

The ability to tolerate the intolerable, to internalize anger, to feel guilt for the acts of others all vary with how you are raised. A healthy, nurtured teenager may have all the angst of adolescent hormonal changes, but she still has a healthy sense of right and wrong. If anything, she can see issues as purely black or white, ignoring the shades of gray so common in everyday life. Moral absolutes seem clear, and moral outrage often bubbles just below the surface.

A teen who has been emotionally battered through neglect, verbal violence, and/or physical assault has a self-worth that is often 180 degrees opposite what a healthy person would see. I long suppressed the reality of my childhood sexual assaults. I did what many small children do in such circumstances: I felt I was undeserving. I must have failed somewhere along the way. I must have somehow brought the violence on myself. I must have done something terrible to experience what occurred, and I certainly failed in not appreciating the reality of my guilt.

> If their [sic] was someone in this world I knew LOVED me and understood at least 1/4 of me, things would be easier to swallow. I really need someone to love. I can't not even on paper, tell you how much. Someone to hold me, won't condemn me, but who would? No one, I know because everyone wants something and someone to be proud of . . . And my Body is nothing to be proud of. I am tired of being ashamed of me. . . .
>
> —*from a letter I wrote*
> *to my doctor when I was fifteen*

☙

I was estranged from Dad, rarely having contact with him despite repeated efforts to write to him or call him. He had an assistant who tried to soothe my feelings when she had to either return my letters or write in Dad's place. He was busy, she explained. He really cared about me but this was a difficult time for him. The lies were gentle, perhaps even loving, yet I understood that they covered his refusal to have anything to do with me, his daughter.

I began running with Stacy, my best friend. She was, and still is, a beautiful girl. A mulatto, she was exotically beautiful to adults but a potential object of ridicule to kids our own age. She was different, and when you're in high school, being different is the social kiss of death.

Stacy and I liked to dress up, go to nightclubs, and flirt with men. We had little interest in anything more than dancing and having a good time, realizing that men in their twenties were strongly attracted to a couple of teenagers. Our favorite place was a club called Hollywood's.

There was a police officer who worked off duty as a bouncer. He was also supposed to make certain that no one underage got into the nightclub. However, both the times and the community were more lax than they are today. If you were an attractive teenage girl who looked older than your years, the bouncer let you inside.

One night during our senior year in high school, Stacy and I went to Hollywood's and tried a new game. If anyone came over, she would pretend to be from a foreign country whose language I spoke fluently. She would talk, making up language she spoke in the type of singsong cadence common in parts of Asia and Africa. The sounds seemed to match her looks, as though if you heard the words you would immediately expect the woman speaking to have the exotic flesh tone and beautiful facial features Stacy had.

The ruse worked, and soon two men were sitting with us. They were taken by Stacy, asking her questions, listening raptly to her answers, and all "translated" through me.

Suddenly I looked across the room at the front entrance. There, coming inside, were Stacy's mom and her aunt. They knew that

Stacy, who had been told there was no way she was going to Hollywood's, was missing—along with me, her cohort in crime.

The moment I saw the two women, I knew our good time had come to an end. "Stacy, your mom is here!" I shouted, and my "Eurasian" beauty became just another American kid in trouble as the two of us raced for the nearest exit.

Dressed to kill, or at least slay the hearts and earn the lust of men we had no interest in pursuing outside the club, we found ourselves wedged in the bushes. We felt like we were Luke and Laura in the soap opera *General Hospital*, who constantly snuck around in order to be together.

But no matter how we fantasized our adventure and escape, we had to face harsh truths. We had no car, no way to escape unseen if pursued by the wrath of a mom. Instead, we hid in the foliage, watching the parking lot and the entrance, waiting to see if anyone emerged. To our great relief, they didn't.

The answer was to go home, something we had not planned on doing and had no easy way to handle. Instead, giddy from the moment, I bet Stacy I could get back inside. After all, her mom didn't care about me and the bouncer had let me in once.

Stacy thought I was nuts, but I was too high on the adrenaline rush of our escape to care. I straightened myself up, brushed leaves and dirt from my clothes, sucked in my stomach, shoved out my chest, and headed for the door.

The bouncer may have been loose, but he wasn't a fool. He was also trained to be observant. I got to the door, he smiled, pointed back the way I came, and I immediately returned to Stacy. There was no returning to the nightclub, no easy way home.

Continuing our degenerating escapade, we accepted a ride from an older man whose main attraction was a Corvette. We thought he would save two damsels in distress. He drove us to his apartment and asked us to come in with him just long enough to pick up something he would need later. He seemed nice enough and there was no reason not to believe him. However, once inside he made it clear that he wanted to have sex with me. When I refused, he threw us out, telling us we would have to walk home from there.

Suddenly we were back on the streets. We were fools, but we weren't stupid.

By the time the evening ended, Stacy was banished for the night from our house and I had walked several miles. I carried my high heels, ruined my stockings, and had to climb through my bedroom window to get into the apartment.

∞

There is an emptiness to rebellion. The adrenaline rush that comes from being naughty, from seeking the cheap thrill of beating the system, gets old fast. I wasn't an adult who could thumb her nose at the dominant culture and become an eccentric woman of the world. I was a kid who, no matter where I ran, no matter what persona I created with my best friend Stacy, still had to return to a familiar bed in a familiar home.

Judy dropped out of high school as part of mishandling her pain. I led my version of a wild nightlife while still focused on graduation. This was not because I was the better of the two but because I knew that I would please my father by being the first person in my family to make the effort to go the twelve years necessary to graduate high school. Thus I was not totally self-destructive, but I needed the reassurance that my future was with Dad, no matter what that meant. As a result, I sat down and wrote him a letter, asking to come see him and begging his forgiveness for past failings.

In my disturbed state, I could only see fault in myself, not in anyone who may have psychologically or physically abused me.

Dad rarely communicated with me, and when I did hear from California, it was almost always from a secretary trying to be nice to what she seemed to suspect was a hurting teenager. There would be apologies and excuses, yet the fact was that Dad had no interest in talking with me. I pushed this to the back of my mind as I sought his forgiveness.

During Christmas 1982 I flew into the Los Angeles International Airport courtesy of my father, who believed my letter but wanted to have a trial visit. The implication was that if I behaved myself, if I showed myself to be a good daughter, he would let me move out there after graduation. I would enroll in UCLA, live in the mansion, and try to get my degree—if everything went well over the holidays.

Every street in the wealthier areas through which I passed in Dad's chauffeur-driven black limousine was decked out for Christmas. A car dealer was selling matching parent/child automobile sets—$30,000 for a fully equipped, high performance Corvette, and another $7,500 for a child-size electric version with working headlights, windshield wiper, and radio. In the window of one store, neckties were on sale for $75.

I arrived in Bel Air to find Dad and Althea truly wrapped in the Hollywood Christmas spirit. He had brought my half brother, Larry, Jr., to be with him in the mansion where my half sister, Theresa, was already living, and the place had been decorated in the spirit of the times.

The wooden banister that rose from the first floor had been decorated with a long line of red bows and real Christmas tree garland. There was one enormous Christmas tree and a rope of firs adorned with silver bells. It was as though Dad had gone to a Beverly Hills boutique and bought Christmas to bring home to his mansion.

My half brother, little Larry, was there, along with Bill and Marsha Rider and their son. There was also Althea's other sister and her son.

My gift to Dad was jointly created with Theresa and Larry, Jr. We went to the boardwalk on Santa Monica pier, and among the rides and games was a photo studio. It was one of those places that had period costumes allowing you to dress up as someone from the Old West, at least the one we see on television. Theresa and I dressed as dance hall girls. Little Larry wore a black suit that made him look like a gambling ne'er-do-well who liked his women loose and his liquor neat. We all stared into the camera, unsmiling, then had the photography studio owner put the picture in one of the cheap frames they had. We were delighted with ourselves, delighted with the humor of the gift, and I think we actually pleased Dad with the present.

Damien, the son of Bill and Marsha Rider, received an oversized plastic bowling game which he proceeded to turn into martial arts weapons. With the boy holding one bowling pin and Dad in his wheelchair holding the other, they proceeded to duel each other around the living room.

Marsha Rider bought me the present Dad gave to me—a set of hot rollers for my hair and a bottle of Ralph Lauren's signature perfume.

Althea brought Dad a present they had received, a painting on what appeared to be velvet. The subject was a black woman with a large Afro hairstyle. As I recall, she was naked and on her knees, her knees spread apart as she leaned backward.

I remember the joy we all felt, including Theresa, whose mother, a drug addict, later overdosed.

☙

What is the matter? Is it just me or the awful world that surrounds me? It has to be me. There is no other solution. But it can't be my fault. Not all of it. I mean, look at my life. What do you see? NOT MUCH! I hurt so bad. Can't someone in this busy world stop what they are doing for a person hurting as internally as I am? I can love. I can laugh. I am alive. I am a human being.

—from a letter I wrote
to my doctor when I was fifteen

CB

There were many memories of those several days in California. Some were of Dad's wealth. Most were of the riches of family which I thought I had found at last.

The wealth was not so ostentatious as some would expect, the result of Althea's rather conservative taste. My bedroom had cushioned fabric wallpaper, at once soft, beautiful, and capable of deadening sound for true quiet. It was blue, gold, and paisley, with a big closet and a 19-inch television set. The brass frame bed had expensive nightstands on each side. There was a telephone in every room with an intercom system throughout the house.

There was a piano in the living room, an elegant baby grand that no one could play. The carpet was off-white, matched by the satin cushions on the chairs. Blues, burgundies, and greens predominated. State of the art electronics provided security. I was led to believe that every room was bugged with hidden cameras and/or listening devices. Bill Rider, who by then was head of security, later claimed the bugging was not so extensive as I remember it. And perhaps my memory is just because I committed whatever "transgressions" Dad caught in rooms that truly were bugged.

There was a security room filled with monitors and recording equipment. Dad was able to view anything that happened in the bugged rooms during the day from the comfort of his bedroom, which had a 500-pound remote-controlled bank-vault door for security.

The luxury extended to Dad's lifestyle. I was accustomed to the world of the family of the overworked, underpaid single mother. Each of us girls had our chores, and the closest we came to family tradition occurred on Saturday. We had neither church nor school nor job pressures affecting our time together, so we made the weekly pilgrimage of so many people in similar circumstances. We went to the Laundromat. We washed, dried, and folded a week's clothing. It was boring drudgery, but it was routine and I never thought that the rest of the world lived much differently. As a result, when I decided to take a bath in the bathroom adjoining my bedroom, I did what I would have done at home. I dropped my clothes figuring I'd pick them up after I soaked for a while. After all, even at Dad's I figured I'd have to do their wash, though I assumed he'd have an indoor washer and dryer.

The first shock came after I announced I was going to relax by taking a long bath. Before I entered the bathroom, the maid had started the water, checked the temperature, and prepared everything I would need.

Relishing this service, I closed my eyes and half-floated in the oversized bath. When my skin began to look like a prune, I reluctantly roused myself from the warmth, dried off with the thick oversized towel that had been arranged for me, and stepped back into my messy bedroom. Except that it wasn't.

Dad's mansion must have had high-speed cleaning and drying units. While I was in the tub, the maid had gathered all the clothing I had so casually dropped, washed it, dried it, ironed it, and hung it in the closet. The room was spotless. I was speechless, part embarrassed and part delighted.

With the exception of the unusual security precautions, including guards toting the same Uzi machine pistols used by the Presidential Security division of the U.S. Secret Service, and the occasional raunchy painting, Dad ran the mansion as though born to wealth. This was even more ironic in that he had purchased the place from the equally flamboyant Sonny Bono.

Years earlier, Bono had married Cher, then a teenage pop singer. They created a successful concert act, with record albums, and a popular television show that eventually included their newborn daughter, Chastity Bono. As time passed, Cher divorced Sonny, enjoying a string of lovers that included rock star Gene Simmons of Kiss. She became an actress acclaimed for her skills while Sonny left show business for politics. He went from being mayor of Palm Springs to serving in the U.S. House of Representatives before his tragic death in a skiing accident. As for Chastity, she announced that she was a lesbian and has now taken a leadership role in areas concerning lesbian rights.

The controversy over the place did not end with the purchase. On February 24, 1986, a rumor made the rounds of the news media that Ronald and Nancy Reagan were planning to buy the mansion for at least $4.9 million. The rumor was unfounded, and the Reagans bought a different house in the same neighborhood. But Dad, delighted with any publicity, commented, "If Reagan buys it, I'll even throw in a bed that sleeps six."

I suppose the mansion and the money implied by the lavish lifestyle Dad enjoyed was seductive. Certainly, like most kids raised in poverty while watching the success of some distant rich relative, I had dreams of wealth. But what made me feel I was home, what caused me to ache with desire and loneliness from the time I returned to Jacksonville until my graduation and a return to Los Angeles, was the personal side of the visit.

Althea, once beautiful, was showing the devastation of her drug abuse. When she went to California she had visions of becoming a movie star. With her looks, brains, and drive, that might have happened had it not been for her devotion to Dad's pornography enterprise. Instead, she deteriorated.

For example, Althea believed that all movie stars had their teeth capped. Rather than waiting to be asked to do it by some producer or director, Althea had every tooth capped while in Columbus. They were pure white and dazzling, a harsh contrast to her very visible gum line, which was an unsightly greenish-black.

Having abandoned her acting plans, she had a Mohawk haircut popular with punked-out druggies. She was also thin as a rail, the result of malnutrition. And she was mainlining heavily, a self-proclaimed junkie who, by the following year, would have an extremely expensive cut-glass candy bowl filled with sterilized syringes and needles to use whenever she desired a fix. But despite all this, she was still the greatest business asset Dad had, his greatest supporter, his ally, and enough in love with him to allow Theresa and me to experience him as a father.

The most enduring memory of those days was when Theresa and I would be in our pajamas in Dad's bedroom, curled up against Dad on his bed. We were like small children who had roused ourselves on a cold winter's day when the sky remained dark, the winds howling ominously, and the chilled air so threatening that only the covers of our parents' bed could provide safety. Theresa and I clung to him, feeling the strength of his arms, reassured by the sound of his beating heart as we placed our heads against his chest.

This was not about sex. This was not about deviance. This was about family, about the nurturing love of togetherness. I had been at war with Mom all of my life. I had viewed Grandma as a thorn constantly pricking my skin. I had seen Judy as an enemy. I had seen the men who came and went from my mother's life as pretenders to a position that would never rightly be theirs.

Perhaps I did have a family in Jacksonville. Perhaps I was loved by all I encountered, each in his or her own way. Yet if that was true, I chose to not see it, not experience it. I had created a psychological wall and I was not going to tear it down.

I left that wall in Florida. I flew to Los Angeles with past scars ripped from still sore flesh. I opened myself as though opening a wound that could fester and sting with the slightest negative touch. And on that bed, in that bedroom, curled up against my father, sharing his love with my half sister, I allowed myself to be at peace. I allowed myself to experience happiness. I fancied myself being at home.

The dream of heaven was forgotten. My faithfulness to God did not waiver. But at that moment, the arms that enveloped me, the quiet that surrounded me, the seeming reality of my private fantasy all were more important than anything else I could think about. I had found serenity, and as though in answer to my long-held prayer, Dad said I could return after graduation.

(Not all would be perfect, though. When I returned, when Theresa and I were again in the warmth of our father's arms, he looked at us and said, "I'm not going to have any fat daughters." He shattered the appropriately intimate moment by shattering our egos, then giving us a goal of a five-pound weight loss each week.)

I returned to a mother eager to hear about Dad, eager to hear what I did, what I got, where I stayed. She was like a schoolgirl whose best friend had an adventure she knew she could only enjoy vicariously. The Larry Flynt we shared was a myth, of course, each of us telling the story in our own way. Mom's myth seemed to be the myth of 1950s television sitcoms, where father knows best and mother is cherished. He goes to work looking handsome in his suit. She stays home, cleaning, cooking, baking, and caring for the kids. She loves his manly presence when he enters the door at the end of the day. He finds endearing the smudge of flour on her cheek, the happy eyes, the rapt attention as she listens to the exciting things he did all day in the city. And at night, when the children are asleep, the rose-covered cottage secure, the dog walked, the cat asleep on the fireplace, they come together in love, physically sharing what words alone cannot express.

My myth remained the knight, the protector, the brave defender of a maiden fair. His love would be all-encompassing, unconditional. I would one day marry another, of course, as he had with Althea. But he would always be present, a force looming in the background—part guardian angel, part Greek god.

The next few months passed agonizingly slowly. I took a job as a cashier with the Pic 'N Save supermarket chain in order to earn money. I hung out with my friends, especially Stacy. But always I was focused on my return.

Graduation was a special day, though not for the reasons it should have been. I was the first child on either side of my family to graduate from high school. I was the first child to be accepted at college, UCLA. I was the first child to lay the groundwork necessary to make a success in the legitimate world the way Dad had turned a strip club magazine into a success in the dark world.

At the same time, my sense of self-worth was so low that I felt myself unworthy of the diploma I was handed. I didn't really belong with the class. And because we were poor, I couldn't share in what was important to all of us kids.

I didn't get a senior class ring. I didn't get my graduation pictures, only the proofs which were all taken by members of my family, leaving me with no visual record of the time. I couldn't go on the senior trip to Disney World, and I could not have afforded to go to the prom if I was asked, which I wasn't.

I wasn't close to anyone. My experiences, both good and bad, seemed unique, light-years from anything to which my classmates could relate. Thus though Mom and my little brother were present, both of them pleased with the success we quietly celebrated together, what mattered to me was going home. Or so I thought at the time.

This time when I arrived at the airport, I embraced the experience of my father's world. I thought I would go to work with him, something with which he disagreed. He was not ready to bring me into his business. Living with him, living as his daughter instead of some distant relative, was all that mattered.

Dad also promised to buy me a car, a critical purchase in the mind of any Los Angeles teenager. It was a promise he had been making since I was eight years old, though I was finally old enough that I was certain he would finally come through.

As Dad's driver approached the St. Cloud Road address of the Bel Air mansion, I looked at the three-story mansion with the remote-controlled gate, the circular drive, the pillars, and the trees and tried to imagine myself coming home after a routine day of work. Instead of being awed by the splendor, I wanted to make it a part of my regular existence. I tried to imagine myself as I would be five years from now, when I would have approached the gate thousands of times, would have glanced at the house and no longer seen a monument to Dad's financial success but the place where I belonged. I wanted to experience it, not as a stranger but as one familiar with every nook and corner.

My room was no longer a guest room, and one of the additions was a gift from Althea, a big picture of Dad, which I placed on my dresser. The maids still serviced my every whim, but Dad made clear that I would have a few chores as well. On the night that the cook was off duty, for example, he expected me to prepare his evening meal. He still loved the kind of cooking on which he had been raised, the kind of cooking my mother had also done when they were briefly married. He assumed she had taught me everything she knew, something that was only partially true. I could cook, and I knew how to make such staples as fried chicken. But the idea of cooking for a man who was used to eating the best of whatever he wanted I found intimidating. Still, this was my home, and the responsibilities I had with my father were far simpler than those I had experienced with my mother and brother.

Not that I didn't make a major production out of the first meal I prepared. I wanted everything to be perfect for my father. I wanted him to be proud of my skills, delighted with the food, perhaps even regretting the six days of professional cook-prepared meals before I would again take over the kitchen.

The first meal Dad desired was pure down-home—meat loaf, milk gravy, fried apples, green beans—all the foods Dad was convinced Mom had taught me how to make. Unfortunately she hadn't.

I tried. I really tried. I called Mom for help. I experimented. And in the end I chickened out.

Taking a Kroger supermarket credit card and the mansion station wagon that was used for hauling groceries and other necessities, I set out on a mission to buy food for the meal. I walked each aisle, carefully planning what I would need. I mixed ingredients in my head. I mentally experimented with recipes, imagining Dad's reaction to each combination. And then I went to the delicatessen, where I bought barbecued ribs and other prepared foods.

I raced home, emptied the boxes onto serving dishes, and added a sauce where I thought I needed to make a change in the taste. Then I made a salad—yes, I actually made the salad—and nervously served the dinner.

I hid the boxes where I knew Dad would never find them, and I nervously watched him put each forkful in his mouth. He chewed thoughtfully before swallowing, seeming to enjoy the meal, never letting on that he probably had a videotape from one of the kitchen surveillance cameras revealing every aspect of my secret. Later I would actually cook on those once-a-week excursions into the kitchen, actually making meat loaf, spaghetti, and similar food. But that first night I simply could not bring myself to risk disappointing him.

There was also one other responsibility, one that in hindsight I find reprehensible. While I would not work for my father's corporation, my father feeling it was inappropriate despite my expectations that one day we would be in business together, I did have a daily chore related to his magazine. I became a movie reviewer of X-rated films.

∞

Most people have never been exposed to hard-core pornography. We know there is something uncomfortable about Calvin Klein "Obsession" advertisements when they involve naked or partially clad very young men and women erotically intertwined in pictures inserted in major magazines. And we are troubled by foul-mouthed rap and rock stars whose song lyrics are antiwomen. But we don't really know the world of hard-core pornography.

Pornography is not about sex. Sex is a gift from God, a joyous activity for procreation and recreation which is enjoyed by many committed couples. When sex is a part of a real relationship, one involving mutual caring, trust, and working together for both common goals and to support individual needs, it is an important factor in sustaining a lifelong marriage.

Pornography makes a mockery of God's gift of sex. The sex pornography encourages is more like masturbation with a mannequin. The sex partner, usually a woman, is an object for male pleasure, not an equal whose involvement comes from intense love. She may be naked. She may be shown in provocative clothing. She may be tied, gagged, chained, handcuffed, suspended, or tortured with such devices as nipple clips. Physical battering may serve as foreplay. Or she may be shown with another woman or second man as a prelude to intercourse. Children may be involved. Animals may be involved. In the extremes, she may be covered with excrement, cut, or urinated on.

The mildest pornography—couples engaged in intercourse—is designed to desensitize the viewer to erotica to such a degree that he or she will begin buying more extreme material. Most people don't realize that the federal obscenity laws allow for the prosecution of people involved with such images if actual penetration is shown, as my father has done in *Hustler*. We have been so inundated with truly violent pictures that we, as a society, generally ignore existing laws when only sexual intercourse is involved. Certainly my father has proven this repeatedly by showing such images without ending up in court.

Hustler offers images of everything from naked women to extreme violence and pain. The success of the publication is based on getting readers to want to see more and more of the same varieties or others sold through advertisements in the magazine. Dad and other publishers don't want their readers to be one-time buyers. They want them to feel the need to look at each new issue, to constantly seek more and different thrills that only come from being a regular reader, a regular buyer of the videos and other merchandise they offer.

Pornography is also about victimizing two different women. The first are the women who pose for the photographs, who participate in the production of films and videos. As I would learn to my horror, some are seemingly willing participants who have turned away from conventional morality in order to make what, to them, is big money, to enjoy free drugs, and to become "famous." They see it as a stepping-stone to Hollywood. But pornography is as much a vehicle for gaining a career in the legitimate film industry as prostitution is a vehicle for being hired as a social worker.

Others are addicts, the victims of extreme abuse leading to an absence of self-worth, and occasionally even forced participants truly functioning against their wills. They are victimized by people who want to use them for what they can offer, then throw them away.

But women outside the pornography industry are victims as well. You and I, the women with whom you work—all of us face the possibility of being treated with violence and/or verbal abuse by dates, lovers, and spouses because of pornography. Far too many men assume that what they view is truly the way women wish to be treated. Reformers decry pornography because psychopathic serial killers like Ted Bundy say they delighted in pornography before their crime sprees. But far more common are men who are jailed because their social skills were learned from pornographic literature. They truly believe that "no" means "yes," and that a woman resisting is a woman aroused, someone who wants to be subdued and entered. By the time they realize that the pornographic sex partner of their fantasy has nothing to do with real life, they are locked away for rape and the woman may have to face months or years of therapy before she can heal enough to trust again.

Pornography is an industry in which the real profit comes from turning a curious man or woman into an obsessive user. The industry would die if people said "no" to even the most casual exposure.

Pornographers get some of the same results by accident that cigarette manufacturers and manufacturers of alcoholic beverages deliberately achieve. Profits come from long-term, heavy use. Cigarettes are sold by the pack and the carton for good reason, the same thinking that goes into beer being sold by the six-pack. Unless someone is a heavy smoker or heavy drinker, profits are diminished. Pornographers do not plan to sell in the same way, but studies of pornography addiction have revealed that the sickness feeds in a similar manner. Use of pornography creates desensitization, causing the viewer to seek more and more. This leads to spending large sums of money for everything from magazines to paying per download of material on the Internet. And for all three societal problems, addiction is the ultimate common denominator.

I was introduced to the real world of pornography and all its extremes by my father, who insisted that if I was going to live in his house, I needed to work as a reviewer. Each night I was to sit in his home office and look at three or four videos sent to his magazines. Some of these were commercial videos with story lines, costumes, and all the structure of a low-budget film. Nudity and a variety of sex acts were obviously key elements, but they were "mild" enough that many would find their way into the "adults only" section of legitimate video stores.

Some of these were homemade tapes, the product of people with high-quality recording equipment and the desire to profit from the sex industry. Fetishism dominated, and the story line, if any, usually had to do with getting to a particular sex act. For example, there might be a kidnapping where the woman would be rendered helpless, then become aroused by the beating her attacker was giving her, the video ending when both the man and woman "enjoyed" his raping her. In the extreme there was no effort to imply that anyone other than the man was enjoying himself. The woman might be severely battered, children might be introduced, and everything filmed was literally a criminal act for which the participants could be jailed.

I don't know if I saw some of the work by one of the most extreme manufacturers of home pornography, but I learned about the business in the news. The pornography came out of northern California, where two men and a woman were making both bondage images to order as well as going out, kidnapping young women, then recording whatever tortures they thought would sell. The victims were frequently the girlfriends of drug dealers and outlaw motorcycle riders, men whose fears of what they faced from law enforcement outweighed their concerns with a missing lover.

The movie producers used a converted van complete with camcorder for imprisoning and torturing their victims on camera for as long as a month before the victim died. Sometimes the film would record the full death. At other times it would be limited to one phase of the torture. Eventually one of the men died, a second was convicted of his crimes, and the woman, an accessory before and after the fact, was given little more than a slap on the wrist in exchange for her gruesome testimony.

Many of the most readily available pornography videos have a number of short scenes involving different types of sexual fetishism, perversion, and violence. The manufacturers know that some scenes may be highly offensive, yet if they are short, the viewer will look at what he or she finds sexually stimulating. The whole leads to a desensitization of pornography in general, an attitude that there is nothing wrong with selective viewing, and a decision to view more. Soon the individual is seeking more and more stimulation from the objectification of women and, at times, men. Relationships suffer. The ability to emotionally commit is stunted. The person becomes as privately obsessed in his home or office cubicle as a drug addict willing to live in the gutter in exchange for one more fix. And since such viewing may take years to impact on the workplace, if ever, no one is likely to realize the terrible changes going on inside the person they do not suspect is in crisis.

As a reviewer, I was expected to watch all these types of films. I saw relatively expensive costume epics that played off real films, like "Flesh Gordon," a satire of sorts on the "Flash Gordon" movies. And I saw the horrors of the damned made by people who used their videos to justify extreme brutality against women. I saw mutilation movies, and the images I described earlier. If it was sent to Dad's publishing company, I was to watch it, then rate it for its sexual appeal.

Later the video would be mentioned in the magazine along with Dad's variation of the Siskel & Ebert "two thumbs up" rating system. Dad noted the best videos as resulting in a full erection. The rest were noted as providing only partial or no arousal.

Dad had me sit in his home office, where he had two high-back hunter green leather chairs with gold buttons, a large television set, his desk, an ottoman or footstool, and shelves of both books and videotapes. The books were all shiny, as though they had been gifts he proudly displayed but never read.

Ironically for a man who had devoured books while in the Navy, Dad seemed to read very little anymore. I never saw him reading a book, though he read newspapers all the time. It was as though the book reading was a formalized self-education program that was ended when Dad felt he had learned what he wanted to know. He had become content with keeping up with the news and exposing himself to extensive pornography.

The films were sick. The forced watching of them was destructive. And the idea of Dad having me review them was a perverted nightmare. I still don't know why he did it, especially since he never made notes or had me fill out some review form. As for me, I was so desperate for his approval, there was no way I was going to say no to him.

Dad also had me look at the cartoons he was offered, the submissions being laid out on the dining room table. I never found funny what Dad enjoyed. It was all demeaning to women and children. It was all humorous only if you were delighted by perversion before you opened the magazine. In fact, a few years earlier he claimed that the cartoons were gross and meant to be social commentary. They were not meant to be funny. However, by the time I was looking at them, either he changed his mind or had degenerated to where he did find them funny.

I looked at the cartoons and, in the majority of instances, found only sickness. I certainly did not laugh. I also made it clear that I did not want to do the job requested. And eventually Dad let me stop. He never thought it was wrong to use a teenager for such a task. He just decided that I lacked a sense of humor. In his mind I was simply his dour, serious child, probably another reason why he seemed to think I might not fit in at his business.

My desire to work with Dad did not come from a desire to become the queen of pornography. I separated Larry Flynt Publications from the realities of his magazines. I think I had created my own ethical walls, deciding which jobs I could do and which I couldn't, enabling me to feel I had a life and career with Dad without looking at the fact that everything about his business was pornography-based.

Moral and ethical issues were not ones I had to resolve right then, though. I got two jobs, a part-time position in a law firm's mail room and a salesclerk job for Judy's dress shop. The latter was work similar to what I had done at the Pic 'N Save supermarket, though with selling added. It did not pay very much money, but that did not matter. I was earning my own way, living with my father, and delighted with my "adult" freedom.

Dad also fulfilled a promise he had been making since I was eight. He agreed to buy me a car (registered in his corporation's name, of course).

There probably isn't a teenager alive who doesn't want a car and the freedom it represents. In Southern California this desire is instantly magnified by the fact that the only way to be cool is to be somewhere else. Nothing ever happens where any teenager lives. Beverly Hills kids have to travel to downtown Los Angeles for excitement, while the downtown L.A. kids are exploring Century City. West Hollywood teens cruise to Malibu, and Malibu teens drive to Hollywood. Everybody has to be somewhere else because where you are is never good enough. And despite a more than adequate system of public transportation, the only means of travel is a car, the more expensive the better.

In Jacksonville I would have settled for anything more reliable than the Green Bomb. In Bel Air I wanted what should have been my birthright, at least by my way of thinking—a Mercedes 450SL convertible. However, Dad was a firm believer in only buying American cars, or so he said when he said no to the high-priced

Mercedes. Instead, with the help of Dad's chief financial adviser, I ended up with the far less expensive but admittedly still cool Mustang GT V8 with a five-liter engine. It was a high performance car just a step down from the old Shelby Cobra, which could do 140 miles an hour without getting warm. It was also used in slightly modified form by the California Highway Patrol, so it was definitely a muscle car. And because Dad authorized his financial adviser to pay cash, he bought it for $4,800 below retail.

Once the sale was complete, the salesman learned who I was. He was livid for making the deal because, at the price that was paid, there was no real money made on the sale. He actually wept in front of me when he realized how much profit he could have made. Yet Dad still felt it was too expensive when he saw it, though he did pronounce it a "nice car," about as enthusiastic as he got over something purchased for me.

∞

There was tension living with Dad, a tension I tried to ignore. The house was luxurious and not ostentatious. The formal dining room had a crystal chandelier. The table used for formal dining had chairs whose seat cushions were covered with satin. The foyer was made of imported Italian marble, and the breakfast room where we usually ate our dinner was larger than the dining room in Jacksonville. There was none of the perverted humor of the Bexley Manor.

At the same time, the mansion that offered so much space and luxury provided neither emotional nor physical privacy. One of the first questions Dad wanted answered was whether or not I was still a virgin. Although I wasn't, having had a brief relationship where I made the mistake of thinking that sex meant love, I did not intend to incur Dad's displeasure. I lied and told him I was still a virgin. He considered this an illness for which I needed an antidote. He told me that if he was my age, he'd be having sex with everyone that he could. The idea of chastity, in his mind, seemed an abomination.

There was another uncomfortable aspect of life with Dad. The house was bugged in ways that went beyond the need for security.

I have been in mansions where security is a concern. Wealthy families are targets for burglars. It is not unusual for the rich to have security guards, as Dad did, and to have closed-circuit cameras supplementing armed patrols. Cameras are usually mounted on the grounds, observing entrances, and at key locations within the house, including in any room where valuables are kept. There may be a security room, as Dad had near the kitchen, where banks of monitors are checked twenty-four hours a day, perhaps with the added protection of film or video set to record a still image every few seconds. This is similar to what is used in banks, and such homes may actually be at greater risk.

Dad's system was different. There were hidden cameras and sound devices everywhere, including in the bedroom and bathroom from what I understood from the bodyguards.

At first I didn't realize the extremes to which Dad had gone. Then I began being summoned to his bedroom as often as once a day.

The routine was always the same. I would come to his door, the 500-pound behemoth that was normally used by banks. Then Dad would use his remote-control device to open it and I would walk in to speak with him.

Dad would have a list of infractions I had committed. Whatever mistake I had made, whenever I had acted in a manner of which he did not approve, he would know and tell me about it. Some things occurred in the bathroom. Some in the bedroom. Most were somewhere else in the house, though the surveillance was so complete that I realized there was no privacy afforded to me. Once, for example, I had been thirsty and taken a soft drink. That night I was berated for drinking a Pepsi instead of a Diet Pepsi.

The surveillance was so pervasive that I realized it was only possible to have privacy in the dark. I found myself closing the bathroom door and turning out the lights before undressing and entering the tub. In my room I changed clothes under the covers, in a closet, or at an hour when, without the light on, it was too dark to see.

From the time I was a little girl, desperately trying to turn a pathetically decorated closet into a private room, I have craved being alone the way a budding flower craves the sunlight. I have needed a personal space, away from prying eyes and ears. I have needed a chance to relax, to cry, to laugh, to dream, to pray without being disturbed.

Dad did not understand the need for other people's privacy, could not understand, and would have been unrelenting in any case. He subjected Althea to the same scrutiny, and while she might have been flattered by his attention, she also knew this was almost as invasive as rape. Together we laughed, making up our own lyrics to a popular song by the rock group The Police—"Every breath you take, every orgasm you fake, I'll be watching you." But our dark humor defused little. I became an emotional wreck, eventually crying myself to sleep on too many nights. Althea was a junkie, her escape coming through a needle, a pill, or a powder.

It would be easy to dismiss Dad's actions as an extreme version of justifiable paranoia. People were physically out to get him, and one man had tried to kill him. There was also an incident a year or two earlier when word went out that he was in trouble and the Los Angeles Police went out to investigate. Unable to get into Dad's room, and apparently unable or unwilling to talk with him other than face to face, the SWAT team scaled the walls of the mansion, convinced there was a good likelihood that he was being drugged and held against his will. They broke open the bedroom door to check on him. He was fine, but the trauma had to have been great.

Yet none of this had to do with watching his teenage daughter naked in the bathtub. Each time the camera recorded my intimate life inside the well-protected mansion, I was psychologically violated. It was as though Dad was doing to my mind what he, Carl, and Mom's relative had done to my body years earlier.

(Discussions between the coauthor of this book and some of the SWAT team members who happened to be in Los Angeles when the incident occurred revealed that they were convinced their actions were a surprise for Dad. They felt the call was legitimate and he did not know what would happen. They were genuinely concerned with his safety regardless of what they thought about him personally. However, Dad was unable or unwilling to believe he could have been caught off guard as he had been when shot, that someone could break into his impregnable bedroom. In what the coauthor suspects was a rationalization not based in fact, Dad was quoted in one newspaper article as saying, "For all of you who thought this was a publicity stunt, it was, and I thank God you all fell for it.")

Not that Dad necessarily thought about any of this. I suspect that the taping meant power to him. He came from a world where the more you knew about someone, the more you could influence their actions or anticipate the problems the person might cause you. He had been shot, confined to a wheelchair, no longer able to react physically as he had during his days running the bars and nightclubs. The elaborate taping system gave him a sense of control over everyone's life.

The idea of Dad's desire to control was reinforced one night when he took me to the movies. The film was a reward for losing weight, another control issue in which Dad delighted.

I have never quite understood why I have periodically let myself get extremely overweight. I have talked with incest and molestation victims who gained weight to reduce their attractiveness to men. They felt that obesity assured they would not be touched again, even though they intellectually knew that rape and incest, especially of a child, have nothing to do with sensuality. They are horrible crimes of violence which the child neither encourages nor enjoys.

Other overweight and extremely underweight individuals have used their bodies to gain attention from a loved one. And certainly my weight quickly became an obsession with Dad and Althea, something they harped on endlessly. Dad went so far as to have the refrigerator chained when not in use, a camera trained on the door in case I tried to open it without permission.

In recent years I have thought about Dad's actions. I think part of him genuinely did not want fat daughters. Each time he was seen with me, with Theresa, with Judy, or any of the other girls who considered him their parent, he had an image in his mind. The girls had to represent the *Hustler* woman, whatever that meant. He bragged that the women in his magazine truly were like the girl next door. Sometimes this was true—some of the girls were plain of face, though always well endowed. At other times the girls were so unusually attractive that they seemed to be the result of God's handiwork—or a plastic surgeon's handiwork, with an artist's airbrushing. And at still other times he glorified the gross, such as one naked model who was white-haired, quite elderly, and so obese I am certain she weighed no less than three hundred pounds. I never could figure out where his daughters were supposed to relate with all this variety, though he made it quite clear that he would not tolerate fat daughters. They seemed to bring him shame, and the last thing I wanted to do was bring him shame, embarrassment, or discomfort.

At the same time, Dad was not against having sadistic "pleasure" at someone else's expense, including his child's. As a result, he played into a problem that many teenage girls had when I was in high school.

Teenage girls obsess about their appearance. Fashion and young adult magazines were using models we kids looked on as ideal. Only years later would we learn that a number of the most successful had severe obsessions with their body weights. A number of them experienced anorexia nervosa, which so weakens the heart that some sufferers, such as singer Karen Carpenter, die from the condition. Many others were addicted to amphetamines in a desperate effort to stay thin. But we didn't know the downside of all this. The girls and young women were shown as idealized bodies in "must have" clothes. As a result, many of us, regardless of appearance, had the same hatred of self, focused on weight. It was a problem for my generation, but while we were experiencing it, no one knew how widespread it was. Even sadder, many of us still struggle with weight issues when, had we not been so psychologically pressured, we would have passed through adolescent turmoil and found our ideal weight, regardless of what the culture may have claimed.

Dad knew how to focus on the emotional weakness of those around him, especially that of his oldest daughter. I've seen pictures of myself at eighteen, and though I may have been a little overweight, the problem was severe only with my self-hate. If my daughter or one of the girls in her class turns eighteen looking like I did back then, I would find them attractive, as would any other objective observer. But Dad had to use my weakness at the same time he was genuinely concerned that I needed to be thinner. It was as though he had an end he thought was good and a means he decided to pervert for his own sadistic pleasure.

Dad knew nothing about nutrition or physical fitness other than fads brought to him by others. He discussed the benefits of fasting put forth by the Cambridge diet, for example. But he also tried odd natural substances outside the mainstream of natural healing and health food practitioners.

Althea was even worse. Although she occasionally managed to put on an attractive face in public, perhaps the result of being extremely healthy when she started on drugs, around the office everyone knew she was physically failing quite rapidly. By 1983 she was an admitted junkie, and she looked miserable. She was as likely to snort a line, pop a pill, or inject herself with one or another substance as she was to eat. She enjoyed a fine meal in an expensive restaurant; she also enjoyed a hot dog with the works. But if she had to choose between eating and taking drugs, she would choose the drugs.

The games over weight were numerous. As I said, the refrigerator was chained, and because the security room was near the kitchen an armed guard usually appeared if I tried to get into the refrigerator without permission. I could not bring in food because I would be caught on one of the monitors. Instead, I had to meet Dad's fantasy goals, goals that seemed based on misleading advertising rather than common sense. I know now that doctors feel that a normal weight loss, including changes in diet and exercise of a modest enough nature to assure long-term lower weight maintenance, is no more than one pound a week. But Dad set goals for me, such as five pounds a week, and I was determined to meet them. If I needed any incentive other than my endless desire to please him, it came from the weekly weigh-ins on the basement scale.

I might have felt differently about myself if the pressure had not been so intense. Dad insisted I drink the Cambridge Liquid diet instead of any meals. Then he would deliberately taunt me by having me sit with him, after weeks without food, my diet drink in hand, watching him savor a big roast beef dinner or some other meal he knew I craved. To this day, almost fifteen years later, I can still smell the aromas of the food arranged on his plate.

Althea joined in the fun by taking me to Barney's Beanery, which offered some of my favorite pig-out foods, as a reward for the weight I had lost. She would choose something she knew was high in calories yet which I loved, then she would order one for herself and one for me. When mine arrived, she told me she would tell Dad if I ate it.

In the midst of this world I tried to tell myself I was happy. I took delight in little treats, such as the night when Dad took me to the movies. The film was *Risky Business*, one he wanted to see and which he truly enjoyed. We traveled in his limousine, and as was usual for a Hollywood area movie theater with a popular film, the line wrapped around the block.

Dad first had stopped by some hamburger joint for a milkshake, burger, and fries. He never asked what I wanted, never intended buying anything other than for himself. Then we went on to the movie theater, the limo pulling up in front. The manager was waiting along with a couple of ushers there to help him. They obviously were expecting him.

Dad's bodyguard got out of the car, took Dad's wheelchair from the trunk of the limo, and brought it to Dad's side. Then, as Dad was being helped, he told me I had to go to the back of the line.

"Why do I have to go to the back of the line?" I asked, surprised. I was wearing a white ruffled dress with large pastel polka dots. "It's raining." "Just do as I told you to do," he said. And so I left the anonymity of the large car with the tinted windows through which I had been looking at the hundreds of people in line trying to see in. My appearance was scrutinized as I stepped out, my every movement noticed. It was as though I had been found wanting by the great man, adding a touch of humiliation to the already miserable evening.

After enduring stares and comments such as "Are you his 'bunny'?" I reached the relative quiet of the back of the line on the other side of the building. From there I waited, wet and unhappy, until finally reaching the front and being allowed to enter the theater to join Dad, comfortably positioned in the back of the house.

I experienced other humiliations as well. On July 4 weekend I went to Disneyland with thirteen-year-old Theresa and Little Larry, who was eleven.

At one point the three of us went into one of the souvenir shops. Theresa and I became engrossed in stuffed animals, while Little Larry became bored. The shop was not like a regular store. There was a back wall, but the other three sides were open, crowds moving in and out everywhere. It was easy to miss Little Larry walking outside to explore other activities in the immediate area while we were absorbed.

At some point I looked up and could not find Little Larry. I panicked. Little Larry was Dad's son and my sacred trust. I had visions of him being kidnapped by bad guys, injured in the parking lot, or otherwise getting in trouble. Without thinking, I raced outside to find him, Theresa close on my heels. In our hands were the souvenirs we planned to buy the moment we found our half brother, but the merchandise was not important right then. Only Little Larry mattered. At least to us. The store security people had a very different idea. They thought we were shoplifting.

For reasons never explained to me, the store management had a policy of prosecuting everyone caught shoplifting. I assume that they saw this as a deterrent. All I know is that we were in trouble before we could find Little Larry, who would have corroborated our story. We left the shop, looking frantically, were grabbed by security and immediately taken to the park's holding facility. Only later did the police find our half brother, and by then we were in serious trouble.

Dad decided to intercede for Theresa but not for me. Again he understood my weakness, my insecurity. He made no effort to get me a lawyer, to help me understand how minor the incident, how innocent I was, and how easy it would have been to convince the judge that there was a mistake. Instead, knowing I was terrified of the future, he played on my insecurities. He and Althea sneered as they both told me I would be going to jail, where I would most certainly be raped by a steel pipe.

I have no idea why they said this. The image seemed to be one from out of a bad B movie shown at a drive-in. Unfortunately, I was unsophisticated and scared enough that it was an image I believed. I was barely in control of my emotions when I went before the judge.

The judge was sympathetic. I was of legal age to represent myself and I think she thought I would say "Not Guilty," explain what had happened, and that would be it. Instead I did what the prosecutor told me to do. Because I had no representation, the prosecutor played a game with me to look good before the judge. He pulled me over to his table and said that if I did not plead guilty, he was going to get me on something and I was going to do a lot of time in jail.

Terrified, I told the judge I was guilty. Between Dad and the various people involved with the arrest—security, police, and prosecutor—I was certain there was no hope. I thought I faced less of a penalty than if I told the truth of my innocence. I thought no one would believe me, and then the judge would throw me in jail for years. I thought Dad knew about the rapes directly from women who had served time.

The judge was shocked and saddened. She had to go along with my decision, but she knew it was the wrong one. I did not have to go to jail, but I was branded a criminal for the first and only time in my life, and it was for something I did not do.

Through all this I tried to tell myself I was happy. I tried to tell myself that negative attention was love. I tried to tell myself it wasn't somehow sick to have to bathe in a darkened bathroom and change clothes under the bedcovers. I tried to tell myself that the sometimes nightly beratings I received for infractions of rules were not unusual for a father-daughter relationship. But in my heart I knew otherwise.

Although I worked hard at my jobs and did whatever was expected at the mansion, there was too much time to think, too much time to reflect on the reality of how I was living. I had made Jacksonville, Florida, and Bel Air, California, into creatures of black and white. Jacksonville had become overwhelmingly bad in my mind. Though I had a couple of friends there, the difficulties with my family, the seeming lack of a future, and the memories of so much pain and loneliness made it a place to which I never planned to return. I never considered how I could make my own way in Jacksonville. I never thought about working my way through school there, sharing an apartment with a friend, or otherwise creating a positive transition for myself.

For years my focus had been on escaping to my father's house. His love and approval were the stepping-stones not only to freedom from Jacksonville but also to a new life where I would have self-respect, a good job, and a future of happiness. California was my promised land. California represented nurturing, safety, a life that would be richly rewarding through meaningful work somehow connected with Dad.

Yet as the days passed into weeks, I found myself crying at night. I found myself feeling as though I was in a house of darkness, the beauty and luxury masking some underlying force of evil. Exploitation was rampant, and though it was far more subtle than the treatment of women in *Hustler*, it was there nonetheless.

For me the final straw came when Madalyn Murray O'Hair was a guest of Dad's in his mansion. I did not realize that Dad was facing more court time for some of his outrageous actions. At the same time, Dad had decided to run for President of the United States.

PRESIDENTIAL PLATFORM

[Larry Flynt's original platform was drafted in 1978 by Dr. G. Ray Motsinger. However, when he actually tried to run in the 1984 election, he wanted to run on the Republican Party ticket, a situation that would have made him follow the platform drafted by members and high officials of the party. Later he decided to run as an Independent. I have no idea what he ultimately considered himself when he made his move six years after the platform was drafted.]

ISSUES

Order:

That we rearrange our Priorities, with more emphasis, empathy and general care, loving and understanding being placed on each Individual within the United States of America; understanding that we all share love and affection for each other and are dependent upon each other for our existence.

1. Adoption—It shall be illegal to raise any adopted child without immediately telling said child that He or She is adopted and who the Natural Parents of said child are.

2. Abortion—Freedom of choice lying with the Pregnant woman and the Father; must have the consent of both within the first three (3) months of Pregnancy, otherwise no abortion.

3. Death— Shall be abolished at the intentional hands of another. Total emphasis being placed on rehabilitation not punishment.

4. Foreign Relations—All Foreign Aid shall cease until every citizen of these United States is comfortable with the necessities of life.

5. Hunger, Disease and Sickness—That by 1982, hunger will be eradicated within the United States forever. That by 1985, all Disease and Sickness will be eradicated within the United States forever.

6. That the President of the United States be elected for one six (6) year term—not to succeed herself or himself. Three four-year terms for representatives, and two six year terms for Senator.

7. Platform of Political Parties—That the proposed Platform of each Political Party be presented to American Public at least 18 months prior to the General election for the Presidency, with a copy of same being distributed to every registered voter in America. That the Final Platform of each Political Party be adopted at least six [months before the general election. Exact wording lost on copy I retained] .

8. Business—That Business in the United States of America shall operate on a Free Enterprise System within the true meaning of the word "Free Enterprise": Free means not controlled by a Foreign Power; not bound by restrictions or regulations; not controlled, restricted or hampered by external agents or influences' given, allowed or provided without charge or cost without encumbrance. Enterprise means business activity; an undertaking involved action or energy. That Compulsory Insurance be abolished.

9. Education—That the Federal Government shall teach all of our People how to survive without killing, without lying, cheating, or stealing and without committing deceit, fraud and deception: This shall be brought about by setting examples at the top level of our Government. That the Federal Government shall take a stronger role in education and research; that we shall have leaders at all levels that we will be proud to learn from in order that we then can be proud of our system; that we shall teach and program how to survive and live, instead of how to kill, hate

and die. That every school child in America be taught how to say "I Love You" in every language in existence on this Earth.

10. Elderly—That a great deal more time, effort, energy and money be spent on our Elder Citizens to insure their health, happiness and welfare and to provide for them Country Club living for those who desire the same. That there shall be no forced retirement at any age.

11. Fiscal Responsibility—Monies shall be diverted from Foreign Aid, Military Spending, and Interest Paid out in order to make the Citizens of this Country comfortable. That we shall put a curb on the two most inflationary items we have, which are the War Budget and the Billions of Dollars Paid out to the rich in interest (which is now Tax free) to finance our Wars. To follow the examples set by our Forefathers the first 125 years of this Nation when we didn't intervene in other Nation's Problems as we haven't been doing too well in solving our own. We are being programed today to believe a strong Defense by killing in this Nation's Heritage—Wrong—this type of programming has been self-serving from those that have stood to gain financially from War and has not benefited 95% of the people of this Country comfortable. [*sic*]

12. Military—There shall be a Drastic cutback in Military Spending, with the full understanding that we do not kill for Peace. That there shall be a gradual withdrawal of United States Troops from all other Countries until all United States Troops are within the United States.

13. Environment and Energy—Our personal energies shall be diverted from trying to figure out how to make bigger and better weapons to kill, to how to make bigger and better methods and means for living. This country has been caught up in how to make bigger and better locks, instead of how to make them unnecessary. Educational emphasis shall be placed on the utilization and

preservation of all our Natural Resources. To build Windmills to utilize the Wind, Waterwheels to utilize the Water and soloray [*sic*] equipment to utilize the Sun and other Stars and the Moon and to work closer with our Family Farmers to better utilize our Earth. Allow free development of energy efficiency systems for transportation and comfort without suppression by established firms.

14. Prayer—That Prayer be put back in our Schools with individual choice being Allowed.

15. Public Officials and Teachers—That we shall raise Public officials and Teachers' salaries and retirement plans as these are positions where we definitely need some of our very best minds and people. That in addition the Standards for these positions be elevated.

16. Busing—That school busing shall continue and be started in those areas where the schools have not been equalized both as to personnel, facilities and equipment. When these standards are equal then busing shall stop and the neighborhood schools be reestablished.

17. Vice President—That the Vice President of the United States in 1980 be a Female.

18. Bankruptcy—That all Bankruptcy Laws be abolished by 1982.

19. Prostitution—That Prostitution be decriminalized.

20. Physical Fitness, Sports—That more emphasis be placed on Physical and Mental Fitness and more energy be placed on our Olympic teams and amateur Sports.

21. Taxes—That the office of the President of the United States run a complete Audit on the entire Tax structure of the United States. That from this Audit the People of the United States will be made aware of who is paying what and a fair structure to all will then be implemented.

༾

Dad was not going to be undone by the issue of inclusion of all Americans in our government. When he announced his candidacy on October 16, 1983, he said he was running as a Republican because he was "wealthy, white" and "pornographic." He promised to "outdo James Watt. I promise to have a black, a woman, two Jews, a cripple, a homosexual, an Oriental . . . and a Mexican in my Cabinet."

The role of Madalyn Murray O'Hair was less clear. Sometimes there was talk of my having some sort of trust fund worth $30 million which she would oversee. Sometimes there was talk of her being involved with Larry Flynt Publications. Sometimes Dad just did things for reasons only he can figure out. Whatever the case, O'Hair showed up at the house for an extended weekend stay.

Madalyn Murray O'Hair was a woman who was either an important leader in the fight to preserve the separation of church and state or a greedy fraud, depending on which stories you believe. She declared herself an atheist and started her own religion. Or was it nonreligion? Or a political organization? It is hard to know. Some of her followers treated her as they might a cult leader. At the same time when her son Bill, the black sheep of the family, declared himself to be a born-again Christian, he noted that he believed his mother believed in God. He was quoted as saying that she used the atheism as a way of getting rich, something my father could certainly respect if true. After all, he believed in pornography but used the First Amendment of the Constitution in order to get rich.

When William J. "Bill" Murray III was forty-three, he gave an interview I later read on the Library NewsBank service. It talked of his break with his mother ten years earlier, his severe drinking problem, and his working in Dallas, where he was getting his personal and religious life together. The article said that he compared his mother's charisma with my Dad's. "She's got the kind of personality that breaks anyone's spirit who comes in contact with her."

The reporter also quoted Madalyn Murray O'Hair as saying, "I have one son who is sane, and then I have the other one [Bill]. There is a bad apple in every barrel."

O'Hair was less careful with her words when she described her relationship with Bill in front of me. Her voice was deep, gravelly. But instead of the dusky voice of an old-time movie actress who sounded like she had sung in too many nightclubs while smoking too many cigarettes and drinking too many glasses of whiskey, her voice seemed that of someone who had visited the depths of hell, liked what she saw, and made frequent return trips. It was a voice I could have believed originated from demon possession. I disliked her instantly.

I don't know what Madalyn Murray O'Hair might have been like as a mother, but I was horrified by the woman. She had a laugh that sounded like a machine gun, the staccato bursts seemingly able to violently penetrate your brain instead of letting you share the humor. She seemed self-centered and was outright nasty. She had high blood pressure and had to watch her sugar intake. When I accidentally brought her Sprite to drink instead of the Diet Sprite she requested to accompany the popcorn she asked for, she exploded at me. It was as though I was a would-be assassin caught in the act rather than the teenage daughter of her host who had made an honest mistake that was corrected before any damage could be done.

I not only had to serve her, I had to listen to Dad questioning her as though she had sense. Her answers were all harsh opinions and foul language. She sounded like a schoolboy trying to be

manly on the playground, mouthing every foul word he knew
while not really comprehending any of them. Yet she was a grandmother at the time, someone who should have had more maturity
and a better vocabulary.

Dad knew that I was a Christian and, as such, would find someone who did not believe in God to be unpleasant to be around at
best, an "enemy" at worst. He also knew that O'Hair loved spar-
ring with Christians even more than Dad did when he tried to take
Bible quotes, misstate them, then take the confused mess out of
context in debates. He delighted in my discomfort with the
woman and was disappointed that neither she nor he could goad
me into a verbal fight.

Eventually O'Hair left the mansion and Dad requested a grilled
cheese sandwich. It was probably the simplest food to make, and as
usual I took my time with it. I carefully spread the butter. I carefully placed the slice of cheese in the center of the bread. I heated
it so the melting would be even, the bread perfectly covered. It was
another of my love offerings to the father whose approval I desperately desired.

Dad ignored the perfection of my sandwich in order to berate
me about how I handled myself with his guest. He knew I was
uncomfortable in her presence, yet I had remained silent. He told
me I should have confronted her, told her how I was raised, and
what I believed in. He said he would have respected me more if I
had had a debate with her.

I did not know what to say. I firmly told Dad the Bible says cast not
your pearls before swine. Then I prayed for guidance, prayed to be a
vehicle for God's word, as Dad whined, "Are you calling her swine?"

Dad showed me a silver atheist medal O'Hair had given him. It
was a little like the old peace symbol, though at the bottom of the
circle, a piece was missing. Dad said it was the atheist symbol,
though I have never learned if that was true. It just seemed odd to

me, uncomfortable, evil in the way that a swastika sends chills up the spines of those who remember the Holocaust.

Dad said, "Let me tell you something, Tonya. When the metal in this circle comes together, then we'll know the truth."

I felt a stirring in my spirit. My voice rose up and I told him, "The Bible said you will know the truth and the truth will set you free. When the metal in that necklace fuses together, you will be in the pit of hell and then it will be too late."

Suddenly we were off. Dad challenged me, including creating his own Bible ideas such as, according to him, the time "when God made them eat their own feces."

I told him that such ideas and stories were not in the Bible, but he would hear none of it. He knew the Bible. He knew of what he was speaking. If he said something, it was so.

Then Dad made a comment I have never forgotten. "The truth won't set you free. The truth will get your ass killed."

We argued all night. Normally if Dad asked me to do anything, I would have tried to find a way to do it, to change myself to his desires. But when it came to matters of faith and God, there was to be no compromise in my life.

I found myself inspired, preaching, teaching, and sharing as I would with someone who was questioning whether or not to come to God. The words I spoke were not my own. The ideas I presented were ones I could not remember ever having thought before. I was as much reaffirming my own faith through recalling the Word of God as I was working to either convert him or get him to walk away from people like O'Hair.

And in the end, he called me his "little Jesus freak" and Theresa his "good little atheist." I knew I had to leave my father's mansion, knew it as I went to work exhausted the next morning. But despite my reminding myself who I was and what was important in life through my many hours' talk with Dad, I still did not go.

In the end, Dad threw me out of the house and sent me to Jacksonville. I had an accident driving into the carport. It was a minor incident, a tiny side dent and slight paint scraping. The repair was a minor one. My speed had been very slow. I had simply misjudged my maneuvering.

The problem was that if Dad saw the damage, I would be in trouble. I believed he would decide I didn't appreciate the car. I believed he would think I was a terrible driver. I believed he would tell me I wasn't worthy to carry his name, a name he had given to Judy but I had achieved through shared blood. I was afraid.

And so I lied. I told him about the dent, claiming it happened when I was shopping in the store. I did not know who had done it. The other car driver did not leave a note or stay around to face me.

The trouble was that I forgot Dad's security and the loyalty of those around him. He quickly learned the truth, knew I had lied, and ordered me to leave.

Once more I had failed. Once more I cried my way back to Jacksonville.

. . . . I must go and not think of it as finding myself but rather learning to be more dependent on myself. To satisfy my need for contentment. Understand I am already thirsting to drink from the well, to fear means consumption. Yet I still partake. To go will leave me hungry, a dull ache and an agony I am unsure if alone I may bear. I will become strong, form a cuticle for future scars to chip. So you see, I must go. I would not love you if I could take from you your soul and have nothing to offer. My heart would not be enough. It is too fragile and would not accept rejection. As I write, I feel the pain all alone. Can you understand? When I see you again, I will be in touch with myself.

—from a letter I wrote myself as a means of trying to cope with the depression and extreme sadness I felt as I flew on the plane back to Jacksonville

9

Home Again?

Sometimes it seems that Dad and I were spiraling downward, seemingly out of control, at exactly the same time. I continued to refuse to deal with the reality of both the man and his empire. I still desperately wanted his approval. I still felt ready to do whatever was necessary to gain his love. I did not realize that my past experiences had gradually caused me to change, that my life was near to hitting bottom. All I thought about was finding a way to make Dad want me back, and toward this end, I wrote a letter to Althea indicating that I had begun working, saving money, planning how to begin my college education. No longer would I ask Dad to pay for tuition, though he had promised to do so. No longer would I try to get back the car Dad retained in Los Angeles after I was banished from his home. I hoped he would support my efforts for education, but if he didn't, the information I provided Althea would give them both an understanding of exactly how I was trying to put my life back together.

As for Dad, a number of factors were working against him, all of his own creation. The most notorious, at least when it went to court and became the subject of a movie, was the parody Campari Liquor advertisement concerning the Reverend Jerry Falwell.

Jerry Falwell's Moral Majority was a controversial organization in 1983. To some people, Reverend Falwell was a dangerous extremist. They worried that a group calling itself the Moral Majority was, by its very name, implying that those who were not members were somehow "immoral." They worried that the group might be exclusive—white, radical right-wing Christians with a political agenda more important than social concerns. They worried that the emphasis on "family values," a new term at the time, might imply the condemnation of single parents trying to raise their children as best as they could. Most important to Dad, Reverend Falwell was getting extensive publicity in the media, most of it positive. Whatever the agendas of the members of the organization, Reverend Falwell appeared to many observers to be genuinely concerned with improving society. This meant everything from issues concerning child rearing to the elimination of pornography from popular culture. Naturally the latter brought him into conflict with my father.

Dad did to Reverend Falwell what he had done and continued to do to others—he used satire as a weapon. At the time there was an advertising campaign for Campari Liquor that talked about a celebrity's "first time." The ad made it clear that the issue was the first time the person had sipped Campari. The innuendo of the term "first time" was that it was about a sexual experience.

The parody Dad's artist and writer created had the Reverend Falwell discuss getting drunk and having sex with his mother in an outhouse. It was crude, disgusting, cruel, and totally lacking in humor. Those who liked it felt that there was always some dirty little secret behind morally righteous individuals and it was important to pop their bubble of pomposity. They figured that a good man was probably a closet sinner, and while the clearly marked parody was so outrageous it could not possibly be believed, it was clearly not satire as normally considered. It was not meant to reveal some hidden truth about the man, his organization, or society as a whole. It was not meant to challenge his work. It was simply a vicious assault, meant to ridicule someone whose ideas Dad apparently found threatening.

Reverend Falwell was stunned by what was done to him in the name of satire. He knew that the attack was meant for ridicule and pain. He also knew that if he had to be treated viciously, it made sense to use his own pain to challenge my father's rights as a publisher. Instead of championing the cause of any of the dozens of other public figures who have been hurt in this manner, remaining silent to avoid talking of his own embarrassment, the Reverend Falwell challenged Dad in his own territory, constitutional law. He sent the thousands of people on his mailing list the brief description of what took place, which I have quoted from his letter. He deliberately exposed himself to still more ridicule to hopefully keep my father from ever again hurting someone else in print.

Here is a fund-raising letter I received from the Moral Majority, dated November 15, 1983:

Dear Friend,
I must defend the honor of my mother.

This time my enemies have gone too far!

"Porno king" Larry Flynt has in my opinion carried his First Amendment rights beyond the limits of civilized discourse . . . and defiled the good name of my dear, godly mother in the process. (Mother died five years ago at age 82.)

Here's the situation . . .

In a recent issue of the pornographic magazine, *Hustler*, publisher Larry Flynt carried out a tasteless and libelous attack on my mother and me.

He printed a so-called "parody" of a liquor advertisement in which the advertising copy told a story of how my mother and I engaged in illicit sexual acts.

At the bottom of the page, the words "not to be taken seriously" appear—as though this excuses going way beyond what the First Amendment intended to protect.

Since you obviously would not subscribe to *Hustler* magazine, you have not seen the awful, full page "advertisement" which attacks my mother and me. There is a large photograph of Jerry Falwell alongside a picture of a bottle of Campari Liquor.

In bold letters the so-called "advertisement" has me describing, as if in an interview, my first experience with Campari Liquor and sex—with my mother. Because of respect for you and your family, I would never repeat the filthy words used in this "advertisement."

In fact, this "advertisement" and others in the magazine were so vile that some magazine distributors refused to sell this issue of *Hustler* magazine.

I'm certain that if you were to read the "advertisement" you would agree with me that it's time to draw the line.

It's time to get tough with these "garbage peddlers" who litter the world with their pornographic trash.

∞

I was less shocked by my father's actions when I received Reverend Falwell's fund-raising letter than I am today. I was eighteen, still in the throes of adolescence, and like most teenagers, totally self-absorbed. For years I had received the same sexually explicit Christmas cards my father mailed to adult friends and business associates. One, for example, was a pop-up card that put a visual sexual twist on the idea that Santa Claus is coming. I was only fourteen or fifteen at the time it was sent to me, far too young for such material, yet that was not the first or last of what would come in the mail. Earlier, when I was probably twelve, a card I was sent showed Santa Claus with his red suit open, a white banner across his penis emblazoned with the words "Happy Holidays."

I still remember the day the card arrived. I was excited to finally receive something from my dad, even a card. And this was one time it wasn't from his secretary, his girlfriend, or Althea. I recognized his handwriting. I knew that Dad truly sent me something for the first time in years.

The front of the card was like any other. There was the house in the woods, the snow, and the words "Santa Claus is coming." But when I opened it, when the visual literally popped out in my face, I was shocked. And then I saw what else he sent: five $100 bills.

I was euphoric. This was one of the worst years we had experienced as a family. Mom had made so little money that we were barely surviving. Then Mom made the decision that she was not going to have a destructive pet around the house tearing up an ottoman she couldn't afford to fix. She secretly gave my dog, my beloved Joshua, to a family who could afford both dog food and vet bills, neither of which were in our budget. But she did not have the courage to tell me the truth. Instead she said the dog had run away, a more difficult idea for me to deal with because I did not know if he was hit by a car, starving, or in some other trouble. I cried deeply, praying constantly to God, never knowing if Joshua was dead or alive, never knowing if I would see him again.

Our family finances also meant that there would be few if any toys and little in the way of a holiday celebration. Christmas presents would be simple, either absolute necessities or little more than the type of items found in discount stores. It was not a happy time, especially when so many of the people I knew from school, from church, and the neighborhood had gaily decorated trees with many presents wrapped and placed beneath them.

And then I got the money, more money than I had seen in my life, probably more money than Mom earned every two weeks. I was thrilled. I knew this was a gift that would make this Christmas the most special of my life.

So why was I hurting? Why was I so scared? My stomach hurt and I felt nauseated. There was something about the card, the money, the past. . . . It made no sense to me. I did not want to think about it, did not want to remember, if remembering would tell me why I was scared. All I knew is that I wanted to both sing with joy and to double over the toilet bowl, vomiting, all at the same time.

Instead I put a mask of happiness on my face and raced to show Mom. I knew she would be happy, even though she was upset with the card. I knew she would share my joy about Christmas. I knew she would think as I did, that the money meant love.

And so I was seduced on a subconscious level in a way that would just add to my troubles when I finally had to face the reality of my father, his money, and his life those several years later. I did not know it then, of course. Instead, I did what I always did. I continued to suppress that which was overwhelming, delighting in the Christmas we all got to enjoy, trying desperately to forget the inappropriate image that accompanied the present.

I had not seen the Reverend Falwell parody, though I did see it later. It was easy for me to dismiss the circumstances as just another of Dad's outrageous actions, never realizing that it would eventually be a factor in changing my life. Not only would the case result in a movie, the publicity for which triggered both memories I had long suppressed and the anger to confront the myth my father was perpetuating, it also would lead me to a deeper study of First Amendment freedoms.

The decision to fight my father was a noble one for Reverend Falwell to make, though its potential for success was questionable from the start. The court challenge to Dad was based on the First Amendment, a difficult area for all of us involved with the fight against pornography. The court issue has recently been clouded when material is clearly presented as parody or satire, no matter how vicious and personally offensive.

The actual First Amendment is not, as some believe, a license to do anything someone wants in print. More important when it comes to my father's work and the publications of others in the same business, obscenity is not protected speech under the First Amendment. In fact, there is much speech that is not protected based on both interpretations of the early drafting of the Constitution and recent court cases.

Miller v. *California* (413 U.S. #15—1973) says, "This much has been categorically settled by the United States Supreme Court, that obscene material is unprotected by the First Amendment." Earlier, in *Roth* v. *The United States* (354 U.S. 476—1957): "We hold that obscenity is not within the area of Constitutionally protected speech or the press."

There are other forms of speech and expression not protected by the First Amendment as my father and his lawyers have learned repeatedly. For example, expressions of contempt in a courtroom are not protected and a judge has the right to send someone such as my father to jail for expressing such contempt.

Among other areas where all journalists, broadcasters, and others in the media know there are constraints and only unsuccessfully challenge them are slander, libel, false advertising, copyright violations, and child pornography. In addition, it is against the law to commit perjury, to falsely yell "fire" in a crowded theater or falsely talk about a bomb, hijacking, or interfering with passengers, crew, or an airline flight in an airport.

Laws can be changed through democratic means, yet the fact that they have not been, that if anything most people have proven to their legislators that they want greater enforcement of existing laws, indicates that obscenity is not desired in America. Equally important is the fact that even those distinguished jurists who disagree with what I feel is national sentiment admit to the seriously harmful effects of pornography and obscenity. For example, Judge Frank Easterbrook of the 7th District U.S. Court of Appeals, a man who, in 1985, felt that pornography should be protected speech, admitted that: "depictions of subordination tend to perpetrate subordination. The subordinate status of women in turn leads to affront and lower pay at work, insult and injury at home, battery and rape on the street."

It should be noted that some people, including so-called legal experts who actually may know that they are misrepresenting the truth, try to equate censorship with anti-obscenity statutes. Censorship only deals with prior restraint (see, for example, the 1993 U.S. Supreme Court decision *Alexander* v. *The United States*). The anti-obscenity laws are concerned with published work. If men such as my father were censored, there would never be a *Hustler* magazine. However, when he is being fought by a community, it is for what he has on the stands. Thus he and other pornographers are being asked by the law to face the consequences of their actions, not to be restricted in the choices they can make concerning what to publish.

Society's tragedy is that so few people understand this. They feel that they dare not be labeled censors, even though it is not censorship those of us working against pornography are seeking. They feel that the laws work against them when the reality is that the law is on their side, just rarely enforced. They give up before the fight because they do not understand the issue. Undereducated and misguided civil libertarians are leading the public astray and making the legitimate enforcement of constitutionally valid laws so uncomfortable that otherwise honorable prosecutors shy away from this issue. It is like the health hazards of cigarettes, a problem discovered at the end of the nineteenth century yet not seriously addressed in the courts for the next hundred years. The truth was known. The enforcers of the publicly approved ordinances chose to shy away from a duty that would have benefited the public's health. The same is true with obscenity.

Pornographers, like cigarette company spokespeople, have their own set of myths they want the public to believe. The first one is that if you are antipornography, you are antisex. You are a prude. And the second is that if you are antipornography, you are anti the First Amendment.

You have seen that the latter issue is not true and the first is equally foolish. Sex is one of the most pleasurable acts God has given us, a joyous experience in a committed relationship. It is for both procreation and recreation, the latter lasting well after a woman's childbearing years as many happy couples in their seventies, eighties, and older will attest.

Pornography is about violence, about rape, subjugation, and pain, at the very least. It is about dominance, not sharing, about casual sex and a "throw the bitch away when done with her" attitude, not working to increase love, joy, and a lifetime of mutual exploration. To link one with the other is as outrageous as linking cigarettes, which slow the cardiovascular system's ability to function, with athletic events where peak functioning is the goal. Yet both myths are perpetuated.

As I have learned from talking with prosecutors and leaders in the fight against pornography and cannot stress enough, the obscenity laws in this country do not work because they are not being enforced. Pornography in all its forms has been called a $12-billion-a-year industry. That means that there is a lot of money for bribes, a lot of money for smoke-screen advertising campaigns giving disinformation about First Amendment issues, a lot of jobs at stake. The fact that the jobs often involve the commission of crimes is too frequently ignored. Equally troublesome is that many people, including prosecutors, confuse freedom of the press with license to break the law if the lawbreaker is using a printing press.

The pornography industry, by producing obscenity, has flagrantly and continuously violated federal, state, and local laws. They have either deliberately or inadvertently been granted immunity by law enforcement. In some instances this might have to do with corruption. In most instances, though, it is because the big lie of pornographers, that stopping obscenity is censorship, has been bought by so many people that they are too naive or too afraid of political backlash to act. They forget that the laws were passed in response to the will of the majority of the people in a community. This failure to do what is right perpetuates a harm that endangers the moral fiber of the nation.

Abraham Lincoln said, "We the people are the rightful masters of both the courts and Congress, not to overthrow the Constitution but overthrow men who pervert the Constitution." As I have shown, pornography as free speech is clearly a perversion of the Constitution. Most people are clearly outraged when they see the readily available excesses of pornography. Yet they have not learned to take control in the manner that Lincoln, a lawyer before becoming president, so well understood could, should, and needed to be done.

When there is blind support for the First Amendment as a defender of all writing, it is frequently because of both knowledge of excesses against communication and the failure to understand the amendment in context. My understanding from experts in Colonial law is that eleven of the thirteen original colonies had obscenity laws when the Constitution and the first Ten Amendments were enacted. These laws remained legally on the books of those regions which had become known as states. The First Amendment to the Constitution did not overturn them. The Founding Fathers did not want a Larry Flynt flaunting perverted excesses any more than they wanted the American political leaders to be able to dictate what could and could not be published.

Today the federal law allows freedom of the press, but existing constitutionally approved city and state laws, currently rarely enforced, can go a long way toward stopping some of the excesses. For example, while it may be legal to publish child pornography under the Constitution, the reality is that it is illegal to take the pictures necessary to have "kiddie porn." A person who photographs children for erotic ends is going to jail, probably without exception. The charges will range from obscenity violations to contributing to the delinquency of a minor. Every major photo lab in the nation has staff members who know to call the police if they encounter film with such images. In a number of regions, librarians, those stalwart defenders of First Amendment freedom, who spot people downloading child pornography when legitimately using the Internet are increasingly calling the police. Arrests are being made. Convictions are being obtained. And courts are upholding these actions. In fact, anyone found with child pornography downloaded from the Internet—whether in the workplace or, given lawful search and seizure, in the home—may be facing court action and possible conviction in much of the country.

There are other aspects of the law that apply to pornography for adults. Prostitution is illegal, and "porn stars" who have sex for pay are violating the law. Since these "actors" regularly appear at adult bookstores to sign their latest videos, it is not hard to make an arrest. And the product they are selling is proof of the illegal action. Yet as I travel around the country, I see that none of the opponents of pornography are using such options.

Other laws also exist, all of them enforceable. Unfortunately, the weakest argument against pornography in the guise of parody is libel. The extremes of such parody are generally held to be legal because the royal families who controlled the American colonies considered any criticism of their rule extremely obscene. Punishment was harsh, ranging from incarceration to beatings, public humiliation, and/or death. In order to have a society in which religious and political discourse can be heard, the Constitution does not allow the federal government to restrict speech. This means that even so sleazy a "parody" as Dad had published to attack Reverend Falwell was likely to be upheld by the courts. Unfortunately the case became a symbol for something it wasn't, and it would give Dad yet another fifteen minutes of fame.

Not that I was about to enter such controversy concerning the Reverend Falwell letter. His case would not seriously matter to me for more than a decade. I was just eighteen and still suppressing too many truths. I was still not ready to tackle what may be the most corrosive evil society faces.

I suspect Dad did not know how the Jerry Falwell libel trial would come out. There are many community-based laws broken each time a new issue of a pornographic publication reaches the stands.

The First Amendment libel issue was the weakest attack that could be brought against a parody, though, and a decision was likely to hinge on a judge and/or jury's attitude toward the two parties involved. Even those who disagree with Reverend Falwell are far more likely to take his side than that of my father, who has become a social pariah.

∽

Dad was in trouble with the law for other reasons, though. And John DeLorean was the reason.

DeLorean had been a brilliant engineer for General Motors. He rose to a position as head of the division accounting for 80 percent of General Motors's profits, was earning $650,000 a year, and was in line to take control of the company. Then he decided to go on his own, creating a high-performance sports car that would compete in price with vehicles such as the Corvette. He arranged to build the car in Northern Ireland, hiring both Catholics and Protestants to work side by side on the assembly line.

But DeLorean entered a violent community where Catholics and Protestants were at each other's throats. Belfast, Northern Ireland, where DeLorean built his plant, was like an armed camp. Endless checkpoints, British soldiers, and terrorist groups all vied for control. The idea that DeLorean could bring two factions together inside his plant was seen by some British leaders as potentially dangerous because it could unite them against British domination.[1]

GM was also concerned with stopping the import of what was seen as a potential rival for its redesigned Corvette, being reintroduced after four years out of production. The company worked through Kingman Brewster, Ambassador to the Court of St. James, to add political pressure, a fairly easy task since then Prime Minister Margaret Thatcher was a friend of then President Ronald Reagan.

Then DeLorean went through a financial crisis. During one hundred days of desperately trying to save his company, he was set up to look like he was involved with drug dealing. Some of the men involved were hoping to become famous by entrapping a "name" with drugs that DeLorean knew nothing about.

Although DeLorean was completely innocent, and eventually fully exonerated both by the courts and the government's own materials (wiretap tapes, testimony of a Drug Enforcement Administration agent who admitted the setup, testimony by an FBI agent who admitted falsifying evidence, and others), in 1983 the story was one of the biggest in the news. Copies of some of the "evidence," especially a videotape of drugs being shown to DeLorean the day of his arrest, were allegedly leaked to some members of the media. Dad got hold of it and began brokering it to the television program *60 Minutes*.

The revelation of potential evidence jeopardized DeLorean's right to a fair trial. Judge Takasugi, who was presiding over the upcoming trial, was livid. Endless rulings show that the Sixth Amendment, an American's right to a fair trial, must always take precedence over freedom of the press. He fined Dad $10,000 per day (later $20,000 per day) to reveal his sources. The fine reached a total of $300,000 with Dad continuing the fight—and getting more and more publicity.

Finally, on November 17, 1983, Dad was ordered to be in court to reveal the name of the source of the tape. It was the same day that photographer Annie Liebowitz was photographing him for the January 1984 issue of the magazine *Vanity Fair*. Dad had long figuratively wrapped himself in the American flag, calling his defense of pornography a defense of the First Amendment. It was nonsense, but Liebowitz had Dad pose on a couch, covered by the American flag.

Dad knew about both the photography session and the court appearance, scheduled for 11 A.M. The court appearance was obviously the more important of the two, but Dad called the judge and asked to have his 11 A.M. appointment rescheduled for 1 P.M. Instead, Judge Takasugi ordered him to be in court in forty-five minutes or be charged with contempt, a jailable offense.

Dad was outraged. He would be in court. He would bring money for his fine. He would also do whatever he could to upset the judge, including arranging for the fine to be delivered by hookers in trash bags filled with $1 bills.

First Dad took the American flag and folded it in the shape of a diaper. Then he put on a bulletproof vest and a metal military hat. Dr. Timothy Leary, a man whose experiments with the hallucinogenic drug LSD were notorious, had given Dad a Purple Heart, the medal awarded to those wounded in battle. Although far from the highest commendation a soldier could receive, it was proof that the recipient had the courage to go into battle, to face the unknown dangers of the enemy, to put his or her life on the line. Dad's outfit was an obvious mockery. It was pure street theater.

The FBI arrested Dad for desecrating the flag, and one of the agents, allegedly infuriated by the mock Purple Heart, slapped Dad's face and ripped the medal from the vest.

Dad was outraged. He began throwing whatever he could get his hands on, screaming at the FBI and court personnel. He was arrested, booked, and placed in jail.

Later Dad would claim that he was forced to go thirteen hours without going to the bathroom, resulting in a urinary tract infection. I don't know if that was true, but he lost any sympathy others might have had when he was hauled before a female federal judge and proceeded to call her a "cunt." (While most people found his actions appalling, there were those who delighted in his antics. They choose to see him as the consummate rebel, not caring what he does so long as those in authority are the subject of his ridicule and escapades—not themselves.)

This was not the first time Dad used such foul language. In fact, Dad was already under a contempt charge from an appearance before the U.S. Supreme Court just five days before his latest confrontation. He was also fighting a libel suit, and though he knew little about libel law, he wanted to defend himself before the highest court in the land. Neither his own lack of knowledge nor the fact that lawyers have to follow a special procedure to be allowed to appear before the U.S. Supreme Court mattered to him. Dad was going to have his way.

Chief Justice Warren Burger made it clear that Dad would have to use a court-appointed attorney if he did not wish to bring someone qualified to represent him. Such a refusal outraged Dad, who claimed that Burger was in on the plot against the late President John Kennedy. According to Dad, former president Richard

Nixon handled the payoffs (was the "bagman") for the Kennedy assassins, and when he appointed Justice Burger to the Supreme Court, the action was meant to protect Nixon. Then Dad referred to the justices as "nine assholes and a token cunt."

Dad was removed to the gallery to watch proceedings handled by a qualified, court appointed attorney. Again outraged, Dad pointed out that he was going to be president, at which time he would have the FBI arrest the justices. He said that he would have a glass cage built to hold them, then make them stay naked in the cage so that people could see what those who perverted the Constitution looked like.

Dad claimed that he was being arrested for doing nothing worse than expressing himself. Magistrate Jean Dwyer did not agree. A hearing was ordered based on the charge of impeding justice. It was that hearing about which Dad was concerned less than a week later when he acted so outrageously.

Later this period would be looked upon by many as a delightfully zany experience where my father, in all his lunacy, was a folk hero. It was as though he played the fool in order to reveal the truth about society. Instead, he defused a much more serious issue by misdirecting attention from the core issues as yet unresolved.

The misdirection and disinformation ignore the first stage of the problem caused by pornography—addiction. People who look at pornography gradually find that this is an important part of their day. More and more time is spent with it. A person who says he is using it to stimulate his sex life is actually avoiding intimacy while entering a world of perverted fantasy.

We see the impact on society in everything from television to advertising. There was a time when a screenwriter or playwright could shock an audience and instantly define a character as evil if he so much as slapped a woman in the face. Today we are exposed to advertisements showing simulated sex, nudity, and violence.

We have television programs and motion pictures where rape is as likely to lead to romance (watch any of the soap operas, for example) as it is to lead to further torture and murder, and all without regard for who is watching.

The addiction is as subtle as Joe Six-Pack's quiet but steady consumption of beer, and it is as blatant as the chain-smoker, the drunk, or the junkie constantly searching for the next high. Even worse, because so much of it is available at little or no cost, such as on the Internet, many people are addicted before they realize it, before their actions begin destroying their relationships, their careers, and their lives.

Next comes the escalation. The person who has been looking at pictures of full frontal nudity, intercourse, and "friendly" variations such as bondage becomes curious about what else is out there. He or she begins exploring sexual violence, bisexual images, and even the use of children with children or children with adults. Material that would once have seemed an abomination is now a curiosity at best, a desired stimulus at worst.

There may be a willing partner in the pornography addiction, but as the escalation of needs increases, the addict is more likely to seek self-stimulation. The partner may be unwilling to engage in the violent and/or bizarre fantasies the addict desires. Or the fantasies may be about sexually related violence so deviant that anyone doing it is at risk for serious injury. Thus masturbation becomes the sexual relief of choice, further isolating the addict not only from loved ones but the world at large.

This is similar to the drug addict's need. After becoming accustomed to what once was a delightful, "recreational" high from crack, cocaine, heroin, or any other drug of choice, the reaction is limited. Variations are desired, sometimes different drugs, sometimes combinations such as heroin and cocaine ("speedballs") and sometimes with increasingly larger doses. The person feels invulnerable to what once was stimulating, never realizing that instead of being a comfortable user, the addict may be one dose away from a heart attack, respiratory failure, or some similar problem. Stroke, mental problems, and death are all too common at this stage, and pornography, though not fatal to view, is just as destructive in its own way during the escalation period. And like the addict who becomes comfortable only with other addicts or alone, the pornography addict escalates to a level where there is no room for a loved one.

Escalation leads to desensitization. The material that once would have been viewed as immoral, dangerously antisocial, and worthy of destruction becomes just another day's viewing. Where once the viewer would have been horrified to think that an individual could inflict such harm and degradation on another human being he no longer thinks about the physical or emotional results. All that matters is ever-greater stimulation, and the values of the past are long forgotten.

And for some, desensitization and isolation from an ongoing partner leads to acting out what has been seen. In the mildest stages, the person becomes promiscuous, voyeuristic, and frequents massage parlors, houses of prostitution, and the like. There may be sex with minor children, at times including immediate family members. There may also be the use of pain during sex, inflicted either on the partner or on one's self.

In the extreme, brutality is routine. A new relationship is coerced into trying what proves to be extremely violent sex. A prostitute is hired to be brutalized. Or an unsuspecting stranger is attacked, the assailant never seeing the individual as a whole person. In fact, when arrested, jailed, and successfully treated, the assailant may live for years with overwhelming guilt and a sense of horror that he ever could have lost control of what had once been core values essential to his life.

The untreated extreme sexual addict will find himself aware of the consequences and still be unable to stop. He will risk the loss of a loved one, the loss of family, of job, of community respect, of positions of power and influence in order to attain his "pleasure." We have seen the most extreme examples even within government, where in the last thirty years, there have been high officials caught repeatedly engaging in promiscuous homosexual sex, violent sex with a waitress in a private Washington, D.C., dining room, and even a man willing to let his mistress listen to his conversations with high government officials. In the latter case, he was so determined to justify the unjustifiable that he went public in a book, which, to the credit of the American people, sold to almost no one.

By November 22, Dad was reeling out of control or very much trying to set up an image of a crazy man. Knowing Dad, he might have been calculating and he might have been erratic, and I'm not certain if anyone could discern the difference.

On the 22nd, twenty years to the day after the assassination of President John Kennedy, Dad poured ketchup on his face and rode the same route as the Presidential motorcade had taken. From there he traveled to Klamath Falls, Oregon, and then, after returning briefly to Los Angeles, he went to Alaska.

The Oregon trip at least made sense. Dad had been in terrible pain, using all manner of drugs to get relief. When nothing worked, he went to Duke University Hospital, where a new surgical procedure enabled him to have the most comfort he had enjoyed since he was shot. After that procedure in 1982, he had explored a number of homeopathic remedies, including something called blue-green algae. It was supposed to cause nerve regeneration, and the distributor lived in Klamath Falls.

The Alaska trip might have been for almost any reason. Dad gave three.

One reason to go to Alaska was to fly the same route as the Korean Airline #858 that had been shot down in 1987. He claimed that he was going to duplicate the flight that had become a major controversy, personally parachuting from the plane over the spot where the airliner went down. A second reason was to duplicate the flight, then throw out one of the men who had shot him in 1978. The fact that there was only one would-be assassin and that man had never been caught was irrelevant. Dad had plans.

The third reason Dad gave for the trip was more elaborate. He had to go see the late Marilyn Monroe.

As Dad later explained, Marilyn Monroe, or someone claiming to be Marilyn Monroe, called him on the telephone. Since Monroe died of a drug overdose and the body was examined by police, Dad did not find the call credible. However, he felt he had to learn the truth and so he went to Dixie Couch, an Iowa cousin of his of whom I have never heard. Supposedly the cousin obtained fingerprints of the woman to try and compare them with the fingerprints of the woman buried in Marilyn's grave. I don't know if he ever had any success because the flesh was undoubtedly long gone from Marilyn's fingers. However, he also used an investigative reporter who allegedly confirmed that the claimant was genuine. What was used for proof I never knew.

Dad was arrested in Alaska, where he appeared before the judge while wearing a Santa Claus outfit. He was returned to California, then tried to fly to Kentucky in December, allegedly to speak in his hometown church. I didn't know he attended one back there, and I certainly doubt that he maintained contact with it over the years. But the reason did not matter. He was under orders not to leave California, so he used a fake name and was arrested in Chicago, apparently as belligerent as ever. The Chicago judge did not believe Dad's real identity until he "cussed her out."[2] He then went before a second judge, who sentenced him to sixty days in jail for contempt of court. However, Dad did not serve the time, instead being sent back to face Judge Takasugi.[3]

∞

I hope that this dishonorable Court does not find that I am showing contempt to the system I have done my damndest [*sic*] to conceal.

I pray to the Lord Jesus Christ that this motion be granted. I have come in peace, but with a big f——ing sword and one hell of a club. To decline this motion would be tantamount to treason, or should I say obstruction of justice. At which time I will order the FBI to arrest every member of this Court and place them in custody with the federal marshals in Washington, D.C.

I am about the Lord's work, you mother f——ers, so move over. I am not the second coming, I would like to emphasize, but I am the new kid on the block and it is not the Last Supper, assholes. It is the morning after and I am his main man.

—*Larry Flynt speaking on his own behalf in the court of the Honorable Frank J. McGarr* [4]

∞

There was arrest after arrest for acts so outrageous that Dad was ordered sent to the U.S. Medical Center for Federal Prisoners in Springfield, Missouri. He arrived on December 21, 1983, and by the second week in January 1984, the report was complete. Although almost certainly suffering from manic states and perhaps from a form of manic-depressive illness, Dad could not be effectively diagnosed. He was what people might describe as either crazy as a bedbug, totally Looney Tunes, three sandwiches shy of a picnic, or an abusive manipulator. Or maybe he was all of the above.

Dad gained a reputation for attacking everyone. He was verbally abusive and foulmouthed. He could be cooperative one minute, refusing to take ordered physiological and psychological tests the next. He talked of the warden's daughter posing nude. He asked staff members to deliberately break his leg in return for a lifetime allowance and the personal chance to sue the institution. And while in a whirlpool bath for treatment he said, "When Mr. Reagan and Jerry Falwell are patients here I want you to put them both in this whirlpool and boil them, and I want you to tell everyone I said that."

Dad constantly berated the staff and the guards with obscenities. He also spoke in a grandiose way about his future, saying such things as, "I'm going to be elected President, you can just go and ask; nine of ten people on the street will tell you they will vote for me."

The days of my separation from my father turned into weeks. I began working in Jacksonville, eventually moving in with a friend. I had my job, saved my money, and dreamed. Until I was contacted by his lawyer.

Dad was to undergo a competency hearing and, for some reason, I was asked to fly to Los Angeles to serve as a character witness. I did not fully understand what they wanted me to do. I was extremely apprehensive, though I was thrilled to have the opportunity. His lawyer was friendly, flirtatious, and teasingly called me "buxom."

This was a man who, after I arrived, would give me the impression that he found me attractive. This was also a man who was close to my father on a day-to-day basis when running the company. To have him find me appealing was beyond my expectations of such a trip and I was delighted to be in his presence. We went to dinner to discuss my role in the courtroom, and it was like being on a date with a stranger who could not take his eyes off me. I was flattered, amazed, and as happy as I could be given the awkwardness of the reason for my trip.

When I arrived in Los Angeles I was met at the airport by a rented limousine with two men in front. Their orders were to drive me to the mansion, where I assumed I would be staying.

The driver and his partner were extremely nice. We had a delightful conversation on the way to Dad's mansion, and they were impressed by the grandeur of the place as we approached the gate. We heard the disembodied voice of whichever security guard was on monitor duty when we pressed the call box to gain admission after I identified myself. But instead of getting inside, the guards approached the limousine with machine guns and told us to leave immediately. They were under orders to shoot us if we did not comply. As the driver nervously put the engine in reverse, waiting for me to tell him what to do, his foot poised over the accelerator pedal, I asked if my Dad was inside. I was told that only Althea was there and that we had to leave immediately. I obviously would not be staying in what I had previously considered to be my home.

Both the drivers were shocked. Eventually arrangements were made for me to stay at the Beverly Hillcrest Hotel, a location just outside of Beverly Hills and within walking distance of many attorneys' offices. I was met by one of Dad's lawyers and was taken to dinner in the rooftop restaurant that overlooked the city. It was there I began to relax, though I did not really understand what was happening.

The lawyer was an overweight, unattractive man who still knew how to touch me in the right ways at the time. He was kind when other men were harsh. He was attentive when other men ignored me or worse. And I was so desperate for someone to love me, someone to care, that I thrilled to have the attentions of this older man who would normally not have appealed to me in any manner whatsoever.

The lawyer reinforced my belief that Dad needed me for the first time in my life. He explained that I would go to court, not saying that I would be driven by a man my Dad told me was an FBI agent in a car with Madalyn Murray O'Hair. He also did not tell me that I might not be called, though in the end the two-day trip was wasted in terms of any meaningful involvement on my part.

The courtroom scene was a shock, yet another instance of reality slapping me in the face.

Althea was a drugged-out mess. She had AIDS. Her face was hollow. Underneath her eyes were gray bags. Her black hair was stringy and unkempt. Her clothing was canary yellow leather with feathers on it. Her thigh high boots were also yellow. As the light hit the material, it made her face look even more sallow and sickly. She was bent over, her head resting on the backrest of the pewlike bench in front of her. And when she tried to talk, she mumbled unintelligibly.

As I recall, when Dad was wheeled into the room, he was wearing a T-shirt and blue pants. It was the first time I had truly related my father to prison life, even though I knew he had been in jail before. I was shocked, saddened, and thought that when he deliberately acted in a manner that put him in jail, he had lost his mind.

Dad was hiding an orange. The judge had not yet arrived, and perhaps the person who gave it to him thought he would be finished before he could be found in contempt of court yet again. I remember Dad holding the orange like a baseball, then shouting, "They say you're known by your fruits. How's this!" And with that he hurled the orange at the district attorney. The DA ducked, the orange splattering against the wall.

Dad then looked at Althea and me. I assumed he recognized us. I assumed he was glad for our support, as sick as Althea was and as emotionally confused about my role in all this as I had been. But if that was the case, he did not show it. He did not show anything. His face remained an impassive blank.

Then I thought about my role in this sick situation. I was supposed to be a character witness, which I presumed meant telling about how stable, intelligent, and good my father was. Yet I had just witnessed him throw an orange at the man charged with prosecuting him, leaving a mess the judge was sure to notice.

I looked over at Althea and wondered why she had tried to get out of bed. Then I rose as the judge entered, sat down when the bailiff instructed us to do so, and proceeded to be horrified by the spectacle of Dad screaming at the judge. He was rude, vulgar, and obscene, the judge giving him six months in jail for contempt.

Dad wasn't finished. "Is that all you've got?" he sneered. "Give me liberty or give me life, you motherf——r."

The judge added six months to Dad's sentence.

Again Dad was belligerent, the sentence finally coming down to fifteen months in jail. And it was all caused by his opening his big mouth to prove some point or other, or so I imagined. None of it made sense to me.

I was driven directly to the airport so I could return to Jacksonville that same day.

Once more I cringed with the familiar pain of helplessness. I had been shown the type of man my father had chosen to become. I went home to frustration and a life that too often involved yearning for the wrong things. What I did not realize was that my Uncle Jimmy would soon be contacting me about taking over Dad's company.

I do not know if my father was crazy, in a manic state because he had chosen not to take his lithium or whatever medication he might have been on, coldly calculating in his actions, or a sociopath with no sense of how others would see the actions he was taking. What I do know is that he got himself so deeply into trouble with his antics that the courts were looking to find him a conservator. Such an individual would take control of his life, including Larry Flynt Publications, having power and wealth limited to only a handful of business executives. My Uncle Jimmy Flynt, Dad's younger brother, had always benefited more from being family than from being an asset to Dad. He was the person who had so upset Mom when she was pregnant and Dad expected her to wait on him. And when he began working for Larry Flynt Publications, he was a yes-man with ambition. He would never make a power play against Dad while Dad was lucid, but when it became clear that Dad's deliberate antics (or insanity, or both, whichever might have been reality at the time) had resulted in Dad's going to jail, he decided he wanted the company.

There were technically two rivals for heading Larry Flynt Publications during this interim period. There was Althea, Dad's wife, who had been so brilliant in the way she understood the business. She should have been the rightful interim CEO because she was someone who had proven her skills to be far superior to Dad's. She was a hard-core junkie by then, but I'm not certain that was even an issue. The concerns were based on conservatorship proceedings after Dad had been sentenced to serve his time in the Butner Federal Correctional Institution in North Carolina, less than a day's drive from Jacksonville.

I was the second logical conservator because I was his eldest daughter and, at eighteen, legally an adult in such matters.

The problem for Dad was that Jimmy was considered third in line, being both his brother and someone active in the day-to-day running of the magazine. If my age and Althea's drug use ever became issues, the court might give conservatorship to Jimmy, something Jimmy strongly desired at the time.

I never discussed Jimmy's motivation for seeking the conservatorship when the issue arose. Jimmy claimed that he wanted to preserve the business Dad had started. At that time many of us believed that Dad might seriously consider giving the entire business to Madalyn Murray O'Hair. Beyond the horror of such a possibility, Jimmy felt that the family, especially himself, should benefit from Dad's labors. I did not want to see the business lost because some stranger was in charge. And I had to admit that Jimmy had a good case for wanting himself in place during Dad's absence.

The trouble was that Dad did not trust Jimmy—and in hindsight, I understand why. Jimmy was not so much concerned with keeping the company successful as he was with making certain he continued to benefit from Dad's money. As I understood it, the conservator was in a position to do anything he or she desired, including selling aspects of the business, changing advertising approaches, working out new distribution deals, and so forth. During the life of the conservatorship arrangement, the conservator would effectively replace Dad on all matters.

I know that Jimmy was anxious to take power, and there was divisiveness among Dad, Jimmy, and Althea. I was seen as someone potentially devoted to Dad and determined to preserve the assets for the family.

I realize this all sounds rather contradictory, but I had not yet looked at my father's world for what it was. I had not done the research necessary to understand the impact of *Hustler* on society. I did not see the hypocrisy that would have existed had I taken control of *Hustler* when I was also trying to be a Christian. There was no way a person of faith could have condoned what that magazine was doing, but I was still naive, still looking at Dad's life with blinders.

∞

"My son, Troy Daniel Dunaway was murdered on August 6, 1981, by the greed and avarice of the publishers of *Hustler* Magazine. *Hustler* Magazine published the article 'Orgasm of Death' in its 1981 edition," explained the boy's mother whose son had been a subscriber to *Hustler*. The boy was a teenager, and though his story made the news media, I did not know about it until later. Yet it was his situation and those of many others that truly defined Dad's business at the time he was ordered imprisoned in Butner.

"My son read the article 'Orgasm of Death,' set up the sexual experiment depicted therein, followed the explicit instructions of the article, and ended up dead. He would still be alive today were he not enticed and incited into this action by *Hustler* Magazine's 'How To Do' August 1981 article; an article which was found at his feet and which directly caused his death."[5]

∽

It was around February of 1984 when Dad asked me to come to Butner. He genuinely wanted to see me, though toward what end I did not know.

Dad seemed to alternate among wanting to be close to me as a person who could have influence on his life through the conservatorship arrangement, wanting to manipulate me, and wanting me as a vehicle for his show. Dad seemed to be trying to have the authorities think he was crazy. One visit he hid under a sheet when wheeled out on a gurney. Another time he embraced Judy when she and I visited, acting as though they were lovers (A photograph taken of the incident shows him holding her and looking as though he is going to French-kiss her). His actions were always meant to shock and/or appear to be those of an irrational man, though this time they went one step further than anyone thought they might. Dad filed for divorce from Althea, an action never completed. Then, while the papers were being processed, he asked Judy to marry him. She was in no way legally related and actually could have married him. Yet the concept was so extremely outrageous that Althea, too drugged out for the judge to allow her to be considered as conservator, sought legal representation to at least protect her interest in the business.

When Dad and I talked, really talked, it was obvious that he was scared of the power play he felt Uncle Jimmy was trying to make. Dad has always had Uncle Jimmy close to him. Even today, when I was in Cincinnati, Ohio, for a press conference at the same time as the opening of Dad's new store, it was Uncle Jimmy who was helping set up the business and coordinating the publicity. It was also Uncle Jimmy who called in to one of the radio shows I was on, alternately mocking me and inviting me over to the store.

During this radio show, in the fall of 1997, Uncle Jimmy denied he knew me. He also told the host not to believe one word that came from my mouth. Then he added that if I had gotten the money I supposedly sought from Dad and him when the movie came out, I wouldn't be harassing them. As he blithered, lied, and contradicted himself, I remembered the times I had visited Uncle Jimmy when I was living with Marsha and Bill Rider. I remembered the conservatorship battle and my time in California at Uncle Jimmy's expense. It was interesting that for a man who claimed to not know me, he was admitting to know so much about me.

And then I realized something else. If my statements were causing Dad and Uncle Jimmy such concern that they had to get on the radio show, that Uncle Jimmy had to lie to stop me, I must be having an impact on their business. The more we fought, the more I felt reinforced in what I was saying, what I was doing, the life I was leading.

When Dad was on the line during that show, he sounded high on drugs, again an interesting situation for a man who no longer was addicted to painkillers. Since the nerve operation at Duke, the only drugs he used that could affect his speech and his mood the way he was acting were "recreational."

Again I felt empowered. I had lived in fear and awe of my father. I had once thought of him with inner trembling.

Now I felt emboldened by the Spirit, and in my courage, in my change, in the righteousness with which I felt I was greeting them, both men fell apart. Dad seemed to have had to reinforce himself with drugs or some other substance. Uncle Jimmy had to challenge truth with lies. And I knew that no matter how long they attacked, they would not win, could not win. I had become the person I never knew I could be.

Dad and Jimmy seemed to work together during that Cincinnati trip, but then, as now, Dad seems to have always treated Jimmy as a beloved dumber brother, the kid you promise your mom you'll watch out for after she's gone because he's not quite bright enough to make it on his own. Many families have their own version of Uncle Jimmy. Few families have the money Dad acquired or get themselves into a situation where the patriarch is in jail and needs a conservator. Dad used one of my weaknesses in trying to bring me over to his side. He promised to have my car shipped to me.

Remember that I never really owned "my car." It was a car registered to the company even though it was selected by and for me. Thus there would always be a control connected with its use. I could never sell it. I could never have it registered in my own name. I would always be at risk of losing it if I incurred Dad's displeasure as occurred before. But these were not concerns just then. I was with Dad, helping him though I wasn't sure to what ends. And he was sending the one possession I treasured above all else.

During this same period I began to hear from Jimmy concerning the conservatorship arrangement. He wanted to be the one running the company and he made a strong case for his takeover. He knew the business, was Dad's brother, had been working with him for several years, and was more stable than Althea. However, I needed to give up my rights to be the conservator if that occurred.

Dad did not want to have a conservator at all, though. He asked me, as a potential conservator, to send a telegram to the judge supporting Althea, the one person who both had the experience to run the company and who was completely dominated by Dad. He stated in his letter to me that if Althea could not have the position, he had instructed the members of the committee to let me be conservator. I don't know if that was true, but I did send the telegram on April 2, 1984. It read: "At this time I don't believe my father, Larry C. Flynt, needs a conservator to his estate. However, if one is to be appointed, I nominate my stepmother Althea Flynt."

By this time I had witnessed Dad's antics and thought he was losing his mind. He had done everything from giving the impression he was trying to have an affair with my sister to deliberately throwing himself off a gurney in order to break his leg. He also tried to give the impression that he was drinking his own urine. Everything was aimed at "proving" he was crazy, even though that could only prolong his stay.

The telegram did not change my legal status, as Jimmy probably well knew. He contacted me, convincing me that he needed me to work in the company. He wanted me to come out, take a job there. Only when I got out there would I learn that he also wanted me to sign some papers which proved to be documents that helped him win the conservatorship. Dad authorized his office to send me my car so I could drive out. Once the Mustang arrived, I felt set to go.

I would be misled about the papers, but I was a naive nineteen-year-old kid who could not be bothered by actually reading them. My foolishness resulted in Jimmy's becoming conservator for what proved to be approximately three months, not long enough for there to be serious trouble anywhere. In fact, of the three of us, he was probably the most capable at the time. This was not praise for Jimmy. It reflected the sad state of Althea, whose drugs were rapidly destroying one of the finest minds in the publishing business.

My trip to California was in almost grand style. I was in my Mustang, accompanied by a drop-dead gorgeous friend, Rebecca, who was determined to become a soap opera star. We had been friends since our mental hospital days together, and now she was about to become more involved with my life than just escaping with me.

Rebecca wanted to act. She wanted to be rich. She wanted to be famous. And together we were going to conquer Hollywood. I would be the queen of the Flynt publishing empire. She would be the star of your favorite afternoon show. Or so we both believed.

I had no money to make the trip, something I told Jimmy. Instead of assuring we could travel easily, Jimmy sent only a hundred dollars. It was barely enough money for gas, and Jimmy knew that when I arrived, I would be totally dependent upon him, a good position for a man who wanted favors from me to give him access to millions.

We had to drive as long as we could without stopping, eat at cheap roadside joints, and mostly sleep in the car. Any roadside motel we might consider would have to be a low-cost dump.

With songs such as "L.A. Woman" and "Hollywood Nights" blasting on the car stereo, Rebecca and I left Jacksonville at five in the morning. We were determined to drive as long and as fast as we could, and as it was, we traveled from Jacksonville to Beverly Hills in just three days. Five days would have been pushing things normally, but with adrenaline flowing through our veins, we had no intention of stopping until we had to.

I put the gas pedal to the floor, ignoring speed limits, racing around other drivers, alert only for police officers who might not agree with my sense of urgency. We were enveloped in the music, the hypnotic attraction of the endless road, and our own fantasies. At last I was going to be someone. I was getting on with my life, leaving Jacksonville far behind. I was needed. I had purpose. I was woman!

We reached San Antonio, Texas, that first day. Long-distance truckers paid solely by the miles they cover rarely drive with as little thought to rest as we did. We stopped off at gas stations, of course, where we tried to use restrooms, though that ultimately became a test of fear.

The first gas station restroom I entered looked as though it was the casting office for the producers who used to make those 1950s horror movies where radiation-mutated insects attack the heroines. I expected flies. I expected the toilet to be less than pristine. I was ready to handle the odor of an uncleaned latrine. But I was not ready for flies that looked to me to be the size of giant beetles. I was not ready for swarms that attacked as though I had entered some secret cult activity and had to die before I could reveal the group's secrets. I was not ready for flies that seemed to form themselves into a shawl that settled over my head and shoulders. And Rebecca was not ready for my piercing scream as I ran terrified from the restroom, still desperate to use the toilet yet now too scared to do anything but endure the pain. Rebecca took one look at the creatures emerging in my wake and agreed that this was not the restroom where we would relieve ourselves. We hurried to the next place where we could pull over, then discovered that the flies had gathered in the first location because it was the cleaner of the two. Finally, unable to contain ourselves any longer, we relieved ourselves in bathroom number 3 of a gas station where we prayed we would not catch some hopelessly fatal disease just from breathing the air.

Exhausted, we found a motel room, where we collapsed without looking around. It was one of those locations where the faucets perpetually leaked muddy brown water whose origins were unknown. The bedspread was worn thin. The towels had long ago given up their nap. And the rug had cigarette burns that predated the Civil War. But we chose not to see any of this. We were safe. There were no flies (they had more self-respect). And we were too tired to do anything but sleep the minimum hours our exhausted bodies had to endure. Then we were back on the road again.

Sometime during the second day on the road, we pulled over at a rest stop. The Mustang was never designed for comfort. It was a high-performance car meant for driving. The seats did not recline. The backseat was relatively short. And in order to sleep in the car, you had to be either very tired or a masochist. We were very tired, were rapidly running out of money, and decided to drop off where we were.

There are two types of highway rest stops. All of them allow you to take a nap during the day because it is safer than having a tired driver on the road. But many do not allow people to spend the night in the parking area because it is unsafe. There are no people around. There is no open coffee shop. What you have is likely to be a dimly lit pullover and maybe a toilet area. It is the ideal location for predators, and the Highway Patrols keep them clear after dark.

I don't know how long we slept. It was dark and we were exhausted when we arrived. It was still dark and we were almost as exhausted when a Highway Patrol officer awakened us by tapping on our car's window. He told us we could not sleep there. He said we would have to drive on. And so we did, arriving at our destination less than three full days after we started.

If you have to go to Los Angeles to conquer the city, as we thought we were doing, the Beverly Hills Ramada Inn is the ideal place to stay. Far newer than such more famous locations as the Beverly Hills Hotel, it actually looks more like Hollywood. Tall, imposing, with a massive entrance and beautifully furnished rooms, the cost per day was as much as many people made in a week. We were given a suite on the twelfth floor, the VIP location, where the singer B.J. Thomas and the musical group Champagne also had a suite.

Suddenly the world really did seem to be ours. We could order room service and charge it to the suite for which Uncle Jimmy was paying. We could eat in the restaurant and never see a check.

For days we deluded ourselves about our importance. Rebecca was determined to parlay her looks into acting jobs.

Image is everything in Hollywood. Who you are. Who you might be. What you own. What connections you have. All these things are coveted more than integrity, intelligence, moral character, and goals unrelated to hedonistic pleasure.

At first we tried to fit into this new, exciting world. I thought I had arrived when I lived in my father's mansion. I quickly discovered that living on the twelfth floor of the Beverly Hills Ramada and being "Miss Flynt" meant far more. Did we want to see the Chippendale's male dance review? There was no problem gaining admission, and, by the way, since we had to walk right by B.J. Thomas's suite on our way to the Ramada elevator, would I like to come in for some champagne?

Me. Tonya. Not the beautiful Rebecca. Larry Flynt's dumpy daughter who Grandma always said wouldn't amount to much of anything. So maybe I was buxom, as the lawyer had said, not the desperate fat kid being weighed on my father's basement scale. Maybe I had a look others found appealing, a style that was both uniquely my own and desirable.

"No thank you, B.J. We have tickets for a show," I told him, though he actually only said his name was Thomas. He sought no formality, only my companionship for the evening.

"Perhaps after the show, Tonya," he said in a way that made me hear the sound of ten thousand hearts breaking as his most adoring fans had to give up their fantasies because, at least for the evening, I was the object of his desire. "Call me."

I didn't, of course. I wasn't that secure. I had just arrived, after all, and I was still in the transitional stage from Jacksonville nobody to the pornographer's daughter.

I went to Chippendale's. I went to the Rainbow Bar & Grill. I went to the places that had a fabled "upstairs," the special star location whispered about by the stylishly dressed, mostly young or carefully dyed, uplifted, liposuctioned, and otherwise enhanced "seasoned" customers. It took a special style to gain admittance to the clubs on their busiest nights, when a bouncer selected just the right blend of revelers from the lines waiting to get in. It required a celebrity connection to go to the private rooms where there was more than loud music, alcohol, and lines of white powder secretly snorted in the public restrooms. And when Rebecca and I would be sent up, all eyes were upon us, those not yet blind and numb from the illicit substances they would be using later in the evening.

Sometimes we danced with "nobodies" like ourselves whose specialness came because they were the daughter, son, spouse, or lover of "someone." At other times we were with the rich, the famous, the people whose good times are chronicled in *People* and whose bad times rate the covers of *National Enquirer*. Both of us met and danced with some of the soap opera stars whose acting roles and bodies Rebecca had coveted. Sometimes we danced with headliners from various clubs.

We became party animals as much as we could, children of the night. And all of this at Jimmy's expense.

I don't remember exactly when things started to change, not just with our daily existence but with my understanding of what was taking place. Certainly a letter I received from my father was part of this.

After writing the telegram he desired, then inadvertently signing the papers that helped assure Uncle Jimmy's brief conservatorship, I got the letter from Dad. It was one of those rambling missives that seemed to tap-dance around any point it might have had. However, one thing was clear. Although Dad had been talking about turning over his publishing empire to Madalyn Murray O'Hair and having her run a $30-million trust for me in the Cayman Islands, he understood my seeming hypocrisy in all this. "What would a good Christian girl like you want with pornography money?" Dad wrote, in part.

It was a statement that brought me up short. The time in school when I am convinced I went to heaven did not change me. The depths of despair in the adolescent psychiatric treatment ward did not change me. The awareness of Madalyn Murray O'Hair's actions being an abomination did not change me. But Dad's letter began to bring me back to Christ.

> What would a good Christian girl like you want with pornography money?

I was never so stunned as when I began to think what all this meant. Not that I was ready to give up the hotel suite, the car, the perks of going to the most famous clubs in Los Angeles. Not yet, anyway. Instead, it was as though my eyes had slowly become scaled over, so I was looking through tiny pinholes that let me see a small fraction of life. Suddenly the scales fell away and I was forced to encounter the full light of day.

I had come to California to help Dad with his publishing empire. Flynt & Daughter would conquer the world. Flynt & Daughter would make millions. We would live well, help others, and have wonderful lives because Dad would be proud of me, would love me at last. And if Larry Flynt didn't love me, the eternal love of God seemed to matter little. Or so I was acting. So, perhaps, Good Lord forgive me, I may have been living.

Nineteen years old, standing in a suite with a view of monuments to money, a phone call away from the fulfillment of every whim, I realized I was on top of nothing. Women had been ridiculed to pay for where I was staying. Women had been debased. Women had been bound, beaten, cut, defecated upon. I was enjoying the good life only because other women my age, younger, and older had been put through hell. Even worse, I realized that God had provided me with Rebecca to show me one more side of Dad's world I did not want to know.

In exchange for money, drugs, the use of a limousine, an affair with a publishing executive, and infamy she never thought would gain national circulation, Rebecca became a porn star.

To be fair, this was an era when, in the land of the flesh obsessed, to be desired as a centerfold was the highest compliment some men could pay a woman. *Playboy* magazine was still sending photographers to different universities in order to do photo shoots of possible centerfolds. This was a continuation of their series on the "girls" of various major schools.

It is easy to get seduced by an industry that makes a young woman feel special the first time she poses. The magazine treats its subjects extremely well, flying them first-class to a resort location in Mexico, supplying whatever food and drink is desired, and helping models relax. Not that Dad was ever linked with drug dealing. In all the time I was out there, I never saw direct involvement. My understanding is that instead of anything official, the model would be befriended by the different people involved with the photo shoot. There was a hairstylist, a makeup artist, and others helping the young woman look her best. The photographer had one or more assistants handling film, lighting, and other needs. It was an experience no different from what a *Vogue* magazine model might enjoy, except instead of being concerned with the garments they had on, they were concerned with the garments they were removing. And from time to time as the shooting was about to begin, someone might just happen to have a pill or a powder to offer. "It will help you relax." "I have some in my purse." "It's no big deal. Some of the models find it helpful."

Was this a helpful assistant trying to assure she would have more work if the session went well? Most of these were freelancers and *Hustler* was just one client. Or was the drug something supplied by the magazine or for which the magazine was paying, the price hidden in an expense sheet? I did not know, nor did I ever hear of a photographer himself making the offer when talking with others. But I know I was routinely offered drugs by a photographer working directly for the magazine, so I have to assume this was a dirty little secret many of the young women enjoyed but did not discuss.

The series of images was always the same. The photographer would have motor-driven cameras, the sound of the shutter click and the whir of the advance mechanism a constant reminder that the model was special.

He would begin in whatever way the model was comfortable. There might be head shots, something with which some of the women were familiar because they needed such portraits in order to seek work as legitimate models and actresses. There might be photos taken either fully clothed or in a bathing suit, lingerie, perhaps something even more sensual.

Eventually, of course, the model would be eased into the reason she was there—stark naked and with her legs spread. The camera would usually take the same view as would be "enjoyed" by a man about to enter her during a time of intimacy. And if you could look at the contact sheet, you would see that often the model had gone from the happy face of the pretty girl next door to a piece of flesh. She would be transformed from a human being to sex object in thirty-six easy images.

That was for the typical model to whom a full photo spread was devoted. Sometimes models posed with clothes on as part of a composite series where some models were dressed, albeit provocatively, and others were either naked or wearing attire obviously meant to facilitate intercourse (e.g., crotchless panties). And sometimes the models agreed to fetish work such as images of sado-masochism. Increasingly there is also computer enhancement of images, some of the more grotesque abuses shown being a combination of photograph and computer technique. However, the nature of the model releases required is such that the model generally knows how she will be shown and agrees to it.

By the end of the first month, it became obvious that Rebecca and I were not going to continue the lifestyle we had begun to enjoy. Uncle Jimmy had his conservatorship. I was increasingly distanced from the business, both because I was not wanted and because Dad's letter was affecting me. We were not worth the money being spent on us. We were told we would have to be responsible for our own bills.

Rebecca was a survivor in a way that troubled me. She would take jobs wherever she could, then frequently have an affair with her boss. She would go home with him, so she didn't need an apartment of her own. She would eat with him, so she didn't need to buy food. She would often have access to his car.

I have no idea what Rebecca thought of these men. She may have genuinely decided she was in love with them, mistaking physical lust for love. She may have felt sex was a small price to pay in exchange for the security they offered. She may have had no respect for herself and not cared how she was used so long as she got hers.

At one point Rebecca had an affair with a married top executive for Dad's company. She spent time at the Plaza Hotel in Century City in the man's suite. They ate together. They shopped together. And according to her, they had sex together.

I asked Rebecca why she was doing it. She was certain, she said, that I wanted to have an affair with the man. As a favor to me, or so she said, Rebecca was going to bed with him so I would know what it was like. The man was related to me. I had done my time in hell through the abuse of male relatives. The last thing I wanted was to have an adult relationship with such a person, either on my own or with the gracious, willing help of my dear friend.

The timing for what happened is a blur. With our instant need for money and Rebecca's connection with *Hustler* management, she informed me that she was going to pose for the magazine. The pay was good, well over a thousand dollars, and they treated her well. They flew her to Mexico, to the resort beaches most people dream about through magazine spreads devoted to the lifestyles of the rich and famous.

I never did learn the full extent of Rebecca's work in the pornography field even though we frequently shared living space. She was embarrassed by what she was doing, yet she loved the money, loved the drugs, and loved such perks as riding in a limousine and drinking expensive champagne.

The story I've heard Rebecca tell is sad, sweet, and noble. We two women were thrown out of our living arrangements without jobs and without savings. We had made friends, some of whom would loan us money to help us, but we were truly helpless. Even my car was owned by someone else, so though we could travel in style, we could not sell the car to meet our needs. Thus, with a crisis facing us, including the impending loss of a roof over our heads, Rebecca started posing for the magazine.

Rebecca did not like admitting how far she had gone, but the nature of pornography work is that you are not wanted in the industry unless you can be marketed as broadly as possible. There would be a time when she and I were living with an old Armenian man in East Los Angeles. I don't know how they met, did not want to know the relationship. His apartment was cheap and filthy beyond the typical bachelor quarters. The aged couch was covered with a filthy white sheet. He flushed the toilet but saw no reason to clean it otherwise. The sink and bathtub were stained, and every time I used the bar of soap, I washed it and washed it to rid it of the surface layer of the man's dirt.

The Armenian enjoyed *Hustler* and bought each new issue. He did not know that Rebecca had posed for the magazine, only that she was a beautiful blond in trouble who might be very grateful for assistance. One day he started laughing as he looked at one of the photo spreads while Rebecca was away from the apartment. He had me look, too, and I was amazed to find pictures of Rebecca cavorting with some man. I knew she was posing, but this was the first time I had ever seen the results of what she was doing. She never described the photo sessions, never explained how she posed. Now I was looking at Rebecca and the man naked on a bed in an explicit photo feature.

Years later, when I was a new bride and my husband, in the Navy, was coming home, a coworker handed me a videotape she thought I should watch. I had already planned a romantic evening with my husband's favorite dinner, champagne, and an outfit I knew he would enjoy. Unfortunately, after everything had been prepared, the food placed on the table, the candles lit, the music playing in the background, I learned that my husband was going to be delayed. Frustrated, bored, and with nothing else to do, I put the video in the VCR. To my shock, it was a porn video in which Rebecca was the star. She entered the screen carrying a golden penis-shaped object, and the best way I can describe the movie is to say that it degenerated from there.

Rebecca also liked the way she could go out alone, say that she was Larry Flynt's daughter, and get everything from free admission to Joan Rivers's show to admission to the private club rooms. She felt that she was treated like a queen and couldn't understand why I increasingly removed myself from such a world.

It was in the midst of all this that we hit our lowest period. We were thrown out of the Ramada, ran out of money, and had to live out of the Mustang. We used gas stations in the Bel Air area for washing up because they were the cleanest we could find. What cash we had went for food until one day, the lowest point we reached, Rebecca and I ran out of all our money. We had a full tank of gas, of course, because in Los Angeles you always feed the car before you feed yourself. But there was nothing else.

I suggested to Rebecca that we should go over to Dad's mansion and beg for food. I thought he might have a change of heart, that he might have the guards let us in. He had been so moody and volatile over the years, I truly believed he might take pity on us when we arrived, hungry and in need. And if he didn't, rejection would not be a new experience.

Dad was back in Los Angeles, having served his jail time, though I believe he had to report to his parole officer until the full sentence was complete. He would be notified of our arrival, hopefully opening his gates and his heart.

We weren't thinking only of being invited inside. This was not the prodigal daughter returning to the loving arms of her father. We knew Dad wanted nothing to do with me, that he was probably furious for my seeming alliance with Uncle Jimmy during the ten to twelve weeks he was under the conservatorship. Still, he had made no effort to make me give back the car. And we really were starving just then.

Rebecca suggested we get tin cups and run them back and forth across the uprights of the fence, like in one of those old prison movies where the inmates run their cups back and forth across the bars of their cell doors, shouting for the warden.

In the end we simply drove to the gate, pressed the buzzer, and waited. Then, when one of the guards asked what we wanted, I said, "This is Tonya, Larry's daughter. We're hungry. We don't have anything to eat. Could you throw out some food? We'll take table scraps. Anything. We're really hungry."

The guard told me to wait a minute while he checked. When he returned to the speaker, his voice was colder. "We've been ordered to shoot to kill if you don't leave immediately," we were told. And I believed him.

Would the men have killed us? I believed it. I've always believed that Dad would turn violent against his family if he became angry enough. As to the guards he hired, I'm sure some were professional. However, there were others who were both loyal without thinking and quite dangerous. Others would do anything Dad ordered, thinking about the possible ramifications later. In fact, I knew of one who committed a rape that was never reported because the victim suspected the guard was ordered to engage in the violent sex act by my father. For reasons too complicated to try to explain here, there was a good chance that the sexual imposition was my father's idea of a "gift" to the victim.

I think I wanted Dad's rejection at this low time in my life. I still thrived on rejection. I could understand people closest to me refusing to meet the necessities of life. In a rather sick way I gained comfort from it the way a small child clings to a raggedy, smelly, foul-looking teddy bear long after everyone else thinks it should go in the trash. That teddy bear shared a life with the child. It was a source of constant familiarity no matter what new places the child visited, no matter what problems might befall the family. Just its presence provided a sense of continuity, of stability, of comfort. And I think I felt the same way about Dad's endless refusals to see me.

Whatever psychological factors may have been involved, at the moment we were threatened with death, we were terrified. I threw the car into reverse and pushed the gas pedal to the floor. We were lucky there was almost no traffic in the area.

The car raced through the streets, emerging at the monument to teenage food lust—McDonald's. I pulled into the parking lot, exhaled, and decided to see if we could get enough coins for anything.

We began scrounging for money, checking the parking lot grounds and then the car. We looked in the glove compartment. We looked on the floor of the front and back seats. We looked under the seats. We felt down in that small space between the rear seat and the trunk. And we examined every inch of the trunk. Finally we had enough pennies and nickels to make 35 cents, the price of one small order of French fries. Delighted by our good fortune, we entered the drive-through line, our sound system blaring, our windows wide open.

The songs were Bob Seger's, the best choice we could have made. We sat, starving, each determined to carefully count the many French fries so we could divide them exactly in half. Rebecca was not going to get a fraction of an inch of potato, grease, and salt more than I got, and she felt the same way.

There was a Corvette in line in front of us. The driver was a young guy, probably our age or a little older. He had his windows down and could hear our music as we inched forward to the order location.

The driver threw open his door, got out, and came up to our window. "I drove here all the way from New York with a broken radio," he told us. "I need some music. My tape player works. I've been listening to your Bob Seger cassette. Do you have any cassettes you would be willing to sell?"

That guy had to have been sent by God. Rebecca and I tried to be cool as I plucked the Seger tape from the cassette player and handed him the box of cassettes I had in the car. He chose carefully, and each time he added one to the pile he was going to pay for, Rebecca and I mentally added to the feast we were about to purchase. It was like Christmas Eve, and we had visions of quarter-pounders dancing in our heads.

Finally we had $10 each. We got quarter-pounders, of course. We got large fries—one each, no sharing. And we got the largest Cokes we could.

Even today I can still taste that meal. When I get to heaven, I will not be surprised if angels drive Corvettes with broken radios and earn their wings by hanging out at McDonald's.

∞

Rebecca developed a cocaine habit while she was working in the pornographic movie business. She claimed at one time that she did not take the coke offered to her when she was posing for my father's magazine, and that may or may not be true. I never asked her where she first began using the drug or when she got hooked. I never tried to find out if this was part of the underworld of the porn industry, the result of her partying at some of the private nightclub rooms, or something she came to enjoy on her own. All I know is that she was making good money, most of the payments in the industry being under the table, and the drug habit became just another part of her lifestyle. Later I understood, though for different reasons. Seeking an escape from my misery, I, too, began using drugs for a while. I tried cocaine for the euphoria, but having little money, I took whatever I could get during my low points. I can only thank God that I had neither the income nor the friends to allow me to go as far as Althea.

Rebecca had a succession of both high-income and low-income boyfriends while I remained for a while longer in the car. Cleaning clothes was difficult. And I was still humiliating myself by washing inside gas station bathrooms. My low point came when I tried to wash my feet.

It was possible to keep your upper body clean washing in a gas station restroom sink. It was possible to maintain enough lower body hygiene not to be obviously foul. But my feet were hot, sweaty, and dirty, and I decided to wash them in the sink.

I plugged the drain, turned on warm water, got some soap, removed my right shoe, and raised my foot over the edge so it was resting in the water. I felt my pants tighten as I lifted my leg, never thinking about the limits of stretch in the fabric. That was when I heard the tear. The seam that ran from my crotch to my butt completely ripped. Even worse, it was my last pair of clean pants.

With nothing more to lose, I scrubbed both my feet, dried them, put the shoes back on, and walked out with as much dignity as possible. I didn't look back.

The jobs I took during this period were an odd mix. The only one that still troubles me came during the first few weeks of my stay. I was with Rebecca over at *Hustler's* photo studio in Culver City, watching the preparations before the private shooting. I was allowed to sit with her as the hairdresser rolled her hair, the makeup artist applied her makeup, the nail technician painted her fingernails, and all with the skill and loving attention of professionals working in a luxury spa. Then came the wardrobe people, who carefully chose the lingerie that she would wear.

There was also a catered lunch available—expensive finger sandwiches, salads, beverages. It was like a movie set in the section reserved for the stars. No expense was spared in an effort to assure that the model would feel the most important woman in the world, at least for the time it took to be photographed.

It was all so glamorous, so exciting, so pampering. And then Rebecca slipped behind a giant curtainlike backdrop. I was excluded from the set in an effort to assure her privacy while she worked. I could not see what was taking place other than the silhouettes of the camera, the lights, the equipment that reminded me of my fantasy of a Hollywood stage set or a fashion shoot for an international magazine.

As I watched Rebecca slip around the curtain, I wondered how she was feeling. I tried to imagine myself in her situation, to imagine if it was me who had moved in front of the camera.

I did not think of this as pornography. I thought of this as glamour. I walked over to the large mirror brought by the makeup artist. It was surrounded by lightbulbs in order to light every pore of the subject's face. I idly picked up one of the brushes, stroking my hair, watching the brush, pretending an expert was doing the work. I tried the makeup, shifting my face from side to side to see the changes.

Unexpectedly one of the photographers working with Rebecca came over to where I was standing. I remember that I was wearing a short-sleeved, pink knitted top and a pair of black slacks. He approached me silently, as though he had been studying me. "Tonya, I've been observing you. *Chic* magazine [*Hustler*'s sister publication] is doing a photo shoot called 'Silken Seduction: A History of Lingerie' for the October 1985 issue, and we don't have time to find someone to pose for the shoot in a lacy corset." It was to be a lingerie shot, and no face being shown. What mattered was that the woman had large breasts. "We won't be able to find someone with such large breasts that are so perfect in the time we have left. Would you consider posing for the magazine?"

I was shocked. I was over there, thinking I was "somebody" being Larry Flynt's daughter, watching at the photo shoot. And now I was being complimented in a way I had never been before.

I told him I didn't know what to say.

Then the photographer said that he would need Dad's approval, but if he agreed, I would be paid well like all their models. This was before Dad's return to Los Angeles from jail, and since Uncle Jimmy had the conservatorship, he was the one who would have to approve.

Before I could agree, Uncle Jimmy told me that he could not give approval until he talked with Dad. As I should have realized, Dad gave his approval. I was finally an intimate part of his world, at least to the extent of a few photographs. And more quickly than I expected, I was being fitted for the wardrobe.

It was *my* fingernails that were being painted. It was *my* body on which a corset was being tried. Yet the glamour was not as great as I had imagined. The large wardrobe room reminded me of Dad's first club, the one where Judy and I had gone into the dressing area to play with the strippers' clothing. The glamour was being subverted by memories I did not want to relive—not then, not ever.

At the same time, I was being told I was beautiful, desirable. Rebecca and I were as giddy as Judy and I had been. We were little kids playing dress up. We were little kids fantasizing we were glamorous. And we both were beautiful in the eyes of the photographer. Or so I thought. So I desperately believed in what was still my quest for love and approval.

Finally I was fitted with a corset. Someone placed a large costume jewelry ring with a design that seemed from the Victorian era on my right ring finger, and a strand of pearls around my neck. Then I was asked to sit on a chair in front of a simple photographer's drop in a portion of the room where everyone could see. Apparently you had to be naked to warrant a hint of privacy before your photos were shown to the world.

I was scared as I sat there, suddenly worried that my face would be recorded, then used for blackmail in the years to come. I was afraid that the small bulge in my belly would be revealed. I was afraid I would look fat over the pants and be embarrassed by being out of shape. What I did not think about was that men would be viewing this in an erotic context, in surroundings that could be obscene. At the same time I had a sense that what I was doing was wrong.

All I could do was concentrate on the money, how desperately I needed it, how much easier life would be for the short term when I was paid the $800. It was more than a month's pay for a real job. I also realized I would never do it again.

What I did not think about was an issue that haunts me today. What I did not think about, what I suspect many women truly in the business do not consider, is that participation in such a photo shoot and the appearance in such a magazine implies approval of pornography that is used against other women.

Some men decide that whatever they see in *Hustler* and similar publications is what women like and want. They might reason this way: "Look at that woman having sex with two men. She's having the time of her life. They wouldn't put pictures like that in a magazine sold on the newsstands if that wasn't normal." Or they might reason this way: "I showed you the pictures. I had you read the article. A normal, healthy woman likes to be forced to have sex. Every time you tell me no, I know you really want me to make you do it."

Law enforcement officers are especially finding problems with Internet users. Men and women with violent fantasies are reinforced by like-minded individuals hundreds or thousands of miles away. There is no censorship. There is no way to know what is being triggered in the mind of the user. But it is happening and has been occurring with magazines as well.

In 1990, in Norman, Oklahoma, a boy walking in a wooded park was attacked. His eyes were gouged and his genitals mutilated. The attack, by a man who claimed he was looking for a lost dog when he approached the child on October 22, was identical to the material detailed in the *Hustler* article "Killer Prose: Mayhem Manual." Even the most extreme material has obviously been a blueprint for sick minds.

Each time women pose for a picture in a magazine whose images are demeaning, violent, and objectifying of women, they are enabling a man they may never meet to abuse a woman they may never hear about. Yes, there are women who are kidnapped or otherwise coerced into performing for sexually explicit material. But there are also women who make a choice seemingly willingly. Sometimes they are willing to do anything asked to "star," as Rebecca seems to have done at least once. And other times they set mental standards, never crossing a certain line, as I did, yet still being guilty of contributing to that which ultimately harms all women and relationships.

∞

The following definition of pornography is excerpted from the model antipornography law proposed by legal scholars Catharine MacKinnon and Andrea Dworkin:

> Pornography is the graphic sexually explicit subordination of women through pictures and/or words that also include one or more of the following:
>
> [i] women are presented dehumanized as sexual objects, things, or commodities, or
>
> [ii] women are presented as sexual objects who enjoy pain or humiliation, or
>
> [iii] women are presented as sexual objects who experience sexual pleasure in being raped; or
>
> [iv] women are presented as sexual objects tied up or cut up or mutilated or bruised or physically hurt, or

[v] women are presented in postures or positions of sexual submission, servility, or display, or

[vi] women's body parts—including but not limited to vaginas, breasts, or buttocks—are exhibited in such a way that women are reduced to those parts; or

[vii] women are presented being penetrated by objects or animals; or

[viii] women are presented in scenarios of degradation, injury, torture, shown as filthy or inferior, bleeding, bruised, or hurt in a context that makes these conditions sexual.

The idea that people claim to not understand the nature of pornography, how demeaning it is to women, children, and, in some circumstances, to men, is outrageous. The Andrea Dworkin/ Catharine MacKinnon definition is clear beyond argument, the reason it is often quoted. But common sense also must prevail. When a woman is portrayed as being an eager, willing participant in anything a man wants to do, regardless of how painful, demeaning, perverted, or violent, gaining sexual pleasure as a result, no one thinking objectively can say this is positive or innocent. Yet that has been the attitude by those who are trying to justify the unjustifiable.

∽

As for my life in California, a one-car accident was about to change everything for me. Not only would I stop coveting my Mustang, I would also be forced to leave an area where the toleration of the intolerable was destroying so many people around me.

With all the rejection, the influence of California cool, and my total dependence on the Mustang for transportation, entertainment, and shelter, I began to worship the car. It meant more to me than anything else in my life. It was stable, always present, and never failed me, concepts I should have been applying to Jesus. And because of that, I feel I was brought up short one night on that part of Wilshire Boulevard that becomes a modestly high-speed eight-lane road.

At the time, I was rooming in a house owned by an old woman. There were two tiny bedrooms, a small kitchen, and a living room. The woman also provided modest meals, and all for $600 a month.

The amount may seem reasonable today, but at the time it seemed expensive. I could barely pay the rent, and there were months when I wasn't sure I could keep the place. Even worse, the woman was less compassionate than my father on his worst days. This was clear to me after my accident.

To this day I do not know exactly what happened. I was not speeding. I was exhausted, and there is a chance that I nodded momentarily, turning the steering wheel and striking a ramped surface that threw the car completely off balance when I overcorrected. Suddenly I found myself upside down, spinning out of control and traveling 175 feet as the roof of the car scraped against the surface of the street.

The car stopped and I somehow got out, propelled as though still in motion inside the vehicle. I raced across all eight lanes, never looking for cars, never seeing anything, almost blind to my circumstances. Then I sat down by a telephone pole, in shock, crying, my cream-colored blouse torn.

I remember someone coming over to try and help. I remember asking someone to call my mother. Or my father. Someone. Eventually I was taken to the hospital, and both parents learned I had a fractured tailbone and other injuries, all minor, but all painful. Mom was in tears, terrified I was more badly hurt than I was, fearful of my future.

Dad was . . . well, Dad. I was told by the police that he said they should have left me by the side of the road to die.

The police officer who investigated noted that I was not intox-icated, though other than that, no one had any more information about the accident than I did. All that was certain was that the car was totaled, and when I went to the wreckage at the impound lot after I was released from the hospital, a bottle of Ralph Lauren perfume I had in the glove compartment was gone. Since that had been my Christmas gift when I made my first trip to see Dad, I sup-pose that was also some sort of message. Maybe someone at the lot got a big kiss from his girlfriend for the nice gift he brought her.

Dad was just as nasty when he talked with me by telephone about the car. He knew what it meant to me and got a certain amount of pleasure in seeing me lose it. "That's what happens, Tonya, when something's ill-got," he said. I wasn't certain what he meant. He had been promising me a car since I was a little girl, originally saying he would get me one for my sixteenth birthday. Perhaps he meant that I had not earned the money myself, that I had somehow blackmailed him over the conservatorship issue when he agreed to ship it to me in Jacksonville. But the truth was that the car was supposed to be a graduation present. I had been shocked when it wasn't registered in my name. I was shocked again by his attitude implying I had black-mailed him into doing what he had promised all along.

I was livid. The accident was my fault. I was behind the wheel, and even if I have no idea how it happened, the driver has to accept responsibility. But I knew there was no divine pun-ishment, no bad Karma paying me back for my actions.

In anger I said to him, "I guess your legs were ill-got, too." He asked me, "What do you mean by that?" And I said, "You can't use them to get you around either."

It was a nasty comment and I knew it.

As for my landlady, she was horrified when I returned to the house in a cab. I explained what happened, explained that I had totaled my car and would have to bus from her place in Westwood to my job. Her reaction? Anger over whether or not I was trying to cheat her by keeping the place when I might have trouble getting to my job since I was hurt. Yet that was not the worst "independent" living arrangement I would endure.

The last two jobs I held in Los Angeles were dead-end ones where I was never happy. One was with a nice place, but it wasn't right for me. The other was working for a nightclub.

The year was 1985 and my California stay was coming to an end. I had a job with a lounge in Westwood, an area frequented by rising stars. I would see people such as Eddie Murphy laughing and chasing after his girlfriend of the moment. The crowd was young, hip, and straight, as was the lounge, which featured music, drinks, food, and a dress code that did not allow the excesses of other such places.

My job was outside the building, on the street. Since you had to go downstairs to get in the lounge, the owner wanted a young woman to stand outside and bring people in.

> Hey come on in. Come see. We've got two for one drinks. Just
> down the stairs. Come on down and see.
>   You ever been down at the club? We've got a live band.
> Come on down. See the lounge. You ever been down here?

I wore nice dresses or slacks and a good blouse. There was nothing seductive. This was not an area like Sunset Boulevard, where mainstream entertainment places mixed with prostitutes and sadomasochistic sex clubs. And the job paid me $150 a week, just enough to get by with an occasional loan from a friend.

Ultimately my limited pay and the conflicts with the landlord led me to an apartment at Hollywood and Vine. This was the "real" Hollywood, a location that combined a chain restaurant where pimps met with their prostitutes whenever the women took breaks from the street, tourist spots, easy access to the Sunset Gower and Paramount Studios, and stores that served the locals. It was not a big money area, and some of the apartments were terrible. I was in one of the latter.

The apartment building itself had a dark, sinister feel to it. Not that it was dangerous, though drug dealers worked from the place. In fact, I had a team of dealers appropriate my apartment to sell their wares without my permission or advance knowledge. They never explained exactly how they got in and I learned not to ask. Worse, I was so beaten down, drugged up, exhausted, scared, and filled with depression that I might as well have been catatonic. I functioned enough to survive, and since they did not try to use me in any way, I neither called the police, fled, nor even expressed outrage.

The problem was that the building had seen too many tears, too many cries of anguish. It was as though the tears of a thousand poverty-stricken, drug-addicted tenants, all feeling defeated by life, had formed the mortar that filled in the bricks. It was as though the poorly lit walls were black from dirt mingled with the blood of overdosing junkies whose last breath of life was taken with a needle in the arm. It was a place where marriages ended, where the depressed would come to feel hopeless. You could clean your suite, and I did, yet the reflection in a spotless mirror was never your own. It was that of a lost soul, desperate to escape yet knowing it was trapped forever.

Rebecca stopped by to see me. She had money again, and each time she was flush, she turned her capital into white powder or crack cocaine which she snorted up her nose or smoked.

Cocaine is supposed to give a rush, and the first use apparently does that. There is a feeling of euphoria greater than anything most people have experienced. Many consider it equivalent to a monumental orgasm, though these are usually people who have never known sex in a committed relationship. Others consider it the equivalent of a spiritual experience, but these are people who have not truly met the Lord in their hearts. Whatever the case, the feeling fades quickly and the addict spends the rest of his or her days chasing elusive feelings.

What is not mentioned is the number of those days. The first jolt of cocaine can kill you—as it did basketball player Len Bias in 1986. For others, death can come after years of use. And a "lucky" few use it into old age.

Not Rebecca. She arrived at my place wired, flying high, sure she was in control, when suddenly she gritted her teeth. She fell to the floor, convulsing in a manner that reminded me of an epileptic fit. Her arms and legs twisted in awkward positions that would have been quite painful had she been conscious of pain. I tried to give her mouth-to-mouth resuscitation, but her jaw was locked.

Desperate, I called 9-1-1 and she was rushed to the hospital. Her life was saved, but the medical report made it clear that Rebecca never dared take a drug again. If she did, she might not survive.

I had almost lost a friend. I had lost the fantasy of my father and had to confront the reality of his empire of pornography. I had lost my car, briefly lost my values, been hungry, homeless, on drugs, and miserable. The only constant had been God, and for months I had refused to admit his presence.

Finally, in that apartment building from hell, I hit bottom. It was time to go home, not just to Jacksonville but to God's love, the one love I had so frequently rejected in the past because I wanted someone human to meet the needs of my soul.

What I did not realize, could not anticipate, was his grace. I would soon find myself in a marriage unlike any experienced in my family, with a daughter I would adore beyond life itself, and a challenge that would bring me into the forefront of the fight against everything my father stood for.

10

Finding Faith, Finding Home

I don't think I had ever heard of the idea of the unlikely vessel of God when I was living in Los Angeles for the final time. And while I had heard of the grace of God, I had little idea what it meant. Yet both realities were to change my life in ways I could not then begin to imagine.

The first concept, that of the unlikely vessel of God, has existed at least since Old Testament times. Many of the prophets fit this category, as did people who became reluctant leaders. Most were humble men, often beaten down by life, their education limited or nonexistent, their jobs so menial as to make them invisible to those around them.

One of the greatest early leaders, Moses, was different in that he was first raised by royalty in Egypt, but by the time God chose him, he had a speech impediment and was living as a sheepherder in self-imposed exile. He also had a quick temper that would get him into trouble for much of his adult life. He was an unlikely vessel for God's use in bringing the Hebrew people out of bondage, through the wilderness, and to the edge of the Promised Land.

David, often considered one of God's most beloved leaders of the early Hebrew people and possible writer of the Psalms, showed God's presence while still a sheepherder. He faced the giant Goliath, a member of the race of Philistines. And though he was small, had never been trained as a fighter, and had no armor, he was able to use the simplest of weapons, a slingshot, to kill the man devastating his people's army. Later he would be an adulterer who arranged for the death of his girlfriend's husband. Yet he remained faithful to God, repeatedly trying to better himself, even as he failed over and over in his lifetime. Few Jews or Christians approve of many of David's actions, but in his willingness to face his sins, to repent, pick himself up, accept responsibility for his own actions, then try to do better while never ceasing to love God, we also witness God's loving grace working in all our lives. God remains constant no matter what we do or fail to do so long as we are trying to strive to follow his way, never letting even a journey into the depths of human hell prevent us from returning to the Lord, whose hand is always reaching out to restore us on the path we should be following.

Too often I find that so-called religious leaders wear blinders when it comes to seeing those touched by and/or used by God. Some practice what is called prosperity theology. They feel that God rewards the good, ignores or punishes those who are not doing his work. The closer someone is to God, this thinking goes, the wealthier, more influential, and/or powerful he or she will be. Thus the CEO of a *Fortune* 500 company is inherently closer to God than a janitor in the same firm. They ignore the fact that the CEO may be an adulterer, amoral in his or her business practices, and unthinking of others unless they can do something he or she values. At the same time, the lowest-paid employee may tutor inner-city children, be active in community housing efforts, and work with those who are hurting, sick, or in trouble. But to Christian leaders practicing prosperity theology, wealth and power equal greatness, a situation that means that if Jesus were preaching and teaching today, he would not be worth such religious leaders' time.

After all, his humble life would relegate him to an inferior position in God's eyes, or so they believe.

Other religious leaders feel that the Word means more than the deed. A marriage in jeopardy, a fire destroying a home, a short-term financial crisis temporarily creating a homeless situation, or some similar need causes some individuals to go to their church, where social outreach is supposedly practiced. These are not strangers about whom nothing is known. These are members of the congregation or regular attendees working to get through a difficult period of life and well known to the parishioners.

I have found that church members may open their hearts on an individual basis. Someone with extra room may provide a day or two of shelter, just long enough to resolve a problem. Yet if the person in trouble goes to the pastor, the help becomes quite different. Instead of a loving hand and real assistance, the person may be met with a line such as, "Do you know Jesus Christ as your Lord and Savior?" The concern is having the person express faith, not helping the person to see Jesus in the loving assistance truly needed. It is like the street-corner evangelist who counts the number of people standing about, listening to the message, as "saved souls." Yet when someone needs real assistance, even if that is only counseling to resolve a moral dilemma, such needs are sometimes ignored.

People who claim to do "good works" but who shy away from real involvement cause all religious leaders to look bad. And tragically, when it comes to pornography and the crusade against it, too many pastors want to pretend it does not exist. The handful who feel they are taking the "high moral road" usually limit themselves to a statement from the pulpit or an hour spent looking somber on a picket line. Truly helping someone overcome such addiction, or taking a moral stance demanding that the police enforce existing laws, a stance that might subject the clergy member to ridicule, is just not done by the vast majority of men and women who should be in the forefront of the fight.

Equally tragic are the number of pastors addicted to pornography, the one vice they feel they cannot mention to anyone, even other clergy they may routinely use for their own spiritual counseling. Today it is all right for a pastor to admit to alcoholism, to seek treatment, to become a part of a local Alcoholics Anonymous group. It is all right to admit addiction to prescription and/or recreational drugs. Again help is available and congregations are likely to applaud the integrity of the clergyperson. But to talk about pornography abuse is to assure the end of a career, isolation from the spiritual community, and total disgrace.

In addition, there are many pastors who refuse to speak about this problem despite the fact that though they do not have it, they know it exists among some of their congregants. They feel that to make parishioners feel uncomfortable about themselves is to risk losing money. Such pastors know which type of sermons will result in the greatest contributions to the collection basket and which will cause them to be short of money. They would rather preach feel-good sermons than gut-level issues that might reduce or end a donation while saving a soul.

But as Paul wrote in Galatians, "My friends, if anyone is detected in a transgression, you who have received the Spirit should restore such a one in a spirit of gentleness. Take care that you yourselves are not tempted. Bear one another's burdens, and in this way you will fulfill the law of Christ" (6:1–2).

Such men and women are the unlikely vessels because their lot normally keeps them separated from the people who must hear God's word—people of power, wealth, prestige, and publicly acknowledged accomplishment. And we tend to listen all the more, to remember what they say, simply because they run counter to our belief that only

those with high social and/or business stature have anything meaningful to offer.

Judy Flynt, my half sister, was one of God's unlikely vessels for
changing my life. She was living and working in California at the
time, dealing with her own concerns about Dad in her own way.
She had been a "secret shopper" for the Radio Shack stores, then
went into armed security work. She had been in and out of trouble, in and out of substance abuse, but she was trying to succeed in
her new field. She was also trying to gain Dad's approval and love
whenever she thought it might be possible, much as I had done.
Still, the two of us could not relate. There was nothing but tension
and animosity between us.

I had hit bottom in my quest for survival after it was obvious
that I would not have my father's love, approval, or respect. I was
living in a nightmare world where drugs, violence, and corruption
made large profits for crooked cops, slum lords, pimps, and hustlers.
I was unable to think about tomorrow because surviving today
required all my effort. And I certainly had no thought of Judy
doing anything other than either criticizing my life or delighting
in my plight. Possibly she didn't either, until touched by God as a
way of reaching me.

I no longer remember the date. I only remember the knock at
my apartment door and the sudden presence of Judy. She had a
one-way plane ticket back to Jacksonville, a flight paid for by her.
She called Mom and asked her to meet me at the airport in Jacksonville. And when she arrived, she stuffed everything of mine
that would fit into the suitcases I owned. The rest was left behind.
(Since Judy was Judy, I suspect that whatever she liked may have
ended up in her own apartment. After all, if she had changed totally, she would not have been my unlikely vessel.)

My first experience with the grace of God had passed without
my being fully aware of it. When I survived the accident with my

Mustang, the police report at first seemed straightforward. The car flipped over, slid 175 feet on the roof, came to a stop, and I fled across the highway. I have always had a fear of dying in a fire, and I was certain from seeing crash scenes in movies that a flipped car would burst into flame. I shouted "God help me!" as the roof crunched against the pavement and began sliding, though I did not think of the implication of that simple prayer. I just later assumed that I had been fortunate to be in a well-made car that protected me until the out-of-control vehicle came to a stop.

Not so, the paramedics said. They had seen similar accidents over the years, including in the same model Mustang I was driving. Based on where they found the car and its appearance, I was the first person they knew to not have his or her upper body turned to hamburger. There should have been no way I could have survived alive. The roof of the car was crushed down to the dashboard. The driver and passenger side doors were impossible to open, and the support bar of the side frame was jammed up over the roof instead of holding it in place. And while the steering wheel was not touching the front seat, it had been jammed forward enough that it should have kept my body from being able to move. Yet somehow I had gotten out.

As I had learned during my dream of heaven, I had something more to do. It was not my time, and the passing of a few years did not change that reality. I survived by the grace of God.

∞

God's grace came in yet another way, and his name was Lawrence Vega. He was the best-looking man I had ever seen in my life. He also wanted me, something I had not been aware of experiencing with another human being my entire life.

Lawrence shared more than the same first name as my father. He was also in the Navy when I met him, but unlike Dad, my future husband had made it his career and found success in the field of aviation hydraulics. He wasn't a hero with a chest full of medals for secret operations behind the enemy lines. But he served his country honorably wherever he was sent, and that included time in both Vietnam and the Gulf War. He certainly did not seek violence. But he liked the work, even when it became dangerous—and on flight deck duty, even in peacetime, his was a physically risky job. One mistake by a pilot and a flight deck crew member can be maimed or killed. There is no place to take cover, no time to react. Despite the risk, he enjoyed his work.

∽

But I was depressed in Jacksonville. My fantasy life was shattered. I was not able to start college. And though I was working, I was staying at home with my mother, in a relationship that was still strained.

I had lived with a close friend after my second visit to California, but when I met Lawrence I was again living with my mother. There was still the tension between us, the overwhelming sense of loneliness, of helplessness, and of failure. I was alive but I wasn't living. I was working, though it was for survival, not for a future I had planned. I knew neither love nor the certainty that I was capable of being loved.

Many nights I cried myself to sleep. I wasn't suicidal, yet I wished that God would cut short my days on this earth. I remembered the dream I had at fifteen, remembered the sense of overwhelming peace, and I longed for that peace to be the whole of my existence.

My friend Karen and I began going out on weekends, frequently to the various naval base recreation clubs such as Cecil Field, the Naval Air Station. Jacksonville is a Navy town with three separate bases. In order to reduce the chance of problems, the bases had their own recreation clubs and Karen had a base sticker from her second husband's Navy days. They had music, dancing, drinks, and all the other activities you would expect from a club catering to people in their early twenties. They also had few problems because the Military Police made certain nothing improper ever went on. Single young women loved to take advantage of the base clubs when they could go there because they were great places to meet guys without worrying about the problems that occur in city bars.

Karen and I were in an off-base club that night, a place called the Gazebo, in September 1986, when I met Lawrence. I had been nervous that night, wanting to make a good impression on someone, yet certain I would not be attractive to anyone in whom I might be interested. Still, hope springs eternal in a woman's makeup chest, and I spent two hours getting ready to go out.

We danced and talked to various men, including Larry. Although nothing happened that night for the two of us—no flashing lights, no fireworks illuminating the sky, no romantic theme music—at the end of the evening I told Karen that I had met the man I was going to marry.

There were a few problems, of course. One was that Larry had to go on a weeklong operations cruise, a ritual shakedown and retraining that everyone knew about. Or so he claimed. Actually he had an old girlfriend scheduled to come for a visit, though to my great relief, she did not. More important, he never had an interest in asking her back again.

The second problem was more of a snag. Lawrence was married.

The marriage was over. The two of them were long separated and just waiting for the divorce to be finalized. But I had seen too much of divorce, been victimized by it as a child, and had also heard that some ministers consider the act a sin.

Still, I was twenty-one and certain I was in love, certain I had found the man for me. I went home and told my grandmother I had met the man I was going to marry. I don't know if she believed me, but she certainly knew I believed what I was saying.

A couple of weeks later he invited me to spend a weekend with him. I was determined to make a good impression. I pulled out one dress after another, one blouse after another, one pair of slacks after another, viewing each one with a critical eye. Would Lawrence like the color? Would he like the style? Would he like the way I looked in it? Would he like the combination?

I looked at my shoes. I needed the right ones for every activity we might try, and the right ones for each of the outfits I considered wearing.

In the end I made the choice that seemed appropriate to my level of desire, anxiety, and insecurity. I carefully packed six large suitcases to handle what I would need for two short days. Then I had to watch the less-than-enthusiastic look on Lawrence's face as he first encountered my load and then had to carry it all up the several flights of steps to my weekend quarters.

Lawrence Vega and I were married on March 29, 1987, and if you ask what our courtship was like, I doubt that I could tell you. I finally understood Mom's reaction when I asked her about the town where Dad was raised which she visited when they were first in love. She was so fixated on her future husband that she had seen almost nothing.

Marilyn was born during our first year of marriage. Rather than complicating a still-emerging relationship, her birth enhanced it. Giving birth is a process that brings us as close to the Creator as we can get. We experience a life created in our own image, yet each child is unique. God gives us the chance to delight in new life, to love unconditionally, to have a physical reminder of the divine in us all.

At the same time, I was humbled by Marilyn's presence in the world. In the Old Testament it is written that a man and woman, by themselves, cannot make a baby. In order for a fetus to come to term and a newborn to grow, there must be a relationship between the man, the woman, and God.

In the New Testament, Jesus talks of adults becoming like children in order to enter the kingdom of heaven. We must accept the miraculous, greeting life with awe and wonder. And of course we must love God above all else.

Marilyn brought me to such realizations. She also taught me that there is nothing more precious than children, that they can be nurtured into strong, caring, loving, morally upright adults, or they can be broken in ways that perhaps can never be fixed. I had to heal for Marilyn. I also had to be certain she was protected from the predators who want to shatter childhood, seducing the innocent and forcing them to have experiences that should be impossible for them to imagine.

Not that life was suddenly perfect. Marilyn was a big baby, 9 pounds, 11 ounces, and had to be delivered by cesarean section. I did not dilate correctly, having had an epidural too early. The pain was intense.

Marilyn was born with long hair and long fingernails. She was the most beautiful baby I had ever seen, yet I was reluctant to take that first look. My heart was pounding and I was ashamed to tell the nurse to keep her away from me. Yet even though I saw her, recognized her beauty, I refused to bond with her. That took several months. I deliberately, though subconsciously, held back my emotions. I was afraid I would abuse her like I was abused, since I knew that child abuse is often multigenerational.

I was also aware that Marilyn was the first responsibility in my life I could not shrug off. This was not a job to which I could call in sick when I wanted to do something else. This was not a school class I could cut. This was not a man I could walk away from. This was a helpless gift of God who needed me for survival twenty-four hours a day, seven days a week. It was a reality that terrified me.

There were other problems, other concerns. Girls who have had their self-esteem trampled by adults, who have been sexually molested and emotionally abused, almost invariably marry one of two types of men. Either the man is verbally and/or physically brutal, or he is so passive there is no possible threat. Lawrence was not passive.

I hesitate to talk of violence in my marriage because it seems to give the impression of myself as a punching bag for an angry, disturbed man. Nothing could be further from the truth.

Lawrence and I found that we both had to learn how to disagree in a committed relationship. There is fighting that is abusive violence by one or both parties. There is fighting that is genuine communication, true give-and-take no matter how emotionally heated, with each party listening to the other. It was the latter we had to learn. We had to work on real dialogue, recognizing that even in anger there was love that needed clarification and nurturing.

Certainly this can be true for couples from healthy environments. But it is more difficult and at least as critical when one or both of the marriage partners has been physically and/or emotionally abused. Fortunately for us, we were both willing to recognize this, both willing to find answers when our first reactions may have been to lash out or separate forever, neither of which would have been right.

Not that we understood this from the beginning. There were even two times when I felt the need to get a restraining order against my husband. Fortunately the second instance was like a healthy slap in the face, a time to stop and reflect which enabled us to both be open to God. We each sought counseling for our individual and mutual problems. Lawrence stopped drinking and learned to appropriately deal with anger. I began to see that I was neither worthless nor in need of some magic armor to keep another person from truly touching my heart. I found that to be vulnerable in love was to be strong, and in that strength, a new, healthy, loving relationship could follow as it has for us today. I have no illusions about the future. I just recognize that, like David, to love God and keep trying is to assure that each day we are trying to do our best for him, for ourselves, and for our daughter.

After I began my healing journey with Lawrence, the more I learned about adult victims of child abuse and molestation, the more I understood why the man to whom I was attracted would have a dark side. I also came to understand that while Lawrence previously acted inappropriately toward me during periods of extreme stress, he did not want to do so. He had to seek a more effective way to deal with life, just as I had to learn to look more objectively at people like my father. Lawrence acted out anger when he should have talked through his, at times, rightful extreme emotions. I internalized anger, creating depression and self-hate when I should have been more appropriately forceful and verbal.

If I had just had a marriage like the one Lawrence and I are experiencing, I would have said that God has given me a new chance at life. I would have understood his grace in forgiving me for the negative actions I took over the years when I was so desperate to achieve my biological father's approval and love. But there was to be more, the reason I decided to write this book, the reason I have become intensely involved with discussing the larger concerns of pornography's influence on society. I went to a movie.

⚭

What we have a right to do and what's right to do are worlds apart.
Just because someone has a right to do something does not mean

that it is right. With every freedom there is a responsibility. All choices have consequences. Exercise a right at the wrong time and/or in the wrong way and the consequences can be tragic. Unfortunately too few people look at the ultimate results possible from the choices they make. We rarely think about the fact that the choices we make have consequences for other people. Worse, there are those who do recognize this and do not care.

—*Tonya Flynt-Vega*
from a fall 1997 college lecture

∽

We are the experts in Hollywood on what you can and can't get away with. Lawyers love us, because we know the rules. And as long as you don't have Jerry Falwell saying something inappropriate, it's cool.

—*Scott Alexander, cowriter of the movie*
The People vs. Larry Flynt, *as quoted by Matt Labash,*
"The Truth vs. Larry Flynt,"
February 17, 1997 The Weekly Standard

∽

I suppose *The People vs. Larry Flynt* was the hip movie of 1996. So many Hollywood stars were there for so slight a picture, the cast seemed to me to be a pickup crew of the talented, the desperate, and the greedy. There were also cameo performances by real-life people pretending to be actors pretending to be real-life people, and all of them sure to gain a nudge in the ribs, a wink, and a nod from knowing viewers sharing their recognition with others in the audience.

For example, there was Courtney Love, hired to play Althea, a part she could well understand. Not only was she a rock singer who, for years, had not known what life was like except when high, her husband, Kurt Cobain, lead singer of the grunge band Nirvana, had committed suicide with a rifle. She was also from Seattle, a city discovered by the Hollywood rich who wanted to raise their children in a clean environment away from L.A.—and then brought with them their own form of pollution through moral corruption and degradation.

There was Donna Hanover, the actress wife of former U.S. attorney and current New York City Mayor Rudolph Giuliani, a man who made his Manhattan reputation on cleaning up the Times Square/42nd Street area. He said that the Times Square adult book stores, including those selling Dad's magazines, were a menace to the community. He said that the live sex shows were wrong. He said that the pornographic movie houses were wrong. What he did not say was that it was wrong for his wife to be in a movie glamorizing a leading member of the industry he was elected, in part, to fight. He did not say that the movie, as originally filmed, risked an X-rating and had to be cut drastically to avoid distribution problems. Or perhaps he justified her actions by thinking of the movie as only another role, even though they both should have known full well that film "truth" is the only reality for many teens. Such is the power, the strength, the value, and the tragedy of how some young people relate to a screen more readily than to real life.

Woody Harrelson played my Dad, and if stories reported off the set were true, perhaps his casting made sense. Not only is he the son of a convicted felon suspected of being one of the three Dallas, Texas, "tramps" possibly connected with the John Kennedy assassination, he also seems to have Dad's interest in handling women. According to Holly Millea writing in the December 1996 issue of *Premiere*: "He [Larry Flynt] readily admits that Love is not one of his favorite people. 'The first time I ever met Courtney, she came here for a script reading. And she was almost three hours late.' Flynt is in his office, sucking on a Cuban cigar. 'Woody was here.' Puff. Puff. 'Woody was mad. She came in and Woody said, "Courtney, when we start shooting, I'll give you a half hour. Anybody deserves a half hour. But don't ever do this to me on the set." And she looked at him and said, "Who the f—— are you?" So, sure enough, Woody jumped up and grabbed her in the air and threw her down on the floor like a professional wrestler. And he got on top of her and put his knees on her arms and she couldn't move. And he said, "Bitch, you're not getting up until you apologize." ' Puff. 'And Courtney apologized.' "[1]

Not that Woody Harrelson is that aggressive with all living things. Although he played a man who promotes pictures of women being sliced, diced, marinated, and eviscerated, in real life Woody relates to trees. He was part of a group of nature lovers who staged a protest that stopped traffic on the Golden Gate Bridge in order to keep axes from touching trees. You can take a blade to your wife, but leave the maples and the oaks alone.

There was Larry Flynt himself, my Dad, playing the judge who tried him—or a composite, anyway. The movie blended two trials into one, misrepresenting them both but enabling the writers to use the Jerry Falwell incident for both laughs and serious purposes. After all, the full First Amendment guarantees freedom of religion, not just the freedom of speech.

There was Milos Forman, the Czechoslovakian director of such previous works as *One Flew over the Cuckoo's Nest*, *Amadeus*, and *Valmont*. He was convinced of the importance of the film based on the free speech issue, which was so critical to his homeland over-run in the 1950s by the Soviet Union. (So important had the arts been in his native land that when the Communists were ousted, the first elected leader, Vaclav Havel, was a playwright.)

There was Douglas Bauer, who acted as Dad's bodyguard on and off screen.

There was James Carville, the key political strategist for President Bill Clinton's 1992 and 1996 presidential campaigns before marrying a Republican strategist and "retiring" to make big money. From posing in an American Express credit card advertisement to a small role in the movie, he was a liberal who seemed to be selling himself to the highest bidder, enjoying his sudden fame.

There was Blaine Nashold, who was Dad's doctor on and off screen.

These were the people connected with a movie one critic considered to be about Larry Flynt as filtered through a writer such as Mark Twain. Dad had become a twentieth-century Huck Finn, a mischievous scamp, a lovable rogue, not the incestuous pornographer and convicted criminal (tax evasion as well as his obscenity and contempt of court problems) he was.

The movie was something else. No one wanted to hear the real story of Larry Flynt. No one wanted to act the truth. It was much simpler to dodge reality and history by creating a lovable scamp who just happens to make millions through booze and broads and an aw-shucks type of demeanor that hides a brilliant mind capable of great speeches.

☙

There was a larger irony to all this, one that has been lost from all but a Julia Duin story in *U.S.A. Today*, a story Oliver Stone said he could not remember when contacted for confirmation. It is also a story I will never forget.

I was twenty years old, talking with Judy, and the two of us felt we should write a book about growing up as Larry Flynt's daughters. I was not thinking of the abuse back then. I was still suppressing the incest memories. I just knew that our lives had been a roller coaster of outrageousness, and between Judy and me, we felt that we could tell a great story about Dad. Others agreed, and eventually we had a contract with a publisher, Grove Press, for a book with the working title, *Our Father Who Art a Hustler*. However, the book was never meant to be. I'm convinced that this was because God knew we were not finished. I needed more experiences, some of them painful, to gain the necessary perspective on my father and his empire.

Despite this, at the time we were riding high. We soon were mingling with some of the Hollywood elite, including Oliver Stone.

Judy knew Barry Fisher, one of the lawyers who had represented Dad while he was in Butner, North Carolina. She and I made an appointment to see him in his Century City office, eventually signing a contract with him on July 12, 1985. Through him we met with Alan Rinsler of Grove Press's San Francisco office, who flew in to see us.

We all got together at the City Restaurant in Los Angeles, where Rinsler decided to make an offer. He returned to his office and promised to send the contract.

We were elated but also nervous. For some reason, I first thought about writing a book about Dad when I was ten years old. Sometime in my teen years I mentioned this to Althea, I believe in Judy's presence. She very seriously said that if we ever wrote such a book about Dad, he would kill us. Certainly we believed her, though I did not know that at least one book had already been written. At Dad's request, Boye De Mente had written an autobiography, extensively interviewing Dad and Althea. Boye considered it the best work he had ever done, and though Dad paid him, Dad also insisted the book not be published. Boye placed the book and all research material in a safe-deposit box, where I presume it still exists.

This would have been different, and while I am not certain how far Dad would have gone to try to stop us at the time, he did not want anything released over which he had no control.

Judy and I never should have tried to work together because it was quickly clear to me that we could not collaborate. She had her own ideas which she aggressively pushed, yet she did not seem focused when trying to work out a structure or document our stories. We quarreled constantly. It was as though she wanted to have written a book but she didn't want to do the work necessary to get it between the covers.

I wrote Barry Fisher after receiving a draft of the possible contract for the book. I was back in Jacksonville, had a better perspective, and realized that everything was wrong, from the contract clauses to trying to work with Judy. I evaluated the contract paragraph by paragraph and explained why it would not work. I also pointed out the conflict I was able to see that had been created by his personal relationship with Judy separate from the business. She was the wrong partner, and because of their past relationship, he was probably the wrong attorney.

After I returned to California, realizing I couldn't work with Judy, I was connected with a ghost writer named Richard Boyle. Boyle was the cowriter of Oliver Stone's movie *Salvador*, the film version of his own life. In the movie, his character was played by James Woods.

In order to bring me into his world and convince me to use him for my book. Richard Boyle invited me to the private screening of *Salvador* at MGM Studios.

In my fantasy, Boyle was going to arrive in a real Hollywood car. Perhaps it would be a Mercedes 450 SL Convertible such as I had always coveted. Perhaps it would be a Rolls. Or it might be a Corvette, top-of-the-line BMW, or some other classy vehicle. Instead it was a variation of Mom's Green Bomb. The muffler was damaged and the engine seemed to have a terminal illness. If it was possible for a car to get tuberculosis, leprosy, and bronchitis all at the same time, this one had it. Even worse, the interior looked as though it had seen long-term use as a shelter for the homeless and a dump site for every fast-food restaurant in Los Angeles.

I had been embarrassed by the fact that I was still living in the low-income neighborhood apartment infested with drug dealers. I had been embarrassed by the fact that I did not have an appropriate outfit for the screening. I had been embarrassed just to be me. Until I saw him arrive. Then I was worried that even the roaches in my building would laugh at me.

I got in the car, driving over with a man who was wearing casual clothes, his car's seat cushions covered with a three-day growth of unidentifiable mold. Yet when we reached the MGM guard shack, we might as well have been in a chauffeur-driven limo. The guard had our names on a list. We were ushered through the stopping point and sent to a prestigious parking spot, just as if we were riding in Cinderella's coach instead of sharing the trip with her mice.

It was a small, dark room which we entered a few minutes late. Screening rooms are glamorous only because most people are denied access to them. They are like a neighborhood theater drastically scaled down and without popcorn or soda pop. I had no idea who was present, and no one turned when we quietly entered.

Once the movie was over, everyone applauded wildly. I didn't think the movie was all that great, but the house was packed with cast members, friends, crew members, and others in the business who expected the same treatment when their work was screened.

But reality meant nothing. I had loved movies all my life. The idea that I was in the midst of the end of a real production was exciting. I read the credits carefully, noting Oliver Stone's name as producer and cowriter, knowing a little about him from magazines such as *People*. There was a glamour even if the man who brought me was rather grungy, though I did worry that I might have to give an honest reaction. Instead I said what everyone else did, that it was "great." And when I just couldn't bring myself to lie, I used that saving face term "interesting."

It was a little like being at the opening of an artist's gallery show where the artist is a jerk, the work pretentious, and yet everyone is supposed to use jargon they don't understand to imply the artist is a genius.

As we left the screening room, Richard introduced me to Oliver Stone. I became light-headed, nervous, scared, and detached. I had lived a fantasy life with men such as Stone being part of the fantasy. I had been caught up in all of Rebecca's movie talk before it was obvious that she was never going to be in a scene that allowed her to keep her clothes on. And here I was with one of the hottest producers in the industry, introduced by a man who had a long-term working relationship with him, a man who might do the same with me. I was overwhelmed.

Oliver Stone took Richard and me to Trump's, a hip nightclub that was extremely expensive to join. Few people got in and even fewer could be guests of the members.

Everyone in the club was beautiful. Everyone was tall, sculpted, without lines, sags, bags, or even pores. They looked as though they had been airbrushed at birth. They looked like money.

I was not just overwhelmed, I was at a loss as to how to talk with them. Not only was my eye level about on a par with most of their navels, I felt as much out of place as a germ in a hospital operating room.

Richard Boyle, Oliver Stone, the director of Far East operations for MGM and her boyfriend, and I all sat at a table. At least with Richard present I knew I would not be asked to leave because I didn't meet the physical standards necessary to enter the room. If anything he seemed more out of place, though he was a bit of an insider because of his work with Stone.

Oliver Stone asked Richard about Boyle's new project. Richard was delighted to discuss the fact that he would be working with me on the book, and soon everyone was asking questions.

I was a bit overwhelmed, feeling unsophisticated and naive. I was just twenty. I was also infatuated with this tall, brilliant, handsome man. Then Oliver asked what the story would be about, and I remember him listening intently, looking as though he was staring through me, seeing the story unfold on a screen, my role being that of narrator.

Later we went to a party in the Hollywood Hills, Richard lighting up a joint on the way to the house. For some reason I believed that drugs were for two types of people. There were those like Althea who were involved with the counterculture. Drugs were for hard-living, early-dying rock musicians and their friends. Or drugs were for the poor, the lost, those with a sense of hopelessness. I firmly believed that no one in the most sophisticated world of the visual arts would use marijuana or other recreational drugs.

Sure, I had done it, but where I lived was an area these people would have been certain made me white trash. Not that he was committing a crime out there. Not that Richard would have been subject to arrest if a police officer saw him driving while smoking. But my values were finally coming together, and the inappropriateness of what he did, the immorality of it all as I saw it, caused me to freak. I knew I would be leaving that writing arrangement even if, as it turned out, the book might be delayed for years.

I was out of place at the party, a puppy available for brief amusement or snide remarks when playing in a different part of the room. I heard small groups of people talking about me as though I was this week's Hollywood curiosity.

At the same time, the people felt they should show their superior knowledge of an industry which, so far as I know, none of them had any connection with. They told me that I should take no less than a $200,000 advance for my book because "you can get it." The fact that this was a year when the book industry was retrenching to be more professional, that advances were down and only a perceived blockbuster might reach six figures, meant nothing. They knew. I felt stupid and out of place. And probably all of us were glad when I left because then they could laugh together, not in small groups wary of my overhearing them.

The book deal went down the tubes, along with my life. I rarely thought about a book again. Until the movie. Until I saw that same producer's name—Oliver Stone. Only this time it was connected with Dad's name, and this time the movie made by a man known as an ardent conspiracy theorist was not just a slanted opinion. It was an outright lie.

The screen lies began with a scene of my Dad, at age ten, selling bootleg whiskey from a wooden cart. (The published screenplay calls this image one of "Huckleberry Finn industriousness.") It was a delightful scene establishing the adorable entrepreneurial *Hustler*. It never happened, though. Dad picked cotton, and when he was a teenager he legally transported whiskey between two counties.

The movie script did not include the story of the chicken, a disgusting image that was limited to Dad's book. In fact, the best comment that can be made was the one Matt Labash used in his *Weekly Standard* article: "The truth is that, scene by scene and line by line, the distortions, omissions, and outright fabrications in *The People vs. Larry Flynt* make it a dishonest piece of work in almost every particular."[2]

One of the high points of the movie deals with Dad (Woody Harrelson) standing in front of a screen where a projector is intercutting images of naked women with the mutilated bodies of victims of

Vietnam War atrocities. The point is a dramatic one. It relates pornography to war, asking which is better. Even this was rigged for visual effect, the images of naked women, usually airbrushed, often soft focused, all very tame. They did not represent what Dad regularly publishes, what pornography is all about. And they were contrasted with pictures of battlefield mutilations and charred remains, in a sense the obscenities of real life. In my mind, though, all I could think about was the fact that with some of the images Dad and others have published, the only difference between pictures of battlefield mutilations and the women on their printed pages is that the victims on the battlefield are dead. (Recently I have learned that some publications have begun showing true crime images of mutilated female corpses. I don't know if this is what the reader is supposed to work toward in his relationships or if this is supposed to bring about a new level of sexual excitement.)

In the movie my dad states emphatically, "This is not a pep rally for pornography. My conviction is simply a reminder that what we fought for two hundred years ago can't be taken for granted!"

The speech causes the members of the audience to be deeply moved. My father goes from a comic, slightly disreputable uncle who is the subject of gossip at family gatherings, to a hero of First Amendment freedoms. It's also a lie. It never happened. The ideas and comments that were expressed and on which the scene was very loosely based involved another man entirely.

In the movie there is a composite lawyer using the name of a real lawyer, Alan Isaacman, who won the 1988 Supreme Court victory over Jerry Falwell. The Supreme Court declared that Falwell was not libeled by the parody advertisement. Earlier, a lower court had ordered Dad to pay Reverend Falwell $200,000 for emotional distress. That decision was also overturned based, according to the decision, on the fact that "The State's interest in protecting public figures from emotional distress is not sufficient to deny First Amendment protection to speech."

The primary lawyer in Dad's life relative to First Amendment issues was Herald Prince Fahringer, a man used in the creation of the composite. His history of representing pornographers dates back more than thirty years, and it was his ideas and his words that were credited to Dad in scenes such as the one with the naked women and mutilated war victims. As he told Matt Labash for the *Weekly Standard* article, "I hope it doesn't sound boastful, but I was certainly the main speaker there. I don't know whether Larry spoke. . . . But all this stuff about the First Amendment with that rear projection behind him, there was none of that, of course."

The movie had one lie piled on another. Dad's many wives were ignored in favor of Althea. His drug abuse seemed related to the shooting, though he has been involved with drug abuse much of his adult life. He was a heavy amphetamine user long before he was shot, and the cocaine and similar illegal drugs he took had nothing to do with pain management.

Althea, according to the movie, was abused by nuns in the orphanage, adding to the acceptance of a promiscuous woman involved with prostitution and the running of a pornography empire. This was just another of Dad's attacks against religion that marked the pages of *Hustler*. In truth, Althea's sister, Marsha Rider, explained that the two orphanages in which the sisters lived were never connected with nuns. One was a Methodist home. The other was a state home. Neither was connected with any religion where nuns were caretakers.

There were other phony details. Althea died in 1987, two years after she allegedly contracted AIDS. In the drama of the movie, Dad discovers Althea having slipped under the water in the bathtub. It was so high, it went over the side and under the door, where Dad supposedly saw it.

The scene is moving. Althea was weakened by drugs or AIDS. She fell asleep or otherwise lost consciousness enough to slip under the water and drown. Then, with the water visible from outside the room, Dad threw open the door, rolled in on his wheelchair, pushed himself out, and sobbed as he used his upper body strength to drag her out onto the floor, where she is dead.

Truth? What is known is that the nurse found Althea's body. Dad was bedridden. The water was also not flooding dramatically, a moment in the picture that I suppose might hearken back to the old gangster films which ended in the rain, a newspaper announcing the death of the gangster as it floats, discarded, down a flooded street and toward a storm sewer waiting to suck it away.

The fact is that the water was shallow, perhaps less than two inches from reports I have since heard. Since Althea was on her back, the idea of her drowning after falling asleep and slipping under water that reached the top of the tub, then poured over the sides, was nonsense. Certainly Althea was heading for an early death because of the drugs. There was nothing taking place at the time of which I am aware that would give a member of Dad's inner circle a reason to want her immediately dead.

The lies and misrepresentations went on and on. But what was troubling was not just that the real story was never told, that the truth of pornography was never hinted at, or that the man on the screen was not really Larry Flynt. Instead, what tore at my heart and frightened me for the future was the way the audience believed what they were watching. Men and women, young and old, were clapping and cheering for Dad. He was a folk hero, the lanky, rawboned frontiersman who speaks straight, shoots straight, and so what if he ends the day with a whiskey, a woman, and a chaw of tobacco. It was as though they were watching Davy Crockett standing against the Mexicans in the Alamo as interpreted by Walt Disney. It was like when Dad and Mom were growing up and the Saturday matinees frequently featured westerns where all the kids cheered the approach of the cavalry saving the fort from an attack by the Indians.

They did not know that it was because of Dad that some of them have been physically hurt and others face a future of violence, at least one time. They were not aware of the interview convicted serial killer and rapist Ted Bundy gave to Dr. James Dobson before Bundy was executed for his crimes in Florida. Bundy told him: "I've lived in prison for a long time now, and I've met a lot of men who were motivated to commit violence just like me, and without exception, every one of them was deeply involved in pornography. Without question. Without exception. Deeply influenced and consumed by an addiction to pornography. There is no question about it . . . . And what scares me is when I see what's on cable TV. Some of the movies that come into homes today was stuff that they wouldn't show in X-rated adult theaters thirty years ago."

They were also not aware of the article in *U.S.A. Today* on Friday, September 26, 1986, which stated: "In a Cincinnati, Ohio, neighborhood where adult bookstores and X-rated theaters were closed, there was an 83 percent decrease in violent crimes such as rape, robbery and assault." It was one of a number of looks at neighborhoods where, though there had been no clear evidence that pornography leads to crime, here was positive proof that eliminating pornography drastically reduced crimes of violence.

They did not know the truth behind the man they suddenly saw as a folk hero, and I knew their positive reaction would influence their thinking about the dangers or lack of them concerning pornography. Someone had to speak out. Someone had to tell the truth. Someone had to risk standing alone, defying family and friends if necessary, to tell what was right as God wants us all to do. What I did not expect was to also realize that I am that someone.

To say that I was cured of my self-hate and desire to defend my father would be untrue. In fact, just a couple of years earlier, on March 27, 1994, I had rushed to his side when he was recovering from still more surgery in Duke University Medical Center. This was the first time I had seen him since he was in the Butner facility, where he left me with his lawyers while he and Judy talked for hours. I didn't know if he was crazy then or just faking it, though he gave Judy detailed instructions about contacting a number of people, several of them dead, others of whom, such as her "Uncle" Teddy Kennedy, had never met either of them. I had been hurt, scared, angry, frustrated, and confused, and then I had begun to get my life together. Now Dad was in Duke for surgery to ease his back pain and I found myself flying to North Carolina.

I made the trip out of fear—and out of the desire to gain his love one last time, the same desire that had caused me so many emotional problems throughout my life. Someone with a spinal injury has problems people who are mobile do not. Everything from bedsores to kidney problems are constant threats to the quality and quantity of life for an individual in a wheelchair. Dad's fluctuating weight, his heavy drug use, and his promiscuous sex life all put him in a high-risk category. Every time he has a serious problem—pneumonia, corrective surgery, or anything else from which the average person Dad's age is expected to recover—Dad may die. It is a reality he has had to face, and so have I.

As doctors have explained to me, any time a patient has full anesthesia, the surgery is no longer minor. The procedure itself may be a simple one, causing trauma that will limit activity for a day or two, but the anesthetic creates its own risk. Dad could die on the table or from complications just because of the damage from the shooting.

I have always believed the extremes when it comes to my Dad. If he says a meal I make is good, and if I am not in one of my self-hating, question everything moods, I will decide it is superior to anything he has ever eaten. And if he says he is going to kill me if I write about him, as has happened more than once, I do not look on the statement as the angry words of a frustrated father. I decide that there may be hit men on every corner.

Now Dad was in the hospital. He was a high-risk patient, and though he was otherwise in good health so far as I knew, the hospital meant death. I had to be by his side. I had to see him one last time.

At the same time, I was feeling like the little girl in trouble. If he died, I would have no one, and that meant that only Dad could be my rescuer, the Dad who was the knight on the white steed charging through Jacksonville to scoop me up in his arms. It was all irrational, especially now that I had Lawrence and Marilyn. Yet there I was at 9 P.M., standing by the airport rental counter, trying to get a car.

I had remembered much of what I needed. I remembered my makeup. I remembered my clothes. In fact, as I had done the weekend I spent in the Navy barracks, I overpacked too many suitcases. That time I took six bags for two days. This time I took four bags for one day. The only thing I forgot was my credit card, a major catastrophe.

I marched over to the car rental place, dragging my suitcases, looking professional in my business suit. I was the typical executive woman in appearance, someone who was equipped to spend a couple of weeks handling whatever problems my boss needed me to tackle in North Carolina. But I was not equipped to do something simple like get a rental car, then go to a hotel for one evening.

The car rental people were sympathetic, but there was nothing they could do. Fifteen-thousand-dollar cars are not handed to women without proof they have a cent to their names, no matter how sophisticated they look. I understood. I really understood. It was a setback I would conquer.

The tears began flowing. Frustrated, terrified that Dad would be dead before I could get out of the airport, alone, knowing no one, I could handle the stress no longer. My cheeks were wet, my nose was red, and I was as miserable as the little girl who was still hiding, alone and terrified, inside the adult woman's body.

Two computer salespeople were in the airport and they came over to see if they could help me. All my life I assumed that men, with the exception of Lawrence, my husband, were out for no good. I thought that every male used and abused the women in their lives. I thought that it was dangerous to trust because I would always be hurt if I did. And then the man offered me a ride, his female companion agreeing, and they took me to a hotel thirty miles out of their way just so I would not have to endure another minute in the airport.

The man and woman, now an hour out of their way, let me out at the hotel. I was late getting there, of course, and I had not made the arrangements needed for a late arrival. All the rooms had been rented.

There was another hotel a few blocks away, and since I had to conserve what little money I had, I began walking. The night was dark, the streetlights casting harsh shadows as dark and frightening as the periodic illumination was comforting. It was as though I was walking in and out of danger, through the valley of the shadow of death, as I made my way to the next hotel. Instead of a rod and a staff, I had four heavy suitcases. And instead of enemies waiting to attack, I had only the demons of my emotionally disturbed thinking. I encountered no danger. There was probably no danger to encounter. Still, I felt like the heroine in a teen horror exploitation film who ignores all warning and is going alone in the area where the deranged slasher is waiting in ambush.

I found a hotel room, and though it was late, I tossed and turned all night. I anticipated a dramatic meeting, a loving embrace, delight that I among all his relatives had rushed to his side in the last hours or days of his life. I cared. He knew. We embraced. Father and daughter at last united.

I arose early, opening the suitcases and laying out clothing. It took six tries to settle on the perfect outfit, another conservative suit. I was the mature Tonya, the woman, not the child. I was married. I had a daughter. I was a responsible adult.

I did not eat because I had been starving myself for two weeks, desperate to lose weight when I heard Dad would have surgery. I was rushing to his bedside, of course, but I wanted to be beautiful when I did it. Thus I was lightheaded from the adrenaline rush and lack of food, but that did not matter. I was on the way to the hospital, which, by chance, was across the street from the hotel I had found.

There was no problem getting to Dad's room. I was his daughter. I was cool. I was professional. I was beloved. I belonged by his side.

I rode the elevator, walked down the hall, found the room, and entered. The only other person present was a nurse who was also his girlfriend, the hopefully future Mrs. Flynt as she saw her life progressing. But she did not matter.

Like an actress in a bad movie, I walked across the room, stood by his bedside, and took Dad's hand in mine. It was warm, the blood flowing freely, his heart obviously in good shape. He obviously couldn't talk, and he had tubes in his nose and in other parts of his body. Still, he would recover. The procedure had been successful.

There was a warmth that filled my soul at that moment. My prayers had been answered, and if Dad was going to live, he also was undoubtedly going to delight in my presence. I was the lone child present. I had not been in a position to afford the flight, yet my husband had been so understanding, he did not care what debts we incurred. And now Dad and I were reunited.

Dad looked at me, his eyes impassive. Then a tear came to the corner of one of his eyes. It moved slowly down his cheek, replaced by another and another.

This was it, I told myself. This was why I had come, what I had sought all my life. And I, too, began to weep.

Then Dad looked toward his nurse, his would-be wife. He slowly lifted his hand, pointing to her, pointing to me, then pointing to the door. Weak though he was, he made certain the woman knew to throw me out.

Even when God's grace is ours for the taking, ours without condition, God still lets us make fools of ourselves if we choose to do so. I knew better. I knew I was unloved and unwanted by my biological father. I knew he was immoral in his actions, a dangerous, devious, at times hypocritical, occasionally dishonest individual capable of justifying anything that gave him pleasure. I had walked away from his world after witnessing Rebecca come close to being destroyed by it. Yet one more time I had denied my knowledge and sought my father. One more time I had been brought up short.

I began crying uncontrollably, and medical personnel came running. Dad apparently had the psychiatric attendants called, and since he was rich, famous, and my father, they wanted to take me to the psychiatric ward for examination. Not that they said that. Instead they asked me to accompany them to the emergency room, where I would be given a drug to help me relax.

Reluctantly following the attendant, I suddenly found myself in a padded room. This was an area where potentially destructive or self-destructive patients could be placed. It was truly padded, meant to absorb the shock of a patient trying to smash his or her head against a wall or floor. The door could be locked. The patient could be observed. And treatment could begin whenever the person calmed down. It was meant for extreme circumstances, and the fact that I was in there terrified me.

The tears stopped. I understood everything, and as quickly as I had fallen apart, I was fine.

I finally got it. I finally knew what the Lord had been trying to show me for well over a decade. I was well dressed, calm, and articulate. When the doctor arrived, I explained that I was back in control after an extremely upsetting encounter with my father. All I wanted to do was return to my hotel room, collect my belongings, and return to my home in Jacksonville.

The doctor wanted me to stay. It was voluntary, of course, and to prove it, he made certain that though I was in the "rubber room," the door was open. I was free to come and go, though obviously I was expected to decide that the comforts of the place and the potential vacation I could receive with evaluation, drugs, and who knew what else, would make me want to stay.

Since this was voluntary, I decided to leave, to get to a telephone, to call my husband. I walked out and encountered a nice-looking man in a suit and tie. I smiled. He scowled. And suddenly I was thrown back into the room and ordered to not leave. A police officer was then asked to stand by the door where I was "voluntarily" resting.

I had visions of a legally sanctioned kidnapping, my father's ultimate revenge. I thought of electric shock treatment. I thought of becoming a zombie from the drugs I would be given. I thought of Lawrence and Marilyn. And then I thought of tomato juice.

"I'm feeling light-headed," I told the police officer. "I haven't eaten and today's been quite traumatic for me. Would you mind getting me some tomato juice with a lot of salt in it?"

The officer agreed, and when he went down the hall, I took off running. The man in the suit started yelling, and I heard the pounding feet of others chasing me. But I had a head start.

I fled the hospital, raced across to my hotel room, and called Lawrence. He told me to drop everything, to take a cab to the airport, and come home. I argued about the cost—$80—and the need to pack.

"Come home," he told me, and I finally agreed. But I could not leave my clothes, not my four essential suitcases. And the time I spent repacking was enough for the hospital personnel to locate me.

Suddenly there was a pounding at the door, and as I asked who was there, the manager opened it with a passkey. Police moved in, guns drawn. I was thrown against the wall, my feet kicked out so I would be off balance if I tried to move. I was frisked, handcuffed, then my luggage checked for weapons or who knew what.

"I am not suicidal," I told them. "If I wanted to die, don't you think I'd be swinging from a chandelier? You've got loaded guns pointed at me. All I'd have to do is scare you enough and you'd kill me. I'm not going to hurt myself."

They ignored me and took me back to Duke.

Just as my position as Larry Flynt's daughter got me in trouble, so the implied notoriety I could generate enabled me to leave. I knew that I had media access whenever I desired it, though at the time I had no reason to exploit this potential.

I was locked in the rubber room for two hours before being placed in a regular room with a telephone. I was given a mild sedative, slept through the night, then called a girlfriend of mine and told her to call the top investigative reporter at the investigative tabloid television program *Inside Edition*. I told her that Duke University did not need any further bad publicity, but they were holding me against my will. I described where I was and how the show could reach me.

When I hung up, I discovered the doctor had been listening at the door. He knew I was serious. He also knew there was no reason to keep me there. He and the rest of the staff could not get me out of there fast enough.

Later I was sent a bill for $11,000 for my night's stay. I kept the bill in case anyone ever challenged my story. I also did not pay it. Instead I had my lawyer send a letter explaining the penalty for false imprisonment. I never heard from the medical staff again.

Conclusion:
The Fight against Pornography

In 1996, with *The People vs. Larry Flynt* receiving so much attention, with lies and distortions about my father and pornography becoming fact in the minds of the American people, I couldn't take it anymore. It was like being witness to the murder of someone, then not coming forward because the police caught the perpetrator seemingly red-handed. Then, over time, the murderer is let go because the law enforcement officials, going against all the evidence, announce that the death was an accident. There was seemingly no witness to contradict the false statement, the silence of the witness assuring the declared innocence of the guilty.

Overwhelmed by the knowledge that my silence could cause such harm, I finally had the strength to assert myself, to say no to the public myth, to set the record straight. I began calling the media, making it clear that I wanted to reveal the truth about my father.

I began by calling Enough Is Enough, a Washington, D.C.–based antipornography group I knew about and respected. Their focus has primarily been on Internet pornography, but their concerns cover the entire industry and I trusted their integrity when I needed help in reaching out to tell my story.

My interviews with various members of the media led to frequent requests to appear before college students and adult groups around the country. At first I used a prepared speech, certain that I was not smart enough, well-versed enough, or suave enough to talk with people better educated than I. Then I realized that I, too, might be an unlikely vessel. And even if I wasn't, I had gained knowledge that few others could ever experience. I had been to hell in California. I had been to heaven through the grace of God. And I was on earth with an increasingly supportive husband, a daughter who needed protection, and a message to deliver.

I began speaking from my heart, relying on experience, talking with others, asking the Lord what I should say. Men and women wept in the audience. Soon I had college girls coming to me with their own stories of degradation, abuse, and one or more family members obsessed with pornography. They confirmed what I knew, told me stories worse than I had experienced, and understood that they were not alone.

Many of them had been abused by their fathers. And while the Columbus Police Department did not have a strong enough case to prosecute my father on molestation charges—charges I filed—I know the truth. Like these young women, I know what pornography can do to a family.

Instead of finding a handful of prudes or religious zealots, as pro-pornography forces are likely to dub those who try to tell the truth, I found liberals *and* conservatives, religious individuals *and* those who had turned away from God. I found rich *and* poor. I found children of CEOs of *Fortune* 500 companies *and* children of ghetto families both telling the same stories. They were finding strength in my words and in my willingness to speak out. And as they began their own healing journeys, I realized I had lost my fear. I had finally embraced the faith that heals, loving God and respecting His creation enough to stand against those who hurt others, who exploit women and children, who debase themselves over and over again.

My walk has been from fear to faith. My crusade is not against my father, but against an evil tearing the very fabric of society.

I have seen the violence of those who are addicted to pornography. But instead of running for cover, I am emboldened. If pornography has taken control of their souls to such a degree, then it is essential they be helped if possible—and, if not, stopped.

Yes, the American people have rights clearly defined by the Constitution. But rights carry responsibilities. Freedom is not license to hurt other people. That which is wrong may be a right, but it is not right to do.

I am the pornographer's daughter. And if I am successful in my lifetime, pornography, at least to some degree, will have stopped with me.

Notes

Chapter 1:
The Country Roads of My Mind

1. USMCFP, Springfield, Missouri, Psychiatric Evaluation of Larry C. Flynt, Reg.#: 78407-012, January 9, 1984, p. 1.
2. Psychological report of Larry Flynt; p. 2; written January 18, 1984, by Christina S. Echols, Ph.D., clinical psychologist, and reviewed by M. A. Conroy, Ph.D., chief of psychology. Document part of the Classification Study for Larry Flynt, Register Number 78407-012; U.S. Department of Justice, Bureau of Prisons, Medical Center for Federal Prisoners, Springfield, Missouri; William S. Logan, M.D., forensic psychiatrist.
3. Ibid., 2.
4. Ibid., 1.
5. Ibid., 12.
6. Ibid., 4.

Chapter 3:
Jacksonville

1. I have eliminated the name of the relative who was the other person to molest me because he is still alive and I have not tried to prosecute him. The man is old, feeble, and not mentally well. Going after him would serve no purpose. He will face judgment by a higher authority than the court system. By contrast, my father has been living a lie, going high profile with the movie, and is still young, with many years to influence the public. I felt I had to take a legal stand against him, not just write a book telling the truth. Thus I have brought charges against him, charges which were still being investigated at this writing. I have not been directly notified of any decisions, though I understand from a reporter that the detective feels there is inadequate evidence to go further. In a "he said-she said" type of case so many years after the fact, the only prosecutorial tool is often

psychiatric evidence of repressed memory. Such information is not available in my case, and though I understand that my allegations were believed, at this time it appears that nothing further will be done.

Chapter 7:
Spiraling Out of Control

1. Psychological report of Flynt, Larry Claxton, DOB: 11-01-42, Reg. No. 78407-012, written January 15, 1984, by Christina S. Echols, Ph.D., clinical psychologist, and reviewed by M. A. Conroy, Ph.D., chief of psychology at the U.S. Medical Center for Federal Prisoners, Springfield, Missouri. Quote from Conclusions statement on p. 9.
2. Joe Holleman and William C. Lhotka, "Cold-Blooded Murders Were Racist and Random Confessed Shooter of Vernon Jordan, Larry Flynt, Others Explains His Choices," *San Francisco Examiner*, June 25, 1995.

Chapter 9:
Home Again?

1. The information concerning the DeLorean incident is from research by coauthor Ted Schwarz, who extensively investigated the case, including interviewing many of those involved, as part of the background check for his as-told-to autobiography of John DeLorean (Grand Rapids: Zondervan Publishing Corp., 1985).
2. Dad's different claims and the quotes concerning the various judges and his actions are taken from his January 9, 1984, Psychiatric Evaluation at the U.S. Medical Center for Federal Prisoners in Springfield, Missouri.
3. The exact chronology of events that led to Dad's going to jail at the end of 1983, after I had returned to Jacksonville, was the following: October 28: Dad played an audiotape conversation between John DeLorean and Special Agent Hoffman. He was then subpoenaed to appear before both the grand jury and Judge Takasugi. He did not appear on October 31 as requested, nor did he appear the next day. However, he finally testified on November 3. November 6: Dad partied, then flew to Washington, D.C. the next day for the appeal in his libel case. On the 8th he cursed the justices for not letting him speak, at which time he was charged with impeding the administration of justice. The next day he went before Judge Jean Dwyer before going to New York City for a business meeting. The following day, November 10, he flew to Las Vegas for the Hagler-Duran boxing match. November 14: Dad had to appear before Judge Takasugi concerning contempt charges for October 31 and November 1, as well as for failing to produce the audiotape. He was charged with civil contempt and fined

$10,000 per day to be paid until he gave the source of the tape. Another $25,000 had to be paid because of the contempt conviction. November 16: Dad paid Judge Takasugi $10,000 in one-dollar bills, the money brought in by prostitutes he hired off the streets. The women were transported by limo, then carried the dollar bills in bulging trash bags. The next day he wore the diaper and purple heart, and eventually was charged with both desecration of the American flag and falsely wearing an American medal. November 18: Dad was late to court and again charged with contempt. November 22: Dad went to Dallas, the next day appearing in Washington, D.C., before Magistrate Dwyer. He was given permission to represent himself at a hearing set for January 19, 1984, for impeding the administration of justice. That same day Dad's fine was raised by Judge Takasugi to $20,000 per day. He went to Klamath Falls, then to Ohio for Thanksgiving on November 24. November 28: Dad was found guilty of contempt for failing to appear on November 18. He was fined $1,500. Dad was also charged with criminal contempt for failing to pay the $20,000 per day fine from November 23 through November 28. His lawyer presented an argument that was successful enough to clear him of the charge. Then Dad contradicted him, said that his actions in not paying were deliberate, and gave the judge no alternative other than to find him guilty. The following day he was also in court, this time rambling on about matters seemingly unrelated to any of the charges. November 30: Dad flew to Alaska, where he was arrested, appearing before the judge in a Santa Claus suit. December 2: Dad was back in California for charges of desecrating the American flag. Bail was revoked and Dad announced he was going to parachute from a plane. December 3: Dad used an assumed name to fly to Chicago, where he was arrested. There was an identity hearing on December 5 where Dad cursed the judge, then threw a Soviet flag at her. Again he made a rambling speech, then finally admitted his true identity. December 6: Dad went before Chicago Judge Frank McGarr on contempt charges. Dad said of throwing the Soviet flag the day before: "The only thing I have to apologize about was that it was an American flag, or that it was a Russian flag, I wish it would have been an American flag so I could have spit on it, and if I had one today I would do it and throw it in your face. Now I want a fair trial." He swore, spat at the judge, then went outside the courtroom and tried to take off his clothes. He was sentenced to sixty days for contempt against Judge McGarr with an additional sentence for the previous week's antics still pending. December 8: Dad returned to Los Angeles, the next day defending himself against civil contempt charges in Judge Takasugi's court. He testified about the tapes and implicated Bill Rider as a critical witness. Bill was provided a lawyer at court expense and appeared on December 13, the day after Dad was arraigned before Judge James McMahon for charges of desecration of the flag and falsely wearing the Purple Heart. Also on the 12th, Dad not only insisted once again upon being his own lawyer but also on having Madalyn Murray O'Hair as a consultant. December 15: Judge Consuello Marshall ordered a psychiatric evaluation of Dad based on the flag

desecration issue. Four days later Judge Takasugi ordered a similar evaluation related to the criminal contempt proceedings and related matters. December 21,
1983: Dad arrived at the U.S. Medical Center for Federal Prisoners in Springfield, Missouri, for evaluation.
4. Quote from pages 9–10 of the Transcript of Proceedings In Re: Larry Flynt, No.
83 CR 0950, U.S. District Court Northern District of Illinois, Eastern Division,
before the Honorable Frank J. McGarr, Chief Judge. Held in the hearing room
of the Metropolitan Correctional Center, Chicago, Illinois 60604, on Tuesday,
the 6th day of December, 1983, at 12 noon.
5. Quote from letter of Diane Herceg dated September 10, 1986, and sent to the
U.S. Justice Department Commission on Pornography.

Chapter 10:
Finding Faith, Finding Home

1. Quote from Larry Flynt in "Warning: Material Is of an Adult Nature. This Literature Is Not Intended for Minors . . ." by Holly Millea in *Premiere*, December 1996.
2. Matt Labash, "The Truth vs. Larry Flynt," *Weekly Standard*, February 17, 1997.

Index